AN IDEA
AND ITS SERVANTS

AN IDEA
AND ITS SERVANTS

UNESCO FROM WITHIN

By

Richard Hoggart

New York

Oxford University Press

1978

ISBN 0 19-520077-2

Library of Congress
Catalog Card Number
78-59766

Printed and bound in Great Britain by
Cox & Wyman Ltd, London, Fakenham and Reading

To those colleagues
at UNESCO who showed
what a good
international civil servant
can achieve

CONTENTS

Words are for those with promises to keep

W. H. AUDEN

ACKNOWLEDGEMENTS

I am very deeply indebted to the following persons and institutions for help with the preparation of this book: Asa Briggs, Catharine Carver, Shirley Guiton, Kenneth Hudson, Richard Jolly and the staff of the Institute of Development Studies at the University of Sussex, Michael Kustow, the Leverhulme Trust, Norman Mackenzie, Ruth Scott, Roy Shaw, some good friends at UNESCO, my daughter Nicola, my sons Simon and Paul, my son-in-law Richard and my wife Mary.

An earlier version of Chapter Four (iii) was published in *The New Universities Quarterly* (30.1, Winter 1975).

Some elements of the discussion of contemporary cultural development in Chapter Eight appeared in *Art, Politics and Will, essays in honour of Lionel Trilling* (1977).

PREFACE

All organisations need regular, frank and fair criticism. The United Nations Educational, Scientific and Cultural Organisation (hereinafter UNESCO) does not get enough of that. One of its great weaknesses is over-defensiveness, unwillingness to listen to criticism. At the official level this often takes the form of invoking Staff Regulation 1.5 against any staff member or former staff member who publishes any critical comment on the Organisation. Here is the text:

Staff Regulations of the United Nations
Scope and Purpose
Article I
Duties, Obligations and Privileges
Regulation 1.5: Staff Members shall exercise the utmost discretion in regard to all matters of official business. They shall not communicate to any person any information known to them by reason of their official position which has not been made public, except in the course of their duties or by authorization of the Secretary-General. Nor shall they at any time use such information to private advantage. The obligations do not cease upon separation from the Secretariat.

Regulation 1.5 is designed, quite properly, to prevent staff members or former staff members from revealing confidential official material acquired in the course of their duties. Throughout this book, I have tried to obey both the letter and spirit of Regulation 1.5. I have, however, criticised (and praised) States by name where this seemed justified. I have also extended the Regulations and not included material which might hurt individuals. I am content to be judged on this approach.

This lesson—of the value of open, critical comment—is one UNESCO really must at last learn, or it will become even more of an enclosed Byzantine system than it is at present. It is, after all, the one UN Agency whose Constitution enshrines the idea of free enquiry. Throughout the world that idea is having a hard time now. UNESCO will not reinforce the idea among its Member States by refusing to honour it internally. It must learn to live less self-protectively, more bravely.

R.H.

I

THE SETTING

It is easy to see, looking back over the years, the major turning points in one's life. Much rarer are those occasions when one feels, at the very moment of living it: 'This is a watershed. Things will never be quite the same again.' One such moment came to us on a bitterly cold Friday in late January 1970 as we—my wife, our younger son and I—walked almost numbly across the tarmac at Birmingham Airport to board a BAC 111 for Paris and a three-year assignment at UNESCO Headquarters there.

We were numb because in the previous few weeks we had been through a most distressing family circumstance—the sudden death of the last grandparent. We had wound up her affairs, sold our own house in Birmingham, packed up somehow—and here we were, leaving at the last minute, so that I could start work as an Assistant Director General on the following Monday.

Paris was bitter too; and when Paris is bitter she is more gauntly, inhumanly chilling to the spirit than London ever is. The wide bare streets, the grey faceless six-storey bourgeois apartment blocks of the 7th Arrondissement don't suggest a warm neighbourhood life. We had been kindly met at the airport by my new administrative officer; that apart, the weekend was a bleak desert; only two and a half days, but it seemed like a year. One could hardly stay in the hotel bedroom so we walked under a sky like lead, simply too sad to do much, to go to a theatre or cinema.

It passed, of course, that mood; but not as quickly as we had expected. People in UNESCO were kind but an ADG is occupationally rather lonely, if he is to do his job properly. One had to learn who were the genuine friends, those who would not take friendship as a way to personal favours. The Organisation as a whole was in a very bad patch, the staff disaffected, the Director General at his most bullying with them. Nor is Paris, for foreigners who live there, an immediately welcoming city. It is a beautiful place, and one does eventually make warm friendships in one's apartment house, among local shopkeepers and bistro owners. By the end of the first year we had come to love the city, especially at weekends when we could walk on the wide boulevards, have a drink, go to a cinema; then, it was like an extended holiday. But for a newcomer the surface public style of Paris is brusque.

So the first months were lonely, especially after our younger son had left for a few months' work in India; and especially for my wife. I was luckier. I had work to engross me—which *had* to engross me if I was to get on top of it—for seventeen hours a day. Luckily, we had made three promises to ourselves before we ever agreed that I should take the job: that whenever any of the three children felt like coming over they were simply to come and we would pay (this ensured constant reunions and some wonderfully gregarious Christmasses, New Years, Easters and the rest); that we would live as near to the centre of Paris as we could possibly afford, since we would not be likely to have such a good salary or to be in such a lovely capital ever again, and since it would be silly to add, to the rigours of my job, a daily drive out from and into the suburbs (we found a very large, shabby, unfurnished flat three hundred yards from the Champs Élysées); and that, so far as ever possible, my wife would come with me on every foreign trip—'mission', in UNESCO's language (we kept that promise, too, and for my part I can hardly bear to think what those missions would have been like without her, personally and professionally).

So things picked up, and by late 1970 we were engrossed in a new world; a new world-world, in fact, since now the perspective was always world-wide. Sometimes, when there came an odd reflective moment free from the multiple telephone calls, cables, telexes, super priority documents, consultations, meetings, I wondered how I'd ever got there at the start of my fifties. I certainly hadn't sought or particularly desired it. I enjoyed being a Professor of Literature at Birmingham, and even more enjoyed work at the postgraduate Centre for Contemporary Cultural Studies which, with Stuart Hall, I had started there; my outside interests were all of a peculiarly English kind or, rather, had a particularly English complexion; they sprang from a special interest in the texture of English provincial life. So the move seemed odd: to us and, I gather, to some of our friends.

It had come about almost by accident; or, better, by the slow accretion of small events. Up to then, the name of UNESCO had not meant a great deal to me, any more than it does to most British academics nowadays. I had had at least a little to do with it, though. The United Kingdom's relations with UNESCO are overseen by a National Commission. When governmental responsibility for UNESCO affairs in the UK was transferred, in the mid-sixties, from the Ministry of Education to the Ministry for Overseas Development, the National Commission and its sub-committees were reorganised. I was asked to join the sub-committee on 'Culture' which met two or at the most three times a year. I wasn't heavily involved; I made a couple of very short trips to UNESCO's General Conference in Paris, in 1966 and 1968; I paid a very brief visit to one of the Executive Board meetings; and I went to a short meeting of 'experts' which was asked to plan a programme for work in 'cultural development'. All in all, it didn't add up to much; it was very much on the margins of my life.

There is a line in Auden about the dramatic force of 'the telephone call from long distance which defines one's future'. In the summer of 1969, at home in Birmingham, I received three such calls in one fortnight, each proposing an interesting job. The third of them asked whether I would be willing to be proposed as a possible ADG at UNESCO. That seemed the most manageable, given family commitments.

As I've said, I was not seeking to leave Birmingham and had certainly made no effort to do so. But there are some propositions one cannot put aside on personal grounds; if they are offered, they have to be taken—not for self-aggrandisement but because someone has to do them, even against the inclination to stay put. When I went to UNESCO I knew I was risking cutting myself off from all those elements in British life which seemed so far to have interested me. But I agreed to stand for the job, and soon had my first meeting with René Maheu, who had by then been Director General for seven years and was to remain so almost until I left UNESCO finally, in 1975.

Assistant Director Generalships are intercontinental and so intensely political appointments; at any one time there are only five or six in the whole Organisation, so the fights to obtain them are fierce. No continent can reasonably hope to have more than one; and for any country to have one is regarded as a distinction. In 1969/70, the British felt it was their turn. I wasn't their first choice; but, when I did become their candidate, they supported me unfussily and effectively. It was a senior civil servant who telephoned me, that day in the summer of '69, and told me the facts and chances as fairly as possible. So I agreed to 'let my name go forward'.

The only elected member of staff in UNESCO is the Director General; everyone else is appointed by him. That at least is the principle; in practice, a Director General—especially when he is appointing to the top posts—has to measure the force of a great many pressures from individual Member States or regions. At the time I became a candidate, Asia felt under-represented on the top Board of Management and was on the whole expected to obtain that Assistant Director Generalship; and that, I gather, was the Director General's own initial inclination. He is required to consult but does not take orders from the Executive Board on such appointments. The Board now comprises forty-five people from all over the world who meet in Paris bi-annually to monitor UNESCO's work. This particular consultation showed—by what complicated political alchemy I do not know—that the Board overwhelmingly favoured me. It would have been difficult for any Director General, even Maheu who had more than his share of stubborn courage, not to appoint a candidate so heavily backed by the Board. Maheu habitually handed out much more criticism than praise, but he had the grace to tell me a few months after I had started that he was glad the Board had pushed him that way.

But those are the outer movements by which we came to Paris; the inner movements are more interesting. For in spite of the little I had seen of the Organisation, and though I knew that it was at that time a very unhappy place, I was more intrigued by it than I knew; and that interest gathered force when the possibility of working there appeared. So many of the things it was doing—in the arts, the social sciences, communications, or about racism or the environment or population issues—were urgent and difficult and important. I can now see that one incident more than any other moved me to drop everything and go; and it had lain dormant for three years. During my two days at the 1966 General Conference, I attended what was called the Culture Commission, whose job it was to discuss and approve the Organisation's programme for the next two years in an area of work which ran from the high arts to anthropology. During a session on the threats to oral cultures the delegate from Mali—himself highly educated in France and also well acquainted with the inside of French gaols, since he had been a fighter for independence—spoke with exceptional eloquence about his country's needs. Unless a great deal is done quickly to collect and transcribe our oral material, he said, we shall be a people without a past. The old men who carry our history in their heads, in songs, stories and all kinds of phrases, are very old now; and the young men are moving to the towns and have other interests. Then he uttered a sentence which stuck in my mind indelibly:

When an old man dies in one of our villages a whole library disappears.

That sentence more than any other took me to UNESCO.

I stayed longer than I had originally intended because I became engrossed and because an ADG needs time to become effective. So we stayed five years and a bit.

I have written this book for two main reasons: first, because the whole experience seemed at the time and still seems quite remarkable and I wanted to see whether I could make sense of it; second, because UNESCO is scarcely thought of in the developed world today and that is a mistake which I would like to help amend. The United Nations system as a whole does not get a good press nowadays. UNESCO more than any other Agency is likely, if it receives any attention at all, to be treated with amused scorn— rather as the Arts Council is treated by the popular press in Britain. That is inevitable: UNESCO is pre-eminently the Agency with intellectual and ethical aims and that has made it, even when it has performed well, a sitting target.

All this is a pity because, though UNESCO has many failings and I don't propose to spare them, it is still important and worthwhile overall. It seemed to me that I could best try to show this not by writing a history or a comprehensive survey of its work but by drawing directly on my own experiences, analysing them and from there moving out into general judgments. This is UNESCO seen from within and near the top of the Secretariat tree and from the heart of its world-wide operations, from that extraordinarily conglomerate Headquarters building just opposite the École Militaire and facing the Place Fontenoy.

The building itself is worth more than a simple mention. It is a sort of Coventry Cathedral among UN Buildings, the one to whose public areas all the continents of the world contributed some of their best-regarded artistry. All these parts are making one great assertion, in addition to the national pride each expresses: that the nations of the world can come together in homage to the idea of intellectual and artistic excellence. As a result, if the delegates pour out of one of the vast and beautiful halls after a debate marked by little vision and much politicking, they look even more stunted by comparison with the high demands of the architecture. In general the building works well in its public areas; they are alive and animated. The great high-windowed main lobby is the intellectual Clapham Junction of the world. Stay there long enough and you will see an unparalleled cross-section of the world's scientists, artists and scholars; and always there are members of the Secretariat threading their way through with the obligatory bunch of documents and preoccupied air.

It is a Y-shaped building, with virtually uniform Secretariat offices piled six storeys high along each arm. For them, the building does not work so well; its shape divides and stratifies an already divided and over-hierarchical administrative structure. By now the Organisation has spread into other large buildings, some up to half a mile away. But it is the original building and its immediate associates which deservedly have a page to themselves in the Michelin guide to Paris and which bring the tourist groups—to see Nervi's soaring main conference hall or the building just outside it which is wholly submerged but light, since it makes inverted use of the principle of the mediaeval cloister and receives its light from a great sunken inner quadrangle open to the sky.

Between two and three thousand members of the Secretariat work at Headquarters; at any one time roughly as many more are scattered about the world pursuing UNESCO's work, promoting education, the natural sciences, cultural and artistic development, modern communications. The Headquarters mail rooms are packed daily with letters and packets from and to all corners of the world; there are diplomatic bags being made up for dispatch to a range of capital cities on a regular schedule; but most graphic of all is the Telex room at 8 in the morning. Since someone somewhere is actually at work for UNESCO every single hour of every day in every year, the Telex machines chatter unattended through the night. When the operators arrive each morning they are likely to find that the continuous rolls of messages have crept down the face of the machine and along the floor.

In my day there were people of about one hundred different nationalities within the Secretariat, which meant that all but thirty or forty Member States were represented there. Each staff member must be able to cope with the two 'working languages', French and English. That is, they must be fluent in one and able to understand the other without interpretation or translation. So UNESCO's internal meetings are almost always bi-lingual; you use the language you are more effective in, but must be able to follow the other. Clearly, this is a harder task for those, the majority, whose native language is neither French nor English. Perhaps this is one of the reasons for the over-representation of France and Britain within the Secretariat, though other reasons—such as the heavily Western European influences on the Organisation at its start— count for more.

Someone should write an essay on the influence of different capital cities on the international organisations established in them. During the whole time I was there UNESCO's executive style was unmistakably French; so much so that one could fancy it had crept up through the floors from the very soil of Paris itself, or along from the nearby Quai d'Orsay. There were two good reasons, one from the bottom and one from the top. The host country provides virtually all of the general servicing personnel—those outside national quotas, the commissionaires, waitresses, security men and the like—and they set the tone at ground level. For instance, the commissionaires' deference for rank was overt to a degree that has not been common in Britain for fifty years. Second, throughout my time the Director General was French and one who represented a distinctive French style within a particularly ambitious personality—driving, tense, aggressive, emotionally super-charged, as likely to blow up violently as to show extreme tenderness, a strange mixture of the great functionary trained by one of the Grandes Écoles and the south-western village boy who had made good by sheer force of brains and drive.

The Director General is very much at the apex of a pyramid and can, if he chooses, run the place with very little consultation, let alone democratic participation. He has his top Board of Management composed of himself, his immediate deputy and the five or six Assistant Directors General; but he may go weeks without calling a Board meeting. In my time four of the six ADGs divided the work of the Organisation between them, not by geography but by subjects, so that each had a world-wide parish in his own areas of work. The fifth ADG looked after all administrative matters; and the sixth handled planning.

So this was my job: to see that a part of the already approved programme was properly carried out, to plan the next programme and to represent the Organisation in my fields of work in Paris or anywhere else in the world, if needed. By the time I arrived the Organisation had a variety of well-established methods for executing its projects: publications, seminars, missions by experts, establishing international or regional institutes, pilot studies in the field, contracts with Member nations or individuals, and so on.

A 'programme' ADG, as they are called, is in a push-pull position, right in the middle of the main pressures. Month by month, and year by year, he is forwarding the execution of the programme, is deeply involved in that and in the personalities of the staff—the dozen or so Directors, the much larger number of programme officers, the secretarial staff—who make up what is known as his Sector. He is probably housed in the middle of the accommodation his Sector occupies. Day by day he is asked for intellectual, administrative and straight human guidance. He soon learns that he needs to support and defend his Sector against pre-dators from outside. He must be ready, if absolutely necessary, to fight the Director General if he thinks his programme is being ill-served. Equally, he must insist that his staff carry out loyally the directives of the Director General, that the programme plans are honoured in the right way, and that so far as ever possible they go along with him psychologically.

But he is also a member of the top Board of Management and so has considerable larger political responsibilities. If he goes into meetings of the Board simply as a spokesman for his Sector he is not meeting the demands of the job. Nor, no matter how intellec-tually demanding his Sector's work may be, can he run it as might, say, the scholarly head of a large University department who tells 'the administration' that he wants no interference from or time-wasting involvement with them, and that all he does want is the money to get on with his programme. A programme ADG must understand the larger political context of the Organisation, must learn how to measure political pressures and how best to execute his programme in the light of or in spite of them.

So the job is full of tensions and paradoxes. But that is UNESCO's character in general; until I began to write this book I had not realised how far paradoxes of all kinds lie at the heart of the place. For me, the tensions were increased because my brief included some of the most politically hot and intellectually tricky issues with which UNESCO is concerned: among other matters, I had responsibilities towards UNESCO's work in philosophy (a remarkably divisive subject), the social sciences, 'culture' in both the Arts Council and the Ancient Monuments senses, the environment, human rights, racism, 'Peace', population and drugs. I had little to do with the 'operational' side; my colleagues in charge of activities in education and in the natural sciences were much more concerned with such projects. But I had the biggest single clutch of intellectual and political briefs.

It is plain that programme ADGs are very lucky. They have a great range of projects to be responsible for, projects which, unless they have themselves been badly chosen, will interest them very much indeed. In spite of all the stresses of the job I never stopped being surprised and pleased that I was involved in such a range of interesting work on a world scale and with colleagues some of whom were quite the best I had ever worked with. Nor did the fact that intellectual issues were made even more complicated by political pressures make for more than intermittent discouragement. Working at those frontiers brought home forcibly that the foundations which the ideals of objectivity and intellectual freedom occupy across the world are slight and tenuous; and all the more important for that.

So the job was continuously engrossing. When I was wondering whether or not to accept the job if it were offered, I had lunch with an Englishman who had spent half a dozen years in UNESCO. He said: 'Go, yes, for a few years. You will be taxed enormously, frustrated and challenged from all angles, especially if you insist on trying to improve its performance. But you'll never be the same again after working there.' He was right, but it is not easy to sum up just what the experience meant or what it gave. Sometimes it comes to me in pictures, pictures which recall the human misery, endurance and courage which we saw spread right across the globe. I remember a group of tiny, pinched, dispossessed young

Indian mothers (perhaps descendants of the Inca empire) standing at the trackside on the vast, bare, majestic altiplano of Peru, way above Cuzco, begging us for a few cents—with eyes that glowed with resentment and anxiety; or a group of Afghan nomads in the wilds above Bamyan—they were begging too, but for aspirins; or a slim chambermaid in an Asian capital who offered to go to bed with the official who was accompanying us and who, when he refused, said she would be willing to show herself naked to him for a shilling; or a group of farmworkers who had—quietly, carefully and because they saw no alternative—taken over a farmstead in Southern Chile in Allende's day. They chose a spokesman who explained their case with great dignity and patent honesty; they had acted when they realised that the owners were preparing to sell the basic farm machinery on which the livelihoods of the men depended and to quit the country. So I gained—and here I have to tread carefully between the clichés about internationalism—a greatly increased sense of the sheer variety of human ways of life and in particular of the many different kinds of strength and resilience people can show. Within that, if it can be winnowed out, is the beginning of a genuine sort of universalism, a sense of common brotherhood.

The air in UNESCO was of its nature heady. One had, simply, to try to think of almost the whole world almost all the time. Back here in England, where I enjoy working and even, in one sense, enjoy the insularity, I still sometimes miss that ever-present sense, sitting at a desk in Paris, that my constituency was world-wide—of wondering what Asia would make of this proposal, whether North America could be persuaded to become involved, how far it would help Latin America, what the attitude of the Eastern European group would be, how it would look to African eyes. In such a perspective, Western Europe is only one element and its attitudes as open to question as those of any other area; and the United Kingdom looks very small and often rather parochial. Above all, I was given an enhanced sense of the struggle of what is euphemistically called 'the developing world'. 'Undeveloped' or 'under-developed' would be more accurate, but neither word is acceptable to the United Nations today. That world too will never go away, out of my consciousness, from now on. No other atmosphere can quite match this at its best, with its sense of operating on a world scale and of being constantly presented with new problems in your field unique in their size and complexity. I found it so absorbing that I almost entirely ceased to think of those aspects of British life with which I had before been very heavily involved.

Finally, in this summary of gains and losses, there was the profound culture shock on a provincial. The experience as a whole exposed and changed me in ways I still only partly understand. It so stretched me that I discovered both strengths I had not suspected, and weaknesses I would never have known about if I hadn't been put to so extreme a test. I hated some of it, but loved more. We came back to England of our own volition and sought no extension; but we do not regret any of the time there.

Debates about UNESCO's value and its weaknesses are endemic to the Organisation; they began when it began, over thirty years ago, and will go on as long as the institution lasts. The burden of this book is that, in spite of all the weaknesses which I describe, UNESCO is still an immensely valuable organisation. I believe it is a sick organisation at present, for a number of reasons which involve all those concerned with it—Member States, the international non-governmental organisations, the world intellectual community as a whole and the Secretariat. I will try to define the sickness and at the same time to indicate UNESCO's value, though in senses not always invoked when justifications are being made.

ii

If 'peoples speak to peoples' this communication must finally include debate on the ultimate issues of life and not meaningless agreement on shallow generalities about the unity of mankind.[1]

UNESCO is a senior member of what is known to the professionals, as the United Nations 'family'. It is by now a sprawling and diverse family and its members' Headquarters can be found in many capital cities. The core, the most important group, is that

1. Reinhold Niebuhr on UNESCO: 'Peace Through Cultural Co-operation', in *Christianity and Crisis*, October 17, 1949.

composed of UN Headquarters in New York (where the General Assembly and the Security Council sit) together with what are generally called the main Specialised Agencies—the International Labour Organisation, the World Health Organisation, the Food and Agriculture Organisation and UNESCO. It is a more loosely-knit family than most outsiders assume. Each Agency has its own Constitution, its own members (there are small but significant differences between the memberships), its own budget drawn directly from its Member States, and so a high degree of autonomy. At meetings of Heads of Agencies the Secretary-General of the UN itself takes the chair; but he is seen as *primus inter pares*. Nor does a Resolution of the UN command a Specialised Agency to undertake any particular task. On the other hand, a UN Resolution urging or asking an Agency to do something is normally acceded to; and UNESCO's constitution specifically enjoins 'effective coopera-tion' with the UN Organisation. Though each member of the family is jealous of its territory and its rights, they are all likely to act as one against threats from outside, or on matters concerning Secretariat status and privileges, or in cases of simple need. One late afternoon my wife and I were flying with three colleagues in a small plane I had hired so as to visit a UNESCO-financed museo-logists' training centre in the Jos Highlands of Nigeria. About a hundred miles short of Lagos on the return leg one of the two engines failed. We managed to glide into the small airfield at Ibadan and there we might have been stuck for hours and probably missed our international flight out of Lagos at six the following morning. But the UNESCO representative for Nigeria, who was with us, remembered that there was a WHO team working in Ibadan and still another Agency also doing something in that town. He made a couple of phone calls and very soon we were picked up, taken to the home of WHO's Head of Project for something to eat and drink and packed into two UN cars for the longish difficult drive to Lagos.

UNESCO was born in Great Britain and the British were very prominent in its conception and birth. The Founding Conference took place in November 1945, at Church House, Westminster. The Constitution could only come into force, however, when twenty Member States had joined; that position was reached in November 1946, so that is the effective starting date of the Organisa-tion. It had had two main godfathers, but godfathers of such different kinds that one may see them as symbolic foreshadowers of the main continuing tensions within the Organisation.

UNESCO's own Founding Conference had been preceded during the war-years by a succession of conferences of Allied Ministers of Education, held in London and including the Ministers of governments in exile in Britain. The stress there was on educational reconstruction, especially within those countries which would at the war's end be liberated from German occupation. Naturally, the Ministers thought expressly in governmental and intergovernmental terms. But their debate widened as it lengthened and took in all the time new strands of thought, especially from the pre-war thinking of a Paris-based body called the International Institute for Intellectual Cooperation, and so arrived eventually at the concept of a UNECO—a United Nations Agency for Education and Culture. The case had been strongly made that thought about educational development would be thin if it did not take cultural issues into account. It took yet more argument for the 'S', for Science, to be added.

The second godfather is the International Institute for Intellectual Cooperation in its own right. It had started after the First World War and was associated with the League of Nations. It was a remarkable forerunner of UNESCO in both general and particular matters. Two of its more important structural inventions, both of which UNESCO took over, were the development of International Non-governmental Organisations and the idea of National Commissions charged with forwarding the Institute's work in their own countries. More detailed initiatives include the encouragement of international cultural and intellectual exchanges, wider cooperation in promoting the natural sciences, the devising of a code of archaeological practice and of a convention on copyright, and the revision of historical textbooks so as to make them less chauvinistic. So the Institute was an impressive body, most of all because it drew on outstanding intellectuals from all over the world; very eminent men indeed, many more than would be found regularly working for UNESCO today. But it was inherently an isolated body in the sense that it did not have organic working relationships with governments severally or grouped.

Hence, at UNESCO's founding two conflicting types of Organisation were proposed. One would have been rather like the Institute: a very high-level forum for objective international intellectual exchanges, as free as possible from political considerations and pressures. The other would be precisely an intergovernmental Agency; that is, one funded by member governments. The main arguments for and against each form can be simply recited. The first body could more easily retain its intellectual eminence, objectivity and independence; but the cost would be small size and isolation—smallness because governments would finance it only grudgingly, isolation because it would be regarded as marginal by those who wield authority and make major public decisions. It would be condemned to a life on the sidelines, to an obscure if elegant sterility. That had indeed been the fate of the Institute itself, as Roger Caillois noted in a speech at the burial of UNESCO's René Maheu, in December 1975:

> At the beginning UNESCO still set great store by the International Institute for Intellectual Cooperation, of which it was the heir. But that was not so much an effective agency as a society of mutual spirits whose members included such personalities as Salvador de Madariaga, Paul Valéry, Albert Einstein, Sigmund Freud and many others. They held impressive dialogues with one another, a very elevated correspondence, but neither activity had much hold on the reality of affairs.

The second type of organisation, the intergovernmental, would run the constant risk of being made the tool of governments, individually or in blocs. On the other hand, it would be likely to have a budget big enough for much useful activity. It would be organically involved with policy makers in work on some important issues. It would, in its involvement with, say, problems of population or human rights or the environment be in a very difficult but worthwhile middle position. It would be like a junction-box connecting and making currents pass along two powerful wires, one running to and from governments, the other to and from the best intellectual and scientific opinion. It would try to bring those opinions to bear on problems which had more than national implications, would present them freely and honestly, in spite of the unwillingness of governments sometimes to face knowledge which runs against their preconceptions, current expediencies or ideologies.

At the Founding Conference the French argued for an organisation which would combine the best of both the above types, with a tripartite supreme governing body: governments, National Commissions and International Non-Governmental Organisations. It is an attractive idea and greatly to the credit of the French participants that they had thought so far into the likely difficulties of a world intellectual organisation and tried to find a structure to resolve or at least reduce them. But in the end it was an organisation basically of the second kind described above which was created: an intergovernmental agency governed by a corporate conference of Member States. Yet it also has some characteristics of the first type of body, some built-in checks and balance not found in more simply functional intergovernmental agencies—notably the network of National Commissions and the body of International Non-Governmental Organisations.

All large institutions, and especially those with more than quantitative purposes, evolve their own languages-to-live-by. UNESCO's original bannerhead phrase, which has all the resounding opacity of such phrases at their most dense (it is the UN's equivalent of the poetry-lover's 'Beauty is truth, truth beauty—that is all ye know on earth, and all ye need to know'), was drafted by Francis Williams and first uttered by Clement Attlee at the Founding Conference and then, modified by Archibald MacLeish, found its way into the Preamble to the Constitution, from which secure eminence it has haunted, inspired or befuddled UNESCO's councils ever since:

> Since wars begin in the minds of men, it is in the minds of men that the defences of peace must be constructed.

The extraordinary assertions within UNESCO's Constitution—that governments will collectively promote the objective pursuit of knowledge and its free circulation—are redolent of their time. The world had just come through a terrible and protracted war, one initiated by false philosophies working on ignorance through massive control of free speech. The impulse, in 1945, to try to ensure that it did not happen again, and that people should *understand* each other better through improved education and all forms of cultural and scientific exchanges, the passionate emphasis on truth, justice, peace and the importance of the individual—these impulses were almost irresistible. Nor was the atmosphere sombre: someone who was present in Church House has told me that the

mood was heady, confident that a new style in international relations really could be learned. It is always easy to laugh, thirty or
so years later, at the difference between founding ideals and present
reality. But no organisation is wrong to aim high at the start, and
UNESCO aimed very high indeed. Reading Julian Huxley,
Jacques Maritain, Torres Bodet, Reinhold Niebuhr or Archibald
MacLeish today is not an amusing but a corrective experience.
They were not vague and rhetorical; they cared for the life of the
mind and for intellectual freedom, and worked hard and precisely
to further those aims.

Of course, disputes set in early; no organisation could continue
in a state of such euphoria. Just as predictably, the first disputes
were about cash, the size of the proposed budget. Those continue
and have been joined by other sources of dissent. All this is
unavoidable and natural to the Organisation. The overriding
question, which will run throughout this book, is at what point
such tensions make the Organisation unable to fulfil its purposes
and, if that point seems near, how one corrects the situation.

The overall shape of the Organisation is simply described. One
can isolate three main groups of interests. First, the Member
States who provide the funds and want to know they are getting
value for money. The pattern of control is basically simple. Every
two years the supreme governing body of the Organisation—the
General Conference of Member States—meets for five or six
weeks, scrutinises the work of the past two years, studies a proposed
programme and budget for the next two years, amends and then
approves them. This is known as the Regular Programme and
Budget. It is nowadays matched, or more than matched, by work
carried out with extra-budgetary funds, under contract; for
instance, from the United Nations Development Programme.

Between General Conferences, Member States have both
individual and corporate arrangements for keeping track of the
Organisation's performance; individually, through their own
Permanent Delegates to UNESCO; corporately, through the
Executive Board, which now numbers forty-five important or
distinguished people drawn from all parts of the globe. The Board
meets approximately every six months for a couple of weeks or so
and thus provides fairly continuous monitoring of the Secretariat's
execution of the programme.

The Secretariat had best be mentioned next, since they at least symbolically inhabit the space between the two other main groups. Their job is to carry out the approved programme and at the same time prepare its successor for submission to the next General Conference. They are of two main kinds, the Professional grades and the General Service grades. The General Service personnel include everyone from the newest messenger to the very highest Personal Secretary. The bulk of the Professional grade is made up of people who are classed as P1's up to P5's. P1's are usually on some sort of probation; by the time a staff member has reached P3 he will usually begin to devote a lot of time to thinking about the next promotion, and when that comes the desire to 'make my P5' is quite likely to become preoccupying. Above that point, and often recruited directly from outside, are two levels of Director, D1 and D2. That is where the career grades, properly so called, end: above, there is only the top Board of Management, the seven or eight full-time officials chaired by the Director General and comprising his immediate Deputy and the five or six Assistant Directors General. These, then, are the day-by-day workers in the Organisation.

The third group of interests are, or should be, not formally governmental; they should represent the international community's free intellectual and scientific interest in UNESCO. They comprise, first, the National Commissions, which began life as UNESCO's National Cooperating Bodies, and should contain the best minds in their countries in UNESCO's fields of interest. Then there are the International Non-Governmental Organisations, the professional bodies which bring together specialists in an enormously wide range of disciplines. In addition, there is an enormous number of experts and consultants whom UNESCO employs year by year, on contracts of very varying lengths, to help execute its work. These last do not in themselves form a coherent community since they do not meet corporately; but they ensure that at any one period right across the world there are many individuals capable of making an informed judgment on UNESCO's performance. Finally, there is general world opinion as expressed through United Nation's Associations, UNESCO clubs, press coverage and the like; but this is the weakest link of all at present.

From all the above, it is possible to construct a fairly simple organisational model; essentially, it is a pattern of scrutinies. At

its centre is the Secretariat, executing the Programme at Headquarters and in the Field. In doing so, it is scrutinised from
several directions at once: by the corporate Member States
through the Biennial General Conference and the Executive
Board; by the Permanent Delegates on the spot in Paris on behalf
of their individual States; by the National Commissions with a
double perspective—as people making free intellectual judgments
and as advisers to the governments which appoint them; by the
NGO's as custodians of specialist and professional interests in a
world context and, finally, by the great range of experts and consultants who also are guardians of intellectual and scientific
standards. Such a model would, then, look something like this:

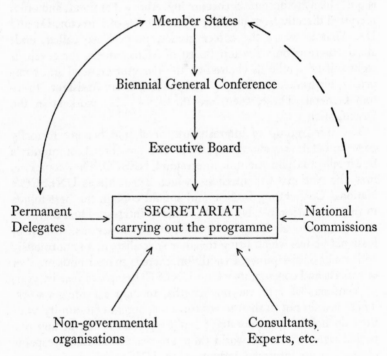

2

INDISPUTABLY USEFUL
ACTIVITIES

It may be helpful, since the developed world knows so little of what UNESCO does, to run through at this point a number of its activities which are plainly useful, which would need doing even if UNESCO itself did not exist.

For a number of substantial reasons, the developing world knows more about UNESCO and respects it more than the developed world. Of these, the prime reason is that UNESCO is from one angle a development agency, that it has money to give either from its Regular Programme or as an agent for UNDP and other aid organisations. Of course, some governments tend to see UNESCO as almost wholly a milch-cow; but in general their attitudes are more respectable and more qualified than that. The 'operational' work of UNESCO, as it is called, effectively came into being about 1960, with the appearance of so many new and formerly colonised nations, especially in Africa and Asia. It was a resolution of the United Kingdom, introduced by a speech of David Eccles, then Minister of Education, which called on the Organisation to set its course much more firmly towards developmental aid, especially for education. UNESCO's main development work is still in that area, in establishing schools, training colleges, technical institutes, schemes for women's education or—largest of all—in mounting elaborate long-term schemes to combat illiteracy. On a smaller scale, much the same could be said about initiatives to develop the pure and applied sciences in the under-developed world, or to establish modern communications systems.

By now there are several networks or near networks of training centres, each of which makes a considerable contribution to its region and which collectively form strong cooperative bonds in their respective disciplines right round the globe. My own responsibilities—and the ADG for Education could have multiplied such a list—included a network of archaeological and museum training centres, a smaller group for the development of the pure and applied social sciences as well as a scatter of centres in other disciplines such as development administration. If necessary, each centre has a different emphasis according to the nature or needs of its region. Thus, of the centres for museological training the one at Chirobusco near Mexico City concentrated on the special needs of Latin America whilst that at Jos in the Nigerian Highlands concentrated on conservation in hot and humid climates. That network is not yet complete but most of its parts are in good working order. Its central spindle is the Rome Centre, a fully intergovernmental, international centre for training in the pre-servation and restoration of 'material cultural property'—stones, woods, fabrics. To obtain a bursary to the Rome Centre is the highest achievement to which a young professional in most countries can aspire. It was steered through its first decade, to the point at which it achieved virtual financial and administrative autonomy from UNESCO, by a former official of the British Museum.

Less tangible but not less important is all the work done, especially in or on behalf of new or developing countries, in the general area of 'culture' where that word is used in its anthro-pological sense: work on the meaning of cultural diversity, on the needs and rights of minorities, and on the pressures on oral cul-tures today. Here UNESCO's record, given the smallness of its budget, is very respectable indeed, whether in long-term projects such as that on mutual understanding between East and West or in the long-haul project on the *History of Africa* (the first such enterprise of that scope and one largely written by Africans, to very severe international criteria) or in its less dramatic but quietly continuing work on such matters as encouraging agreements to winnow loaded history from school and college textbooks. These kinds of thing are unlikely to be undertaken by any national uni-versity or Foreign Ministry. And so one could go on, with list after list.

It will be seen that, since most of UNESCO's budget and most of the funds it receives under contract for development work comes from the rich countries and is spent in the poor, it is for much of the time engaged in a Robin Hood act. This is all perfectly clear when you are inside the Organisation and much less ambiguous than many other matters on which it is engaged. The main dispute, and it is a quite strong and continuing dispute, about the justification for UNESCO's aid to development is not so much internal as external, and comes from the Member States. It is the argument about the relative merits of international aid such as UNESCO provides and bilateral aid, from one State to another.

It is good that the developed nations have over the last few decades recognised something of their economic responsibilities towards the developing nations, even though the recognition is not yet thorough enough: and they do tend to have things very much their own way since they are, through one channel or another, the providers of almost all such funds. It is certainly true that the Agencies themselves are not backward in making claims for the value of their own contributions to aid. But they know how hard they have to press to keep up some flow into international rather than bilateral channels. The developed nations put money into UNDP; but the amounts they put into bilateral aid almost always thoroughly dwarf their international contributions. They usually justify this on the grounds that the UN Agencies are neither as professionally effective nor as economical as they are, especially since they have Civil Services used to scrutinising expenditure tightly; and there may be something in this. But the issue has not yet been fully proved either way. What can be said with confidence is that national States simply do not like their money being spent outside their own jurisdiction, that they are sometimes jealous of the Agencies and accuse them of wastefulness on little evidence, and that the distribution of their own bilateral aid to development is often inspired by a narrow sense of national self-interest, that their impulses include a mixture of neo-colonialism and the hard-headedness of a competitive chain-store operator distributing to the provinces from his London base. No wonder Andrew Shonfield could say at the start of the sixties that countries naturally prefer to spend most of their money bilaterally and that they will go on ensuring that the amount of their money spent by international agencies is smaller.[1] That is still true today.

But there is another side to the account. The Agencies can claim that their aid is free from the suspicion of neo-colonialism, that they are not wooing the States within which they work so as to keep them within a particular political orbit or to bind them by, for example, providing sophisticated equipment copyrighted in the country offering the aid and not compatible with equipment

1. See A. Shonfield, *The Attack on World Poverty*, London, 1960.

available from elsewhere; that the Agencies are not, therefore, as suspect to the receivers of aid as are national providers of bilateral aid and that—much as the more highly-developed countries might not wish to admit it—the Agencies can on occasion draw upon a wider range of skills from all over the world than can almost any single nation.

Probably the best known of UNESCO's forms of good work, and certainly the one which it has itself done most to publicise, is the enlisting of international support to save some of the world's greatest cultural monuments when these are threatened with destruction or simply collapse. Wealthy countries can usually afford to care for their own great monuments; but some of the most impressive and hitherto least known monuments are in countries which can hardly afford to educate their people or build roads and so have neither the money nor the skilled battalions to do such jobs. Hence UNESCO's great appeals for funds over the last fifteen or twenty years to what it always calls 'the international community' so that some huge monument to a faith or a long-dead dynasty may be put into reasonable shape. It was the fourth Director General, the Italian Vittorio Veronese, who at the turn into the sixties inspired the first of these great 'cultural campaigns', that intended to save the monuments of Nubia. It was Veronese's successor, Maheu, who pushed that and other campaigns through unceasingly. Nubia is still the greatest of them all by its sheer scope and boldness. The whole region, with its temples and villages and towns, was to be submerged by the waters building up behind the High Dam. Within that area the greatest single monument was the Temple of Abu Simbel; most of the literate world knows how that Temple was hewn out of the solid rock and re-established hundreds of feet higher, away from the maximum water line, in a spot landscaped to look just like its original site. That cost tens of millions of dollars, so complex were the engineering operations involved. But this was only the most striking part of a most elaborate set of political and logistic operations which involved, for instance, nations literally taking the smaller temples from just ahead of the rising waters and rebuilding them in their own capitals, where one can see them, looking slightly startling, today. The last great operation in this long campaign is that which has pumped dry the Island of Philae, right at the bottom end of the dam system, lifted its multiple temples and re-established them, looking virtually as they were before, on a nearby promontory well above water level. So most of the objects of major value have been saved. What has been lost is a country, a region: Nubia, with its own styles of life and rhythms; and that could neither be saved nor replaced. You have only to go way up the Nile into the high desert and look across that vast new Lake Nasser, whose farther shores you cannot see, and which stretches for tens of miles along what was the Nile bed, to recollect that for centuries a coherent culture existed under those waters—and you feel with unforgettable force what the clash of traditional 'backward' cultures with modern technological needs means, what it costs. Perhaps the Nasser Dam had to be built, so that the standard of living of Egypt's millions should improve, if that will really be the outcome. But, to repeat, let us recognise what was destroyed in the process: Nubia and the Nubians as a people in their own right—a land and a people which have haunted British explorers—exist no more. What UNESCO brought about cost a fortune but could not touch these other issues; still, it was well worth doing. The Nubian campaign, then, can stand for the others UNESCO has mounted, the other monuments and sites it has saved or is trying to save: Borobodur, Bamyan, Carthage, Kathmandu, Mohenjodoro, Venice, the Acropolis.

UNESCO is also a world resource centre, a complex of information banks, a set of clearing houses—to use the language of modern information services. On a scale no other institution can quite match (except for some national institutions within the two major powers, and they do not quite have UNESCO's catholicity) it collects facts from all over the world, in all aspects of what it calls its 'areas of competence'. It sets out to standardise those facts so that they are uniformly and internationally available; it then circulates them, and thus keeps in motion a great swirl of publications—statistical abstracts, up-dated annual year-books, periodic returns, comparative statistics—and a seemingly endless succession of scholarly meetings where this information is analysed, interpreted in new ways and then set in motion across the world again. The great Assembly Halls on the ground floor in the Place de Fontenoy building are for the major governmental occasions and those are periodic; down below in six or seven smaller air-conditioned meeting rooms, week after week and year after year, the experts of the world bend their attention to the latest problems before their disciplines. UNESCO is a great market for the traffic of knowledge. I was tempted to say 'for the intellectual life', but that would be claiming too much. Such meetings tend to succeed best where they can be given a functional character; intelligence— very high intelligence, often—thrives in them rather than intellectuality, speculation.

That is why some of the more successful of UNESCO's long-term projects in sustained international cooperation have been in difficult but essentially practical areas, areas in which differing values, differing ideologies, did not have to come to the forefront. One might say, recalling the success of the great cultural campaigns, that UNESCO most easily succeeds where she can call upon either general gestures of common goodwill or precise agreement on practical needs. Hence such programmes as those in Oceanography, Hydrology, Man and the Biosphere, the Arid Zones, Seismology. I am not saying that these programmes can altogether steer clear of political issues, and some meet them quite heavily; but that kind of politics is hardly perceptible when compared with the political intensity of those programmes which cannot avoid a direct confrontation with differences in value-systems.

UNESCO is also important as a centre for international dialogue among experts of all kinds and also, to some degree, among intellectuals as such. This may at first seem a supererogatory function to intellectuals in the West and North America; any even moderately successful professional in these areas can enjoy all the dialogue he can cope with, through correspondence, through professional journals, through the stream of visiting specialists who pass through his university or institute all the time and through his own visits to conferences, seminars, colloquia at home or abroad. But his is, on a world view, an exceptionally favoured situation. In many other places neither the level of prosperity nor, therefore, the forces of the market will ensure such a generous level of exchange-facilities for intellectuals, scholars, scientists. The professionals in vast areas of Africa and Asia are often deeply isolated; individuals or small groups are scattered around subcontinents with literally hundreds of miles separating them from their nearest colleagues or the nearest adequate library, let alone from a computer or any other kind of adequate storage and retrieval system. It may be almost impossible, unless one's family is to be deprived, to buy the essential journals. In these circumstances quite simple arrangements can be life-lines, such as the UNESCO book coupons scheme. It provides hard-currency coupons for book purchases against soft currency provided by the scholar, so that books can be bought from, say, the United States. I had thought the scheme had died years ago, I supposed not long after it ceased to be needed by British scholars. That was insular and myopic; it is still greatly in demand and, if more funds were put into it, the demand would grow even further.

A different but no less important case can be made for UNESCO's work in improving professional debate between East and West Europe. There is no need to describe the obstacles to that debate. But UNESCO, simply because it is an international body in moderately good standing in Eastern Europe, can promote some exchanges which otherwise would not take place at all. These are very highly valued indeed by the Eastern European scholars lucky enough to be allowed to make use of them and especially by those from countries in the Western arc around the Soviet Union, such as Poland and Hungary. The Vienna Centre for Documentation and Research in the Social Sciences, which was established by UNESCO (the location was not an accident) and is now a free-standing international institution, was designed precisely to be an East/West meeting place, and it works well. Inevitably, it is much more valued by Eastern European scholars than by Western; in fact, some Western governments and some Western scholars make a habit of belittling it, rather as a well-fed man refuses a plain dish. But, as well as helping their colleagues in Eastern European countries, they could learn something at the Vienna Centre about ways of coping with their disciplines in other circumstances than their own. Of course, there are limits to what the Vienna Centre can undertake if it is to preserve the precarious balance between contributing Member States within which only it can live; but a lot of useful work can be done before those limits are reached, and its scholars themselves have learned to live right up on the frontiers.

I am deliberately understating this record of useful achievements, partly because UNESCO itself tends to make very large claims for them and, more important, because though they are undoubtedly valuable they are not either the most valuable or the most difficult things UNESCO is called upon to do. And, even in a particular general area, there are usually more and less difficult things to undertake. This is nowhere more evident than in

UNESCO's work in 'standard setting', establishing international norms. The hardest of all the Organisation's work is in inching towards norms on issues which cannot avoid bringing ideologies into play. Before that point is reached there is a great range of 'normative' work to be done of an extremely valuable kind, work scarcely known except in the professional circles to which particular Declarations, Recommendations or Conventions apply.

Those are the three main types of international instrument which UNESCO promotes and constantly offers for signature to her Member States; and they have varying degrees of force. A Declaration is an international statement of good intent; it is not signed and has no legal force. A Recommendation is also voluntary. It is likely to be more detailed and precise than a Declaration (which deals with large general issues). A Recommendation may, in detail, suggest how well-behaved Member States should set about preserving their ancient monuments; how they should distinguish between good preservation and deceptive reconstruction, and so on. It is a code of good practice and can have a lot of force if the specialists concerned in each country get together, probably through their international non-governmental organisation, to persuade each other and their governments to follow the Recommendation's precepts.

Governments do not greatly dislike Recommendations, since they do not have to be signed or formally adhered to; they give them room for manoeuvre and selective application. But Secretariat members and the experts in each discipline tend to prefer the third type of instrument, the Convention. A Convention is binding on the governments which sign it, once a number of ratifications have been received sufficient to bring the instrument into force. Then it has the force of international law; or should have. It is not surprising that governments tend to dislike Conventions. Federal governments particularly dislike them, since they have great difficulty in persuading their almost-autonomous Provinces or States to agree that the Federal body shall on their behalf sign away some of their freedom.

In addition to these three main forms, there are many kinds of other, more or less ad hoc, types of agreement and the range of subjects covered is remarkably wide. As I left UNESCO the number of instruments of various kinds which were being prepared was at a record level, and it grows biennium by biennium. To take only one of the areas with which I was concerned, that which has to do with 'the protection of cultural property'. Over twenty years, the instruments have included:

1954 Convention for the Protection of Cultural Property in the event of armed conflict.

1956 Recommendation on International Principles applicable to Archaeological Excavations.

1960 Recommendation concerning the most effective means of rendering museums accessible to everyone.

1962 Recommendation concerning the safeguarding of the beauty and character of landscapes and sites.

1964 Recommendation on the means of prohibiting and preventing the illicit export, import and transfer of ownership of cultural property.

1968 Recommendation concerning the preservation of cultural property endangered by public or private works.

1970 Convention on the means of prohibiting and preventing the illicit import, export and transfer of ownership of cultural property.

1972 Recommendation concerning the protection, at national level, of the cultural and natural heritage.

1972 Convention concerning the protection of the world cultural and natural heritage.

The 1976 General Conference alone adopted new instruments on adult education, the international exchange of cultural property, the safeguarding of historic areas, the legal protection and status of translators, and the standardisation of radio and television statistics. The Conference also adopted a Protocol to the Florence agreement of a quarter of a century ago, on duty-free entry to contracting States of a wide range of articles of an educational, scientific or cultural character; this brought the Agreement up-to-date by taking into account technical developments of the intervening years. Two contentious instruments were shelved for the time being. Approval was given for yet more instruments to be prepared, including one on scientific and technological statistics, one on the prevention and coverage of risks to 'movable cultural property' and one which would revise existing recommendations on educational statistics.

There are instruments against discrimination in education, on

balancing the international exchange of skilled workers, on preventing the double taxation of royalties, on the Universal Copyright
Convention and so on. The record is impressive if one takes it at
face value. When one examines how many Member States have
actually signed these instruments, how long it takes to bring most
Conventions into force, how often the instruments are flouted by
States which have signed them or at least publicly associated themselves with their sentiments, the record is less impressive. It then
sometimes looks more like an exercise in international public
relations than a genuine advance in world law. Sovereign States are
easily resentful. They are likely to resist, for example, the stipula-
tion that, if they have adhered to an international agreement, they
must report at each General Conference on their actions in response
to it; and they often renege on that requirement. It is no wonder
that many specialists in international relations are convinced of the
futility of all such instruments. Since they cannot be enforced it
would be better, the argument goes, not to bother going through
the motions; after all, it is the States themselves, whose delegations
agree to the creation of such instruments, who sign them, and then
subsequently violate them.[2] Similarly, some international lawyers—
again probably a majority—call for more 'realism', and describe
almost all such instruments as eyewash.[3]

I am not convinced, after seeing these strange exercises being
gone through for several years and very close up, that they are
quite so futile. I believe—just—in the slow growth and building
up of what has been called 'collective legitimisation'.[4] But the
question is posed at its hardest when one is considering instruments which bring into play differences of ideology. Instruments
of the sort I have just listed are, quite simply, relatively innocuous.
I will return to the harder aspects of 'collective legitimisation'
when discussing the kinds of instrument which touch UNESCO
on the very nerve of its Constitution, which involve questions of
objectivity, freedom and value-judgments. There the waters
become very much muddier than they have been so far.

2. See H. G. Nicholas, *The U.N. as a Political Institution*, London,
OUP 1959.
3. See Clive Parry, 'The International Civil Service', *The Listener*,
August 18, 1955, pp. 243–5.
4. See N. J. Padelford and Leland M. Goodrich, *The United Nations in
the Balance*, New York, Praeger, 1965, p. 479.

Nevertheless, these instruments and the other work I have described—all of it only indicative—adds up to a great deal of useful and almost unique international activity. But it would hardly justify those majestic halls on the Left Bank or the symbolic assertions they make in concrete and glass about the grandeur of the Constitution. That Constitution calls on the Organisation not only to do more but to *be* more. Similarly the people who serve it, the Secretariat, are by their oath required to be much more than faithful functionaries. It is when we get away from the comparatively bread-and-butter level of undisputed good works, when we reach the areas where politics and ideology predominate, that the Organisation and its servants meet their real tests.

3

TWO FINE FICTIONS

The basic fictitious notion about these Organisations . . .
(is) . . . that they are something more than their component
parts, something above the individual states.'[1]

Gunnar Myrdal might have gone further, especially since the
above passage occurs in a lecture about the role of the Secretariat,
and said that there are *two* basic fictitious notions about international organisations: not only that they are 'something more . . .'
than a congeries of Member States because they have Constitutions with purposes beyond national politics, but also that they
are supposed to be served by people who act, in their professional
lives, as neutral international civil servants rather than as 'nationals'
of particular States.

I imagine Myrdal was using the idea of fiction in its low sense,
to mean an easily-gratifying untruth. It can also mean a pointing-
towards a difficult but worthwhile ideal. More even than the rest
of the UN, UNESCO must live on the assumption that the two
fictions are not untruths but symbolic statements of what may be
sometimes achieved and is always to be worked for. In relation to
its own Constitution, UNESCO is like a well-meaning but physically ill-coordinated man who has been required to skate on thin
ice for a good cause. By brio alone he gets so far at great speed, and
then falls flat. He tries again but now someone throws a brick on
the ice and he falls through. He climbs out and tries again; and so
on.

i

The Constitution itself defines quite firmly the duties of the
Secretariat and of Member States towards them:

1. Gunnar Myrdal: *The International Organisations and the Role of
their Secretariats*. Lecture to The Institute of Public Administration of
Canada, Toronto, 1969.

The responsibilities of the Director-General and of the staff shall be exclusively international in character. In the discharge of their duties they shall not seek or receive instructions from any Government or from any authority alien to the Organisation. They shall refrain from any action which might prejudice their position as international officials. Each State Member of the Organisation undertakes to respect the international character of the responsibilities of the Director-General and the staff, and not to seek to influence them in the discharge of their duties.[2]

Twenty years later ICSAB, the International Civil Service Advisory Board, attempted even more exact descriptions:

Integrity, while perhaps not subject to exhaustive and precise definition, must be judged on the basis of the total behaviour of the person concerned. Such elementary personal or private qualities as honesty, truthfulness, fidelity, probity and freedom from corrupting influences, are clearly included. For the international official, however, the Charter also required integrity as a *public* official, and especially as an *international* public official.[3]

The basic idea and style of the international civil service owes most to the League of Nations and to Sir Eric Drummond (later Lord Perth), the League's first Secretary General. At the birth of the League there was, inevitably, argument about whether the Secretariat should be composed of nominees and representatives of Member States or of 'neutral' people. The second concept won and presumably the fair success of League practice helped persuade the UN to choose that system, and to appoint some former League servants. Years later, Hammarskjöld praised Drummond's strength of purpose.

Yet it is a very strange concept indeed, that the full-time officials serve, not their own nor any other State or group of States, but the 'idea' of the institution itself, the corporate body, the Constitution; and some intelligent people will have none of it. Conor Cruise O'Brien concluded from experience that it would be

2. Constitution, Art. VI–5. See Appendix.
3. (*Report on Standards of Conduct in the International Civil Service, 1954*, UN.N Intern. Civil Service Advisory Board. COORD/Civil Service/5. 1965 ed., para 4.)

preferable to be frank about the way in which many members of the Secretariat actually behaved; and to let them be explicitly representatives and consulters of their governments. Hammarskjöld, on the other hand, kept on trying to refine and improve the practice:

> While it may be true that no man is neutral in the sense that he is without opinion or ideals, it is just as true that in spite of this a neutral Secretariat is possible. Anyone of integrity, not subjected to undue pressures, can, regardless of his own views, readily act in an 'exclusively international' spirit and can be guided in his actions on behalf of the Organisation solely by its interests and principles, and by the instructions of its organs.[4]

Just as personal convictions can be a source of strength so long as they do not bring bias into professional judgments, so a firm rooting in one's own culture can be invaluable; the many different cultural backgrounds of Secretariat members can enrich the Organisation's work as a whole. If Secretariat members become progressively 'rootless cosmopolitans'—in the sense of having no colour, styles, attitudes, sources of imaginative response from their own backgrounds—they are then as empty and ineffectual as people who have never known personal convictions or the force of an idea.

Few States are enthusiastic about the idea of an international civil service, and their disbelief shows in three main ways. The first kind of response is cynical, unable to conceive that anyone can even intermittently act neutrally. Partly, this is because so many countries do not themselves expect neutral civil services. So this is not an ideological position; it is, rather, based on an assumed fact of life, a blank assurance that self-interest will always out, that in the end and sooner rather than later all such affairs come down to patronage. Hence it is assumed that posts in the Secretariat just as much as any other perks are to be spread among those who can bring influence to bear, that if there is an expert's contract available, Mr X in the Secretariat will remain loyal to his country, his friends, the home network. Since in most countries the people who are in line for positions such as these tend to be

4. Introduction to the Annual Report of the Secretary General for 1960–1, p. 6.

drawn from a small and privileged class, this whole tendency is intensified.

The second criticism is subtler, an instance of high national self-regard, and one finds it particularly in some new nations. The idea of a neutral civil service, it is argued, is a characteristic product of the Western or Northern hemispheres. It is a form of neo-colonialism, an attempt to mute the energies and unique cultural strengths of other nations by making everyone conform to a drab, neutralising, mechanical, ratiocinative Western style. The concept of a neutral civil service is certainly, as is the UN itself, a product of this hemisphere; its brief and practice do have distinct cultural origins. It would be difficult to know what other criteria or forms could be used to run such complex organisations; but those criteria will nevertheless be attacked on cultural grounds.

The third objection is plainly ideological. It was expressed most dramatically by Krushchev in 1961 at the UN, when he declared that there are 'no neutral men'. No doubt he was helped towards this view by the knowledge that the USA and Western Europe had concerted to keep Soviet citizens out of sensitive posts. The phrase can have two meanings: that Secretariat members will inevitably be working consciously for their governments; and, more subtly, that in spite of all their efforts at objectivity every staff member—including Sir Eric Drummond and Dag Hammarskjöld—will be so deeply conditioned by their cultures that they will simply not be able to be unbiased. Hence Krushchev's disabling—and rejected—proposal that the Secretary Generalship should be shared by a troika, three men representing the main political regions of the world.

The Soviets do find it almost impossible to believe that a member of the Secretariat is not also a member of his national civil service, or at the least a dutiful mouthpiece and reporter. Once, the UK representative on the Executive Board tried to defend me, in a debate on a hot issue, against such an accusation and insisted that his government would never try to influence me; nor, if they had tried, did he think I would have been influenced. This was widely regarded as a rich example of British cunning; the only remaining question was whether the UK delegate had acted unprompted, or whether I was secretly so important a British official that I had ordered him to speak in that way.

It follows that almost all staff members from Communist

countries, and many from others, are ideologically wholly reliable. This means also that they are often dull, unimaginative, concerned chiefly to keep their noses clean so that, when they go home after three or four years, they will be in good standing. But if they are quite high up or well-connected they may have a degree of freedom denied to most. They can then be excellent colleagues so long as you both recognise the limits within which you work. They may sometimes be embarrassed by a silly national brief and will give you a wry look; and you must take care not to rub it in or invite them to join in a discussion. They can also be useful channels of communication with the powers back home. But if an official from such a country is lazy or face-saving it is best, once direct discussion with him has failed, to urge his delegation to send someone better, for their sake as much as UNESCO's; with time, the change will be made. It is better to act like this than to practise the old UN habit of freezing out certain staff members because they were known to be immediately passing on all confidential information; or to render them impotent by swamping them with pointless and unreadable documents.

The claims for fair 'geographical spread' within the Secretariat are the most difficult of all to assess fairly. Roughly, the system works as follows. Each Member State can claim a certain number of posts within the Organisation. That number is expressed as a 'range', by two figures. If the number of posts held by any State falls below the lower of its two figures, it is 'under-represented'; if it has more posts than the upper of the two figures, it is 'over-represented' and should mark time before having more staff members. Within the two figures, a State is said to be 'within range'. Each Member State's range is decided by its contribution to the Organisation's regular budget; and this in its turn is decided by a complex calculation in which, to omit all sorts of qualifications, the dominant factors are gross national product and size of population. Hence, the USA and the USSR pay very large dues and their ranges of available posts are high. The USA's payment and staff range are much higher than those of the Soviet Union since the USA has much the larger GNP. The most important weighting factor is GNP rather than population, and this rightly disturbs some analysts, even if they have no political axes to grind. To take a fairly random pair of nations, India and Belgium. In 1976, India paid 1·19 per cent of the Organisation's budget and had a staffing range from 6 to 10 (she actually had fourteen staff members). Belgium paid 1·04 per cent of the budget and her range was from 5 to 9 (she actually had fifteen staff members).

Few issues are as much argued over as this. The case in favour of a geographically-distributed staff includes such arguments as: that since the Organisation deals with issues which often must become political the staff should represent all main ideological, cultural and geographic forms, or it will be mistrusted and less able to work effectively; that the Organisation should for its own intellectual health represent as wide a range as possible of different cultural and intellectual approaches; that great prestige is involved, especially for some newer States, in having staff within the UN system, and this need should be honoured so that the largest possible number of States may be involved in and loyal to the system. To these arguments it is replied that smaller and newer nations do not yet have enough people trained to the level of executive competence needed at the UN; that their good men are needed at home, to help build their nations, rather than being lost within the UN system for several years at the least. To which it is, in turn, rejoined that a few years in UN service can give such talented people invaluable international, high level, executive experience; and that, even though the UN system's style is Western European, the best Secretariat members—once they have learned the methods—may have come from literally any part of the globe. This is true: the best staff members I worked with included Africans, Asians, Latin Americans, Arabs and Eastern Europeans. Certain nationalities do, it is true, seem at first sight to have been ordained by nature to provide exemplary international civil servants. Switzerland, for instance, has a particularly solid civil service tradition, no imperial past, a reputation for hard work and for achieving compromise and balance within a federal and linguistically-differentiated State. Still, in general, it is short-sighted to equate Secretariat ability with geography or history.

On the other hand, the case against geographical spread as it is at present practised is weighty. Some nations employ their staffing range as a useful form of patronage, or a convenient refuge for the otherwise unplaceable. It is harder for the Director General to resist the claims being made for the Minister's cousin, whom he knows to be lazy and corrupt, if the Minister's country is under-represented; harder still if the DG has promised to 'regularise' the under-representation as soon as possible but has already refused one or more earlier nominees: his options are narrowing all the time. Such elaborate formalities in making appointments through a series of complex manoeuvres not mainly connected with the needs of a particular job are probably common to the internal procedures of more States than not; so this is the way they will act, whatever an international Organisation's Regulations may say. Even the fairest and strongest-minded DG must sometimes feel that the strain is hardly worthwhile. The new nations never cease to complain that they are short of Secretariat members; they are right, since some other nations had a fifteen year start on them. Some of the original Member States, such as Britain and France, have been heavily over-represented for years; but this is not sinister—they are close to Paris and have lots of trained people available. Their governments tend to leave their nationals alone, so they stay if they like the work. Conversely, the USSR and most Eastern European states rotate their staff members at three to five year intervals. They are thus permanently under-represented, always half-emptying the pot about which they claim that it is never full. They will remain in that condition until either they or the Regulations change.

Other nations congenitally under-represented include some so prosperous or so far away, or both, that work in Paris attracts few: the USA, Japan and Western Germany fall in this category. Then there are habitually over-represented nations, among whom the most striking are some—such as Egypt and India—which are populous, under-developed economically but relatively highly-developed educationally. So they become exporters not of raw materials but of brains. They may badly need those brains at home, but they cannot find jobs for all of them or pay those in work more than a pittance. A vacancy for, say, an economist within UNESCO will usually bring more applications from Egypt and India than from all other nations; and the applicants will include some very good scholars indeed.

It was predictable that some Member States would sooner or later try to push 'geographical spread' down to lower levels, would argue that each sub-unit of the Organisation should represent the main divisions of the world. There is a valid point hidden here: a Department of Culture which was wholly Western European or wholly anything else, geographical or ideological, would be ill-balanced, and the Director-General must take care that does not happen. But this is different from arguing on national or bloc grounds—that is, merely politically—that geographical spread should as a general rule operate in horizontal layers right through the staffing structure.

Similar considerations apply on promotion. If France has not only far more members of the Secretariat than geographic spread would make reasonable, but also very many at Director level, then the DG must think twice about appointing more French citizens, and also about making more French Directors, whether by appointment from outside or by promotion from within. And French members of the Secretariat should, if regretfully, accept this limitation. But it can bear hard on a really good career international civil servant, especially if someone manifestly less competent is appointed over his head, whether from inside or outside, because he has a favourable nationality. Indeed, the whole matter of inside-or-outside recruitment is bound to be vexed. Recruitment from outside can bring new blood and more up-to-date specialisms; but it may block justifiable or even better-qualified promotions from within. Promotions from within, unless they are wantonly political, are popular with the staff, who then feel that after all there really is something not altogether nebulous about an international career civil service. But too much internal promotion would eventually produce an Organisation whose staff were chiefly devoted to maintaining the existing structure.

So the Director General must be continuously striking balances, trying to reach the best possible combination of compromises for furthering the Organisation's larger purposes. His job would be easier if Member States trusted him more and reduced their constant calls for almost immediately improved geographical distribution (no matter what the human cost to those displaced), and if the Staff Association (the professional union) took a less narrowly protectionist view. Neither of these changes of heart seems likely to come about soon.

But the greatest obstacle to the emergence of a secure and true international civil service is the 'clearance' system. Within that system the most inglorious procedure is that practised by the USA. Before any American can join the staff or even work temporarily for the UN, the 'advice' of the US government has to be sought; weeks pass, presumably whilst the FBI are making their enquiries, and then the message comes back that, in respect of 'X': 'a favourable (or unfavourable) advisory determination has been received'. The language is pure 1984; they mean that the applicant has or has not been politically cleared. The worst word is 'advisory'; they do not intend an 'unfavourable determination' to be advisory; they mean it to be at the least a fierce shot across the Organisation's bows and at the worst a clear order. It is, apologetic officials will tell you, a left-over, a remnant of McCarthyism enshrined in a US Executive Order dated 1953 which successive Presidents have been too busy to be able to annul. Apart from its inherent evil, it gives the USSR splendid grounds for rejecting any complaints about their own more rigid practices in relation to the Secretariat. That none of their nationals who are not approved by the government ever work for the UN or even leave Russia is well known; but those practices are not openly embodied in a governmental order.

But the American way is only the most egregious of clearance procedures, and matters do not generally improve. Over the years I was at UNESCO I saw the phenomenon of creeping clearance not only creep but begin to race ahead. By now it is for the Secretariat a very complicated business indeed to hire any expert, to remember which countries have explicit clearance procedures, which say they do not but really do, and exactly what different routines for clearance are practised by each Member State. This applies to many 'democratic' societies as well as to totalitarian, and to developed as to developing countries. The core of an independent and academically sound Secretariat has been progressively reduced by formal and informal clearance procedures; an increasing number of posts at all levels are being deliberately filled by government candidates who are in effect direct government representatives and sometimes spies. They are likely to represent the most conservative strands in their government's thinking; they are establishment men or party hacks. Increasingly, when posts are filled competence is not the primary requirement. This decline has been going on for years and seems to be intensifying.

The survivors of the early international civil service—and there are still some even at high levels—should challenge the process more than they do. At their age, they have little to lose; and they might shame some Member States, those who have lazily slid into clearance procedures but are not ideologically committed to them, into going back to a more liberal line. Whenever such a suggestion is made it is said that to inspire a full debate among Permanent Delegates or in the Executive Board or at the General Conference would do more harm than good, that it would show some States who have been dormant in the matter how far others have gone in increasing political control of their nationals and would inspire them to do likewise. But that is the classic argument of the fearful.

In spite of all I have said about weaknesses and obstacles, the idea and the practice of an independent international civil service survive in some people. Each year in which the concept survives and is honoured by some people is a year gained, so that it may eventually be put on an unshakeable footing. It took decades for the Member States of the UN to agree to establish an International Civil Service Commission; but it exists now and will be increasingly influential. The idea itself is so surprising, so much against nature to most government officials, and the practice of it so difficult even for devoted staff members, that it will clearly need decades to come into full being. The seventies have seen a decline in both the strength of the idea and the extent of its practice; but if enough people recognise this, the eighties could see the service move near maturity.

ii

The second fine fiction at the heart of UNESCO is contained in the Preamble to the Constitution itself:

> The States Parties to this Constitution, believing in full and equal opportunities for education for all, in the unrestricted pursuit of objective truth, and in the free exchange of ideas and knowledge, are agreed and determined to develop and to increase the means of communication between their peoples and to employ these means for the purposes of mutual understanding and a truer and more perfect knowledge of each other's lives.

So the Constitution has a double core: the free pursuit of objective truth and the free exchange of knowledge. Yet it is not in the nature of governments to believe in such things; they are more likely to find such ideas suspect and often embarrassing. At those moments their instinct is to clamp down, or wish they had the powers to clamp down. Most governments must regard UNESCO as small and unimportant, a tiny part of the complicated international jigsaw they study and try to fit nearer their own purposes each day. This highlights yet another of the working paradoxes of UNESCO in its relations to Member States. The Constitution calls for steady assent to two fixed principles. But governments habitually live pragmatically, by bargains, if necessary at the expense of objectivity and the free movement of ideas; they are professional relativists. In their foreign relations States habitually have particular purposes, immediate or long-term; they pursue those ends, singly or in blocs, purposively and pragmatically. They thus strive to see all outside elements as 'instruments' of their purposes, to take a word from R. W. Cox. But UNESCO is, in this driven, executive sense, purposeless; purposeless yet full of high ideals and not easily converted into a simple instrument. This is the meeting of oil and water. The Constitution makes a series of general assertions about the nature of and about duties towards the corporate body governments have together created; it aims to be morally inviolate, not the tool of anything outside. To work in UNESCO is sometimes to feel as though you live in an unprotected territory of boundless good intentions, pressed in from all sides by bodies with other, more practical, forceful and precise purposes.

These attitudes in most Foreign Ministries towards the one intellectual inter-governmental agency are not necessarily sinister. Foreign Ministries contain many fine intelligences but are not much given to free intellectual speculation. So they do not often feel the inwardness of what UNESCO was set up to achieve. The history of the social sciences in UNESCO shows that as well as anything. Social scientists are at one and the same time over- and under-valued. They are mistrusted as dismemberers of society and authority, their departments as breeding grounds for dissidents and revolutionaries—especially in parts of Latin America where, together with the Law Faculties, social scientists provided recruits for the radical movements. Almost no official loves a theoretical social scientist. On the other hand, the social sciences regarded as problem solvers are over-valued. They are cast as magicians or social plumbers, to be called in to fix whatever may be the latest social smell or leak, whether it be drugs or racism or teenage violence. If a State has already spent a great deal of money in tackling such problems, this is almost certainly an augury that it will propose a Resolution at UNESCO's next General Conference proposing that the Social Science Department economically solve the problem and report to the next General Conference.

To certain other countries the concepts of objectivity and the free movement of ideas as fundamental values are at best unintelligible and at worst a poor joke; and they have little intention of honouring them. They therefore restrict their interpretation of these concepts to the view that UNESCO has the duty to offer factual, neutral, technical knowledge for the benefit of individual governments, who will then each decide how far those offerings will be circulated. They do not include in their definitions the idea of freely-distributed political, religious or philosophical comment.

Other countries adopt an even stronger form of that position, because they have stronger ideologies. They do not even accept the idea of an agency which aims to keep the level of *direct* political intervention low so that useful work can be done. For them, the whole of life is political, cannot avoid being political and should be political. Thus there cannot be for them any 'objective' knowledge except in a narrowly material or 'natural sciences' sense. Nor do they recognise the right of the individual to free speculation and comment outside the approved orthodoxies; such a notion, which may seem to others the breath of life, seems to them an aberration. So they are likely to carry the ideological pattern into every aspect of UNESCO. In my own early days, for example, the Soviet Ambassador to UNESCO was Professor Sobakin, a very intelligent international lawyer and a man of great charm; you could deal directly with him so long as you recognised the stakes. Some members of the Secretariat, in that self-deluding way one can so easily fall into, used to express their appreciation of Sobakin by calling him 'really a Westerner': flexible, open, ironic. He was all those things, within the limits of a main drive which never wavered. The book he wrote about UNESCO after he left proves this: it is cogent, firm, well-argued, absolutely correct in its Marxist–Leninist stance.[5]

5. V. Sobakin, *L'UNESCO: Problèmes et Perspectives*, Moscow, Novosti.

Or consider the position of Soviet representatives at UNESCO meetings on issues which, for the West, are matters for intense speculation. Except for those who keep a dignified silence or merely read set pieces tonelessly, the tone most often adopted by Soviet delegates is strong assertion, as befits those who hurl the tablets of truth at a corrupt or weak outer world. Raymond Aron noted this characteristic as long ago as 1957:

> They have retained the right to indignation, but only at the expense of the capitalist world which they are not free to know objectively or to visit.[6]

All this points to what Dallin calls 'the Soviet Predicament at the UN: the problem of a State with a "two camp" world view trying to operate in a "one-world" organisation.'[7] In principle, that is certainly a predicament; in practice, the senior Soviet officials with whom I had to deal on UNESCO matters had accommodated themselves very well to their predicament and had even learned sometimes to make capital from it.

All in all, one of the strongest lessons to be learned at UNESCO is that very few governments respect the objective search for truth, free speculation or the integrity of the individual conscience; and that very few countries have those interlaced middle layers of critical comment which give a characteristic texture to societies which claim to be democratic. Perhaps one in six of all the nation states of the world has these qualities. Hence yet another of UNESCO's many paradoxes:

> Those responsible for the conduct of UNESCO affairs are faced by the paradox that they have to apply a constitution based on liberal principles in a world almost destitute of liberal governments.[8]

Two regulations make it even more difficult to fulfil the aims of the Constitution. One, in the directions on publishing, forbids any reference which might give offence to a Member State. This

6. Raymond Aron, *The Opium of the Intellectuals*, trans. T. Kilmartin, London, Secker and Warburg, 1957, p. 125.
7. Alexander Dallin, *The Soviet Union at the U.N.*, New York, Praeger, 1962.
8. A Loveday, *Reflections on International Administration*, Oxford, The Clarendon Press, 1956, p. 223.

regulation was removed by the 1976 General Conference but no doubt some Permanent Delegates will try still to enforce it by insistent visits to Secretariat offices; and some senior staff members will anticipate their demands. It has had a most inhibiting effect on the staff and, not surprisingly, infuriated contracted writers who found their texts carefully combed free of any passages which might by any stretch of the imagination be thought likely to give offence to any single Member State.

The second rule, Article 1–3 of the Constitution, is even tougher and, in my experience, more often invoked:

> With a view to preserving the independence, integrity and fruitful diversity of the cultures and educational systems of the States members of this Organisation, *the Organisation is prohibited from intervening in matters which are essentially within their domestic jurisdiction.* [my italics]

The paradoxes will remain. On the one hand, UNESCO is the creation of and exists only with the continued support of sovereign States. On the other hand, its Constitution gives it purposes beyond those which nation States often concern themselves with (if they do not, as is often the case, reject such purposes within their own borders). The aims of the chartered whole are greater than those of the individual parts. In joining UNESCO, Member States have in a sense voluntarily surrendered a small part of their sovereignty; but hardly one of them is willing to recognise this except very rarely and slowly.

At the beginning of this chapter I quoted Gunnar Myrdal dismissing the idea that the whole can be more than the parts as a fiction behind all the UN Agencies. For him, the reality is very much smaller and dryer:

> When an inter-governmental organisation is set up, this implies nothing more than that between the States a limited agreement has been reached upon an institutional form for multilateral conduct of State activity in a certain field.[9]

That is a healthy reminder, particularly for those Agencies which have a body of hard knowledge around which to discuss cooperation before one reaches areas where differences of politics

9. Gunnar Myrdal, 'Realities and Illusions in Regard to International Organisations', Hobhouse Memorial Lecture, London, OUP, 1955, p. 5.

and values show. But in most of UNESCO's main areas (the chief exception is the natural sciences) there is no body of sure knowledge and so no prior agreed ground. At this point the basic paradox of UNESCO is most glaring. It is as though a group of men agreed to go on a journey together but did not admit to each other beforehand that, though certainly they were all willing to set out somewhere, their choices of destination went to all points of the compass. So they spend most of their time arguing, not so much about differences of aim as about formal procedures, before starting any 'discussion of substance'; this is the impression UNESCO's General Conference often gives.

Writing about the UN, Inis L. Claude puts a view close to Myrdal's.[10] It has not, he argues, and cannot have purposes of its own; it is a tool with possibilities and limitations but no purposes. This usefully deflates excessive pretensions by UNESCO, but if it is wholly accepted it denies the clearly stated aims of the Constitutions and reduces UNESCO to a pretence. There are people who believe that this is exactly UNESCO's position and sometimes, when the Organisation commits a particularly egregious intellectual fraud, even its supporters feel like settling for Myrdal's and Claude's view. Then one recalls some of the good things it has done in line with its own high purposes and feels hopeful again.

To do that kind of work the Organisation must have the support of the intellectual community. It will not have that support unless it commands respect; that respect will not be given unless it is seen to be trying to fulfil its purposes, to be aiming at objectivity and at the free flow of knowledge. Since, as we have seen, those aims clash with the general character of governments, there is bound to be tension—unless the institution presses its claims so insistently that Member States leave and it collapses, or unless it progressively lets its ideals slide in the interests of keeping constituent governments happy. It is useful to be reminded regularly that UNESCO is an inter-governmental agency, not a self-sustaining international power; but those who recall this should in turn be reminded that this particular international agency does have very important, agreed, intellectual purposes. Dag Hammarskjöld, too, noted that the principles of the UN Charter itself were far greater than the Organisation in which they had become incor-

10. Inis L. Claude Jnr., *The Changing UN*, New York, Random House, 1967, p. XVII.

porated. More than any other Secretary General, he tried to make the parent Organisation more nearly exemplify its Charter's principles; he kept at the frontiers, learning bit by bit how far it was possible to go at any one time on any one issue. Much the same applies to UNESCO. In these matters an unexpectant disillusion is not necessarily more sensible than a sober idealism.

iii

These—the concept of a neutral international civil service and the commitment to objectivity and the free exchange of ideas—are the two nice fictions on which UNESCO rests, the two assertions meant to guide and sustain the Organisation's work day by day, to be beacons to the General Conference, the Executive Board and the Secretariat. There are many reasons why the life of UNESCO, life in and at UNESCO, is tense, hardly ever less than dramatic and often melodramatic; but these are the most important causes. Were the drafters of the Constitution, it may be asked, quite out of touch with the realities of national power and international relationships? I do not think so; I think they knew very well what they were about. They knew that the twin assertions were neither true at the time nor likely to be easily realised. But they regarded them as desirable long-term aims; they thought it would be valuable if governments did more often honour them; and they believed it would be a useful start to at least put those assertions into a Constitution which every State joining the Organisation had to accept. Even more, they recognised that those two claims were essential props for the full-time staff. Without them, the Secretariat would have no general guiding principles within which to frame their work, and in the light of which to resist improper pressures.

To those who would like to think of UNESCO as a body which serves truth and freedom in a totally idealistic and aseptic world, all this will be a great disappointment. But they are mistaken. Just as too much politics at the expense of intellectual honesty is a mockery, so intellectual freedom which did not have to fight for its ground would have no working relationship to the centres of power and decision. Other, non-governmental, organisations can be more freely intellectual; there is still a need for this one. UNESCO cannot avoid being a political as well as an intellectual body, and all can gain from the dialectic. If political ends are pursued wantonly and regardless of the evidence, then 'politicisation'—the distortion of debate by the *irrelevant* introduction of political issues—sets in, and that can be toxic. The last few years have brought UNESCO much nearer the toxic level. Ironically, the conventional assumption that UNESCO is little more than a vague talking-shop, a home for the rhetoric of lost and over-idealised international causes, is far from the truth today. More and more, its chief areas of interest—educational, scientific, communications or cultural policies; the environment; population questions and, above all, human rights—are receiving high-level political attention; UNESCO is no longer in a backwater.

4

THE FIRST CONSTITUENCY
GOVERNMENTS

I must confess that I have no faith whatever in the concerted action of intellectuals or in the good will of the 'civilized world'. The mind cannot be measured in terms of quantity, and whether ten or a hundred 'leading lights' appeal to the mighty to do or not to do something, such an appeal is equally hopeless. I regard every 'spiritual' pseudo-action, every plea, sermon, or threat addressed by intellectuals to the lords of the earth, as false, as harmful and demeaning to the spirit, as something to be avoided under all circumstances. Our kingdom, my dear Max Brod, is simply 'not of this world'. Our business is not to preach or to command or to plead but to stand fast amid hells and devils. We cannot expect to exert the least influence through our fame or through the concerted action of the greatest possible number of our fellows. In the long view, to be sure, we shall always be the winners, something of us will remain when all the ministers and generals of today have been forgotten. But in the short view, in the here and now, we are poor devils, and the world wouldn't dream of letting us join in its game. If we poets and thinkers are of any importance, it is solely because we are human beings, because for all our failings we have hearts and minds and a brotherly understanding of everything that is natural and organic. The power of the ministers and other policy-makers is based not on heart or mind but on the masses whose 'representatives' they are. They operate with something that we neither can nor should operate with, with number, with quantity, and that is a field we must leave to them. They too have no easy time of it, we must not forget that, actually they are worse off than we are, because they have not an intelligence, a rest and unrest, and equilibrium of their own, but are carried along, buffeted, and in the end wiped away by the millions of their electorate. Nor are they unmoved by the hideous things that go on under their eyes and partly as a result of their mistakes; they are very much bewildered. They have their house rules that cover them and perhaps make their responsibility more bearable. We guardians of the spiritual substance, we servants of the word and of truth, watch them with as much pity as horror. But our house rules, they are true commandments, eternal and divine laws. Our mission is to safeguard them, and we endanger it every time we agree, even with the noblest intentions, to play by their 'rules'.[1]

UNESCO lives on two fictions, and has two constituencies. So it has always to keep a workable balance between competing claims. One constituency is the Member States, expressing their interests through the General Conference, the Executive Board and their Permanent Delegations in Paris. The other constituency is made up of groups of institutions and individuals who are concerned to keep UNESCO up to the mark in its intellectual and scientific work. Between these two constituencies, inescapably involved with both, is the Secretariat.

i

For a Secretariat member there are several different ways of subdividing the total body of Member States. There are, of course, some fairly stable ideological or geographic groupings: the 'Group of 77' developing nations, the Western group of developed countries, the Latin Americans, the South-East Asians, the Arab bloc, the African States, the East European Socialist bloc. But none of these is quite watertight and there is a certain amount of overlapping and shifting of allegiances. Here, I shall use a very simple fourfold division into the prosperous and developed market economies, the Eastern Europeans, the new nations and China.

1. Hermann Hesse to Max Brod, 25 May 1948 in *If The War Goes On— Reflections on War and Politics.*

In the first group the most important member, in financial terms, is the USA. If secondary checks were not built into the method of determining contributions the USA would pay even more than the 25 per cent of the total budget which Congress decided some years ago would be the maximum American contribution to any UN body. So the American delegation is large and busy. But most of the time it seems unsure and ill at ease. Members of the delegation try to respect the Organisation's intellectual rôle but that doesn't always sit easily with the State Department's view of UNESCO's place in its overall foreign policy pattern. They talk often about the need for economy and are joined in this by most of the larger contributors, especially the Soviet Union. It is the small contributors, chiefly the new developing nations, who vote for large budget increases. At such times there is a well-understood formal game, in which the wealthy countries half-threaten to pull out but eventually accept a compromise they have probably agreed in advance with their authorities back home.

The USA also regularly regrets nowadays the politicisation of UNESCO, and talks eloquently about the greater effectiveness of Agencies which attend to technical rather than politically divisive issues. No doubt they and others also feel that the relative amateurs—academics, artists, specialists of all kinds—who attend UNESCO's seminars may find themselves unknowingly agreeing to some politically tendentious document; and this can happen.

Of the other wealthy Western nations, the Federal Republic of Germany is much the best behaved. This may well be partly because for a good many years Western Germany did not have a place at the UN in New York, so its membership of the Agencies was the more important. But Germany does not give the impression of wishing to exploit the Organisation politically. Nor does Italy; Italy is rather engaging and slightly embarrassing since it has not yet been able to convince the Organisation, which is much involved with the international effort to save Venice, that the intense regional disputes which stand in the way can be settled.

There is no need to say much about the smaller developed Western European nations; almost all of them are for most of the time reasonably faithful to the Constitution, because they are neither too tightly bound in big bloc politics nor seeking aid from the Organisation. They can therefore be very useful middle-men for the Secretariat when it is seeking one of its workable compromises. They tend to be generous in giving development aid, their experts are particularly acceptable in formerly-colonised territories and for politically tricky specialist missions, they supply very good members of the Secretariat, and they have some active and intelligent National Commissions.

At UNESCO's founding meeting the French showed themselves deeply anxious to be the host country, and in that effort Léon Blum made a remarkable speech; remarkable because it lacked the cultural arrogance which the French have often shown and still sometimes show. France's record remains ambiguous. They assume a right to many top jobs and in meetings often act with concerted chauvinism. But they have honoured their commitments very well in other respects, notably in the succession of brilliant Frenchmen and women who have over the years supported the Organisation whether as full-time staff members or from outside.

The United Kingdom's record is more patchy. In the early years its contribution was second to none and full of imaginative energy. Britain has provided some fine Executive Board members and excellent career international civil servants. The latter, most of whom are now retired or nearing retirement, became some of the grand pillars of the system. In the two UK Ministries successively responsible for UNESCO affairs there have been consistently helpful national civil servants, though they have been of unduly low rank.

But nowadays one does not gain a sense that the UK is taking the Organisation seriously. Her most public commitment to the institution—the Delegation in Paris—has been notoriously under-staffed for years and, though since 1976 there have been two officials there instead of one, is still undermanned and under-graded. The diplomatic world is always ready to read deep meanings into appearances, and British casualness in this is usually assumed to be a studied insult. The general situation is so dis-couraging that H. G. Nicholas once remarked that for a Britisher to work for UNESCO is positively dangerous.

British officials contributing to UNESCO meetings are likely to exhibit a slightly nervous unintellectualism and lack of artistic pretension; but that is a long-standing habit. Viscount Cecil[2] noted that, in its relations with the League of Nations, Great Britain talked much more about money than about aims or the

2. Viscount Cecil: *A Great Experiment*, London, Cape, 1941.

programme. This is a pity, because many other nations expect a lot from Britain; she has a stock of goodwill with them, more than her present record deserves. She is respected for just some of the qualities the British ascribe to themselves in their more self-congratulatory moments: fairness, good sense, tolerance, objectivity, humour. In the detailed practice of committee work, her representatives do often show these unusual virtues; it is the larger perspective which is lacking and that must come from Whitehall, or from the National Commission. On Human Rights matters, I should add, the British record is good; and that is more important than any other issue in the UNESCO canon. That is, her own accord with international agreements is better than the average; but she is not inclined to take more general initiatives. All in all it would be good if she could break out of her self-imposed and restricting parochialism and un-intellectualism. There are now, however, a few signs that interest may be being revived; the 1976 General Conference may yet be seen as a modest turning-point.

The large Delegation and steady flow of visitors from home ensure that the Soviet Union's presence is very strongly felt in UNESCO. They create an impression at one and the same time of confidence and thin-skinnedness, of violence and warm gentleness; and overwhelmingly one is aware that they have been trained to make political capital out of each issue. They will side with the Arab States in accusing Israel of blatant offences against human rights; they will join with the new nations in any anti-colonialist resolution; they will take every opportunity to criticise the USA as a capitalist super-state. This last procedure has been inhibited since the entry of mainland China, whose representatives insert in every speech a fierce reference to 'the hegemony of the super powers, the USSR and the USA'.

Russian violence in debate is clearly a national style and not to be read as though it came from a Western European. It is a physical style; they do not hesitate to press heavily on individuals if they think it will work. They will not accept the convention that the Organisation's mistakes are made by the Director General and that, in criticising those mistakes, they should not directly name his subordinates. Once, in my day, they were caught tampering with the matrix of UNESCO's international journal, *Courier*. An essay on pollution listed the Volga, along with rivers in the United

States and elsewhere, as polluted; the Russians deleted the reference to the Volga in the Soviet edition. Their tactic when they were challenged was true to form; they attacked personally the editor of the international matrix; he was a good and experienced international civil servant, but he was also an American.

The tactics of the moment dominate. It is assumed that almost anything can be said if it suits the brief, no matter how painful it may be to someone. The brusqueness is also informed by the conviction that they, the Soviets, are going the way the world is going and that everyone else is simply out of step. Once this is recognised, the attacks need not be worrying; and whatever their force, most Soviet delegates forget them the moment they have been delivered and are likely to smile broadly outside the conference room. If, after years of doubt, they decide that a member of the Secretariat really is acting in accordance with his own sense of his duty rather than on the orders of his Foreign Ministry, they become consistently amused and amiable.

An interesting variant to the Eastern European picture, not a crack in the bloc but a shoot of independence and intransigence, has emerged in the insistence by some of the satellites on putting resolutions before UNESCO which assert the importance of, and the right to, 'national cultural life' and the survival of minorities. Thus, Poland uses UNESCO as a means to define more sharply its cultural differences from the Soviet Union. Such Polish resolutions which are usually long and wordy, see their culture as static and traditional; but that is almost inevitable; they are trying to reassert 'Polishness' against both the unifying, technocratic force of bloc politics and the threat of being swamped by Russianness.

The new nations, who were in general creations of the early sixties, tend to take the UN seriously though ambiguously. Since the UN was set up by the victorious allied powers, it has the stamp of Western ways of thinking. On the other hand, its record in anti-colonialism is good and it has made a considerable contribution to the emergence of some new states. Their relationship to the UN is therefore rich in ambiguities.

The UN is, and this has often been noted, very useful to them as a forum where their grievances, aspirations, demands can be aired in a world context; and all the more important since most new countries cannot afford to have large embassies in many countries. It is important to them also in their movement towards a secure national identity and in the complex relations of that movement to their increasing regional sense. They are often suspicious of each other and in particular suspicious of the big fish in each regional pond: Egypt or Nigeria or India or Brazil. They simply have to create a sense of national unity, often almost from scratch. Calvocoressi rightly points to the lack of internal symbols in such states; to create symbols which will reverberate nationally is a first consideration.[3]

No wonder the representatives of many new States are tender and over-ready to take offence, especially from a Westerner. I imagine this is what Shils had in mind when he described some intellectuals from new countries as 'uncivil'; he was, I think, being exact not insulting, pointing to a deliberate unwillingness to use the civilities associated with the diplomatic or intellectual styles of the West.[4] Shils, again, remarks on the key rôle played by intellectuals in the creation of many new nations. This gives them an edge and temper in debate which Westerners rarely have.

Any remarks about the Chinese presence in UNESCO must be provisional, since mainland China has been there only a few years. Its behaviour quickly became disappointingly predictable. The Chinese seem to have decided to play themselves in with a few set exercises, such as the habit I have mentioned of blaming the two super-powers for any ill in the world, including environmental, population or human rights problems. They publicly excoriate the 'Chiang Kai-shek clique' on every possible occasion. Meanwhile, in the background their officials have combed UNESCO's publications from years back in search of objectionable elements. Any reference to Formosa as 'China' is deemed objectionable and representations are made to have that publication withdrawn. On the other hand, there has so far been no attempt to place many mainland Chinese citizens in the Secretariat and the existing 'Chinese' (Formosan) members have not been harassed. One thing we may be sure of: that we have so far seen only the quiet early stages of China's participation in the UN as a whole.

3. See P. Calvocoressi, *World Order and New States*, Chatto and Windus for the Institute of Strategic Studies, London, 1962.
4. See E. Shils, 'The Intellectuals in the Political Development of the New States', *World Politics*, XII, No. 3, pp. 329–68, April 1960.

ii

Politics, to one degree or another, have figured in UNESCO's life from the beginning. One can distinguish four main phases, each the result of a shift in power and influence as new groups of nations came in and the original forty or so rose to the present one hundred and forty or thereabouts.

The first phase was dominated by Western European and North American influences. The Soviet Union was not yet a member and even those Eastern European nations which were members at the start tended to come out under Soviet influence, not to return till the Soviet Union herself entered. UNESCO's intellectual, non-political honeymoon was short. As the Cold War began in earnest, the USA chose to push the new Agency and other parts of the system, ostensibly on the highest intellectual and ethical grounds, into support for her side. Aid to her Korean war effort was put on the agenda of the Executive Board and approved.

When the USSR, and gradually also the other East European Socialist powers, finally entered, the first main polarisation within the Agency came into being. Given the firm belief of the Soviet bloc that there can be no non-political issues, this was inescapable. But the Soviets no doubt remembered America's conduct over Korea and certainly could soon point out that during the McCarthy period FBI men were allowed office space in UN premises so that they could screen US nationals; nor did they forget that in the early days at the UN in New York Trygve Lie loaded things against them within the Secretariat. So both their hard experience of what others would do, in spite of their democratic professions, and their own ideology disposed the Soviets to find the political kernel in almost any issue. They will not make that distinction in rôles which the USA tends to ask for nowadays.

It has been argued that the threat by the emerging new nations to throw in their lot with Eastern Europe accelerated the death of the colonial idea. Certainly, the biggest shift within the history of UNESCO came when the bulk of the new nations entered. The centre of gravity shifted; the East/West polarisation gave way to the North/South. UNESCO altered internally to a degree she has still not fully measured. Pre-eminently, the shift was from intellectual matters to development. Whatever else it was, UNESCO was henceforth a major development agency, disbursing large sums under contract. She also became more politicised, though with new emphases. This was chiefly due to the new States' sustained use of the Organisation for attacks on the remnants of colonialism. Above all, it was due to the African States' justifiably preoccupying anger at racism and apartheid

The most recent phase in UNESCO's main political history came with the concerted use by the Arab States, with Soviet support, of their oil weapon against Israel. This is a particularly complex story which I was able to follow at close quarters within UNESCO; it reveals most aspects of the increasing politicisation of the institution and so puts the main theme of this chapter into high relief. It seems best therefore to describe it at the very end of the chapter.

More generally, two main tendencies promote politicisation in the UN today, nationalism and regionalism. The revival of nationalism, so striking a feature of the post-war period, shows no sign of weakening; and the arrival of the new nations has given it fresh life. We experience now what Cox calls 'micro-nationalism', the nationalism of very small States, and that is a peculiarly intense form.[5] The UN and its agencies are useful arenas for the exercise of this kind of nationalism. It is not surprising that the Permanent Delegates of new, small States are often among the most active. Though they usually understand the Constitution at least as well as representatives of developed States, they are often expected to persuade the Secretariat to bend the programme, the budget and the structure itself in their direction, whether as concerns the number of their nationals employed in the Secretariat or their share of development funds.

The call for regionalism is twin brother to that for nationalism. Regionalism also tries to use the UN system to further its own ends; it too is particularly strong among nations with ideology or religion in common and among the new nations. Like nationalism, it is growing stronger all the time. It has been noted that the growth of specifically regional intergovernmental organisations has kept pace over the last two or three decades with that of the number of international organisations.

Regionalism is often confused with decentralisation and this is

5. See bibliography for several relevant entries.

a pity, since decentralisation is a useful idea. It is based on a structural argument, on the reasonable assertion that not all parts of UNESCO need be in Paris, that whole areas of work, each retaining its fully international character, could with profit be based in other parts of the world. By contrast regionalism does not ask for the resiting of complete parts of UNESCO's international programme, such as work in the natural sciences or in mass communications. It wishes to split the total programme and budget into regional units, to hand out the pieces so that the regions can carry out a whole programme themselves. To States who resent the dominance of Headquarters or who like to think that ex-colonial powers have too large a say in the distribution of funds, this is an attractive idea.

But the result would damage some of UNESCO's best work—such as that in the natural sciences, which must have a constant international perspective. Some countries would especially like to regionalise certain issues—say, population matters or environmental matters or, above all, questions of human rights—precisely because they find international perspectives embarrassing and implicitly critical of their own performances. With regionalism, UNESCO's capacity to affect some important problems before all nations would be greatly reduced.

There is, however, an argument in favour of regionalism which is put not by States but by individuals who care about the development of good intergovernmental practices. Lord Franks once described regionalism as 'a halfway house at a time when single nations are no longer viable and the world is not ready to become one'.[6] His case was that in some matters we would do well to start with regional arrangements, since we are more likely to work amicably on a regional than on an international level; that regional groupings which are more or less culturally coherent within themselves get further sooner. Certainly, the European Convention on Human Rights has some successes to show and is more effective than the UN. But it has an easier brief. And how much is it likely to influence practice in other areas? Unless other initiatives are taken it will be isolatet, neither a model nor a thread, a sort of Radio Three of human rights precepts and practices. The two

6. In N. J. Padelford and L. M. Goodrich, *The U.N.: Accomplishments and Prospects*, International Organisation—Vol. XIX, No. 3, Summer 1965, World Peace Foundation, Boston, Mass., p. 811.

forms of advance, international and regional, are not mutually exclusive. For the UN, problems must always come in their most unaccommodating forms.

To all the above, there is added the increasing use of the bloc vote on behalf of a succession of aggressively political resolutions, resolutions which do not easily leave scope for the usual Conference understanding that, rather than push a divisive statement to a vote, all sides will work hard to arrive at an agreed text. Certainly, the UN voting system is peculiar. Each country has one vote, since in theory all are equal. But of course they are not equal in power or influence. Heretofore the wealthier nations could rest assured that, because of their economic power, their backstage influence would have considerable effect. So one had groupings, sometimes on old colonial lines, sometimes on modern spheres-of-influence lines, sometimes related directly to modern bilateral aid programmes. And this, say those who regret the passing of that system, was a reasonable check on the one-man-one-vote system, in which Togoland has theoretically as much power as the USA. It was, they add, a necessary check to a situation in which 10 per cent of the world's population, with 5 per cent of its output, have a two-thirds majority in the General Assembly:

> Today, the core of a typical voting majority of the General Assembly is composed of mini-states who are lacking in all or most attributes of nationhood, who enjoy the semblance of sovereignty only by courtesy of the world community and who could not exist even in their precarious state without foreign subsidies. Their votes in the General Assembly do not represent as such a substantial interest of the world community nor are they supported by anything even faintly approaching substantial power. Resolutions which owe their support to these mini-state votes are either nothing more than rhetorical proclamations . . . or they serve the purposes of other powerful states or groups of states, such as the Soviet or Arab blocs, who pay for the voting support of the mini-states with economic and political aid.[7]

7. Hans J. Morgenthau, Testimony before a Committee of The House of Representatives, 4 February 1975, cit. by William Korey in 'The Arab Grand Design in the U.N.', *Midstream*, October 1975.

That is as tough a statement as one is likely to read (outside the merely prejudiced and blustering) of the unfashionable position. I understand it, but do not wholly share it, wonder about a US pot calling the kettle black in the matter of economic aid with political strings, and doubt the reduction of the issues to 'rhetorical proclamations' or bloc politics alone. But much else in the passage is accurate.

The behaviour of the new small States is more complex than that passage implies. They are so anxious to stand on their own feet that they will at times vote against their own economic interests, simply to show that they are no longer anyone's slave. A bloc, therefore, especially a large bloc of new and developing countries, gives small nations more confidence than they have when isolated. Nor are their positions then always rhetorical or self-interested. They sometimes stand up for the idea of a greater moral centre in international life. One might reply that it is easier to be moralistic when one is not a great power and so concerned all the time to maintain a precarious balance of forces. Nevertheless, some of the things the new nations are saying, especially about greater global distributive justice, badly need saying and it would be good if the West itself said them more often and with conviction.

One or two commentators, among them Andrew Boyd, argue that the incidence of voting in solid and fixed blocs is greatly exaggerated.[8] Groups, as they prefer to call them, are more likely to re-form from vote to vote as the need demands, they say. Some also argue that the only genuine bloc—as distinct from shifting groups—is that of the Eastern European Socialist states, since they agree in advance on a single line for voting on any important issue. The distinction between a bloc and a group is a useful one; but I believe that in the last few years both bloc and group voting practices have considerably hardened.

There have naturally been all sorts of attempts to devise a more satisfactory system, with the idea of some sort of weighted voting (say, by population) as a favourite. None of them seems likely to work more effectively than the present system, or for that matter to be accepted. Apart from all else, a full single vote—a vote equal to that of the Soviet Union or of the USA—means too much to the self-image of the new nations to be surrendered easily. As to the actual procedures for voting, it might just be possible to induce

8. See A. Boyd, *United Nations : Piety, Myth and Truth*, London, 1964.

some improvements. For instance, the distinction between real majorities (of all Member States) and voting majorities (of those present) might provide one possible point of entry.

In all these movements one is bound to wonder what happened to the principle of universality as well as to that of internationalism, for the two are indissolubly bound together. When the UN was created some of the founding fathers wished it to be a club of virtuous nations to which any nation might aspire, but before which each would have to establish its right to join. Others argued that the whole meaning of such an international organisation demanded membership open to all, with suspension from membership used only as a very last resort. Wilfred Jenks, an outstanding international civil servant,[9] was one of the strongest advocates of this second and dominant view. He argued not only that universality was a primary concept but that no nation should ever be ejected or even be able to withdraw (they should still be regarded as members, no matter what they themselves said; their chair, like that of the erring son, would always be at the table). Article II–5 of UNESCO's Constitution rules that 'Members of the Organisation which are expelled from the United Nations Organisation shall automatically cease to be members of this Organisation'. But the UN's rules on expulsion are very tight. Article 6 of the UN Charter rules that a Member State which has persistently violated the principles of the Charter may be expelled, certainly; but the General Assembly can only do that upon the recommendation of the Security Council (and this, given the composition and rules of procedure of the Council, is hardly likely ever to happen).

The difficulty is that certain groups of Member States are finding ways of circumventing Article 6 so as to produce the effect of an expulsion. The Constitution is bent so as to win a political point. This is quite different from the occasions when a Member State, because the evidence shows it to be violating the principles of the Charter, and because it has been justly criticised, withdraws on the grounds that its sovereignty has been insulted. It was thus that South Africa left UNESCO, on the apartheid issue, where plain questions of human rights were involved; much the same happened with Portugal before the coup.

These are the deeper, long term, trends towards increasing politicisation. In its day-by-day work the Secretariat meets that

9. C. W. Jenks, *A New World of Law*, London, Longmans, 1969.

pressure regularly. It meets it most of all through the Permanent Delegates, who are themselves fed with regular instructions from their home Ministers.

The life of an Ambassador, any kind of Ambassador, has little to recommend it unless it is a short stage in an increasingly glowing career or at times when relations between the country to which one is accredited and one's own country are at an especially challenging phase. Otherwise, one is a gramophone record or message bearer. Ambassadors used to be able to influence policy by making brilliant reports to the Foreign Minister; instant communications have almost eliminated that rôle. Certainly, the Ambassadors and Permanent Delegates to UNESCO can scarcely ever have the pleasure of assuming that their summaries of the state of affairs in Paris are likely to reach the eyes of the Minister or influence policy. They are treated in strikingly different ways by their governments. Some are asked to combine their work with that of, say, Cultural Attaché in their country's Embassy to France; others have senior Ambassadorial rank and occupy vastly expensive flats in the Avenue Foch; sometimes the size of the flat is in inverse relation to the wealth of the country concerned.

Obviously, UNESCO ambassadorships are usually minor posts; so they act as safety nets for a mixed set of people: many are elderly people delighted to bring their professional days to an end in UNESCO, and often able to give it much; or they are elderly people who have become lazy and have little to give; others are younger people who are being trained for, say, work on the International Agencies' desk in their Foreign Ministries; and there are some of all ages who have been given the post as a piece of patronage. If it is set about conscientiously it can be a demanding post. An interested and effective ambassador will quickly learn the art of private international corridor-diplomacy and can be invaluable when the Organisation reaches an impasse (so long as his Foreign Ministry allows him to play that rôle). Such people help the Secretariat to uphold the Constitution. Others let the Secretariat lobby them, persuade them to plant resolutions which the Secretariat cannot present itself; and then expect a quid pro quo.

The general levels of competence among Permanent Delegates is not high. Too many think only of their country or bloc. So the Secretariat is not encouraged to allow them to come close to the actual working of the Organisation, in spite of their day-by-day proximity. The conditions for a useful exchange are not present. Winchmore has argued, apropos the UN itself, that the Delegations should be closer to the Secretary-General since his own officers, by their status as international civil servants, cannot give the inwardness of their governments' position.[10] Certainly the Permanent Delegate is his government's mouthpiece to the Organisation; but that is not his only function. Explicitly to embody that part of his rôle would be almost as damaging as dropping the idea of a neutral civil service and letting each Secretariat member represent his country.

Sir Eric Drummond saw the problem early and clearly. He saw that Permanent Delegations would be bound to try to put pressure on the Secretariat to advance their own country's interests (or their region's interests, you would have to add today, since they now often move in groups), and that this would fragment the Organisation's purposes; that, especially where pressure fell on a Secretariat member who was from the same country as the Delegate concerned, such a member would be led to make engagements (not necessarily written, of course, but no less effective) which would seriously damage the overall execution of the planned and formally-approved programme.

When I think of these and other bad habits, I also remember that some Permanent Delegates worked very well indeed and were as admirable as the best international civil servants. But, overall, relationships between the Secretariat and the bulk of the Permanent Delegates are not happy; there are too many attempts to lean heavily from one side and too much nervous readiness to yield on the other.

I saw over the years a whole procession of protesting Ambassadors or Permanent Delegates each calling to complain about a slight to his country's household gods: about insults in a book written by someone from another country, about the inclusion in an anthology of a writer who no longer officially exists, about phrasing which indicates political bias, about criticisms of their internal practices. One could not help feeling sorry that men and women with such grand titles and appearances should be the carriers of such threadbare messages; it wasn't even up to the

10. See Padelford and Goodrich, *The U.N.: Accomplishments and Prospects*, Boston, 1965.

level of: 'An ambassador is an honest man sent to lie abroad for the good of his country.' There is a phrase much used in the Secretariat, indeed over-used, by way of self-excuse: 'Why should we be more royalist than the King?'—which is said as they yield to yet another unfair demand by a Member State. The phrase is misapplied; their 'King' is not any particular Member State; it is the corporate body and its Constitution. Still, one sees how such a reaction is provoked. You can never be sure, no matter how correct you may feel your own position to be or how flexible your own attitude, of reaching an agreed solution with a complaining Permanent Delegate. Sometimes they have been given no fall-back position, and are too timid to refer home or know it would do no good. At such times one has to face trouble unless one is in the end prepared to capitulate, no matter how ill-founded a criticism may be.

What is known as the Participation Programme also brings out some of the worst nationalistic characteristics of Member States. By this system UNESCO gives money so as to stimulate good ideas among its members. It is particularly useful in those parts of the programme where development aid is not readily available, such as the arts and social sciences. The experiments thus supported should seem likely to be useful pilots for other countries. Thus, a State might wish to encourage new ideas for cheap mobile theatres, or experimental educational work in remote rural areas. The initiating countries are given a UNESCO grant and the Organisation's formal support; they are expected to put at least as much into the projects themselves. These are valuable, seed potato grants; in principle, it is an excellent scheme.

The practice is not so cheering. There are States who ask for little, put much into projects, report promptly on results and generally behave with a high degree of responsibility. Others ask for more than they could ever be reasonably granted, put pressures on the Secretariat to get the money, make transparently self-interested requests (on behalf of a favoured individual) and have no intention of supplying their share of the cost. Among some Permanent Delegates and some members of staff PP, as it is known, has become a form of personal patronage. There is much jealous comparison of levels of grant as between nations or regions. The effort required from the Secretariat is all the time increasing and by now is quite out of proportion to the benefits. PP has become a bad programme and encourages the more small-minded aspects of nationalism and regionalism.

It is a main theme of this book that politicisation in UNESCO is increasing. Some States are driven by ideology, some by expediency; but the results are similar. With each General Conference the number of long, often muddled, political resolution increases. Then there are the relevant resolutions of the General Assembly in New York. The number and kind of resolutions relevant to UNESCO alone which were passed at the UN's XVIII General Assembly speaks for itself:

3057 Racism
3075 Arms race, peace and security
3106 International Law
3118 Colonialism and independence
3128 Human settlements [promising to become a matter of the Third World versus the rest]
3133 Marine Environment [as above]
3140 Youth
3141 Youth
3148 Cultural values [smaller nations not wanting to be swamped by bigger neighbours]
3150 Science and Peace
3174 Least Developed Countries
3182 Peace, etc.

Since the budget will not be increased to provide for the execution of such resolutions, it is the carefully planned Regular Programme which is cut to accommodate transient political interests.

iii

What came to be known as the 'Israel Resolutions' of the 1974 General Conference marked a main moment in this accelerated, planned and strong politicisation of the Organisation at the expense of any serious attempt at objectivity. The 'Israel Resolutions' were about, respectively, Jerusalem, the occupied Arab territories and

UNESCO's regional groups. In brief, the Jerusalem resolution asserted that UNESCO should continue to have a 'presence' in Jerusalem, condemned Israel for 'its persistence in altering the historical features of the City of Jerusalem and undertaking excavations which constitute a danger to its monuments, subsequent to its illegal occupation of this city', and invited the Director General 'to withhold assistance from Israel' until she adhered to this and earlier resolutions on the subject.

This third paragraph went further than any previous request to the Director General on Jerusalem. But it was not very clear. What exactly did 'withholding assistance' mean? Most outsiders, not used to the intricacies of UNESCO's language and modes of operation, understandably interpreted it broadly and assumed that it demanded a virtual cut-off of Israel's involvement with the Organisation's work. A really narrow interpretation would give the clause an internal, technical meaning and take it to say that the Director General should not allot funds to Israel under the Participation Programme. To cut Israel off from this would at the time have amounted to withholding about $25,000 of aid (which is very much less than Israel pays in contributions to the Organisation). This narrow interpretation was publicly adopted by the Secretariat at the time of voting, and was not challenged by the Resolution's sponsors.

The events leading to this late '74 resolution begin just after the 1967 War, and the UNESCO debates on Jerusalem have continued since then. Their overwhelming theme has been that Israel is damaging the cultural heritage of Jerusalem, especially by her archaeological work. The resolutions asked the Director General to ensure 'UNESCO's presence' in Jerusalem, and that has been done (obviously, with the agreement and assistance of the Israeli authorities) through periodic inspection visits. Apart from earlier visitors, Professor Lemaire of Louvain, then Secretary-General of the International Council of Monuments and Sites, and now its President, has made several visits in recent years.

In general, the findings were that Israeli archaeological work is directed towards rediscovering early Jewish history (for example, disengaging the Wailing Wall and uncovering the Temple of Solomon), that the work is on the whole of very high quality by international standards, that in one place there has been some rather 'ruthless' clearance and some disturbance and damage to

Arab dwellings and to the urban tissue. But the work does not at all deserve the wholesale condemnation it received during the UNESCO debates. By contrast, the reports sometimes criticised Arab conservation work in very severe terms.

Over the years, the debates nevertheless gathered momentum and heat. Yet the concentration on the charge that Israeli excavations were a severe danger to Jerusalem's monuments took attention away from a more disturbing aspect of Israeli activity in the city, her altering of the urban landscape, especially by high-rise building. Why was this not put at the heart of the debates? Perhaps because the archaeological charge seemed more relevant to UNESCO. Perhaps because an imputed threat to a religious site rouses feeling more quickly than most other issues. Perhaps because, if damage to a historic skyline were made an international offence, few countries would escape whipping. Perhaps because the damage to Jerusalem's skyline began before 1967; the Intercontinental Hotel, which dominates the Mount of Olives, was built by agreement with the Jordanian authorities who then ruled the city.

This particular resolution presented the Director General with a tricky paradox. He was asked to continue to ensure UNESCO's presence in Jerusalem (which he can only do with Israel's agreement); he was also asked to 'withhold assistance'. Even though that clause was interpreted in the very narrow sense described above it was still a slap in the face for Israel, and so unlikely to encourage her to admit any more UNESCO observers.

The second 'Israel resolution' of the 1974 General Conference had a history going back two years, to the previous or 17th Conference. That Conference passed a resolution asking the Director General to: 'assemble information by all available means at his disposal on the national education and the cultural life of the populations in the occupied Arab territories.' To meet this intensely difficult prescription the then Director General engaged in elaborate written enquiries, sent a mission to the occupied territories and so produced a report for the 18th Conference. In sum, the results of his enquiries were: that the Arabs naturally hate being occupied, that there are some difficulties with Israeli censorship and particular problems in certain fields (e.g. school textbooks, higher education arrangements); but there is no evidence of an attempt by the Israeli authorities to damage Arab education, culture and religion in themselves. The military's overall brief, which seems to be respected, enjoins: 'Non-presence, non-interference, open bridges.'

But Arab cultural life is certainly going through an upheaval. The presence of a Western-type industrialised state, which inevitably sucks into its own service great numbers of Arab workers (for example, busloads each day leave the Gaza strip to work on Israeli projects, receive wages which are, by local standards, unusually high, and so inject into hitherto fairly-closed communities quite different styles of life). This is happening at speed and through the activities of an alien force; it is bound to be deeply resented, especially by those who feel themselves to be the traditional guardians of Arab culture.

Most speakers in the 1974 debates gave their contributions without close reference to the relatively mild report of the Director General. The resolution which was thereupon passed invited the Director General to: 'exercise full supervision of the operation of educational and cultural institutions in the occupied Arab territories. . . .' Again, a very difficult demand, and one the Director General cannot fulfil without Israeli agreement.

But it was the third of November 1974's Israel resolutions which did most to make Israel's further cooperation look unlikely. Increasingly, UNESCO is doing work of a regional or continental kind. For such work the Member States have, traditionally but loosely, been each assigned to a region. It was decided that this situation should be put in order at the 1974 General Conference and each Member State then firmly allotted to a region. With the great bulk of states there was no problem: Britain is in the European region, Japan in Asia and so on. But there were ambiguous cases, such as those of States who belong culturally to regions of which they are not geographically part. There were about half a dozen of these.

My impression is that there was not a preconceived plan to humble Israel in the debate on this issue, but that a situation which emerged in the course of the debate was exploited so as to discriminate against her. One or two States, notably France, objected in principle to any state 'belonging' to a region of which it is not physically a part (this may have been directed against the USA and Canada, who both asked to join the European region). Then, individual votes were demanded on each affected Member

State—and the necessary opening had been made. In the final voting each Member State was placed where it had asked to be placed, except for Israel. Israel became therefore the only Member State without voting rights in any of the regional activities of UNESCO (she could, as can any other Member State, go as an observer to regional meetings). This under a resolution whose preambular paragraphs state that: 'Every Member State has the right and duty to participate fully and regularly in the Organisation's regional and international activities.'

The swings in the voting were even more revealing. In the first vote in Commission (the organ immediately below Plenary), the votes for and against Israel were equal. That was on the usual quick show of hands, on which the exact vote of each Member State is not recorded. A delegate then asked that the required second vote be by roll-call (each State declaring its vote publicly and by name). On that vote the number for Israel's admission dropped, those against increased and the abstentions rose greatly. Public positions often differ from private. There is a further complication. These issues are voted on by all Member States, not simply by those from the region whose composition is being decided. Even in the subsequent voting in Plenary, at which Israel was once again voted out of Europe and so out of any region, a majority of the European States voting favoured Israel's admittance. The global figures were: 48 against, 38 for, 31 abstentions. Of 29 European states voting, 14 were for, 11 against and 4 abstained: Western Europe was virtually solid for Israel's admission.

It will be obvious why Israel found this the most humiliating of all three resolutions. It was brought about by the exploiting of an unpremeditated situation, and left her in an invidiously isolated position. One can see why the requirements placed on the Director General by the other two resolutions were hardly likely to be responded to warmly by Israel. Nor was the even harsher resolution of the General Assembly a year later, which declared that 'Zionism is a form of racism and racial discrimination'.

The great stir caused by these resolutions revealed two opposed positions. Many people said the votes showed that UNESCO is now a wholly political body which has fallen from its purposes as one international agency dedicated to the pursuit of objective intellectual exchange. To others, such arguments are childish; they argued that UNESCO is, *of course*, and always has been, political and cannot avoid being so; and that today's situation merely dramatises this fact of life.

As we have already seen, the reality is more interesting. UNESCO is an intergovernmental agency and so—even though they have all accepted her idealistic constitution—subject to pressures from one hundred and thirty-odd Foreign Ministers and any number of blocs and groupings. Yet the Constitution postulates the disinterested exchange of knowledge, internationally; and that is not popular with governments. This is the paradox of UNESCO and the tension inseparable from its work. The Organisation's only real justification lies in being able to claim that it does much of the time preserve that precarious balance within which it can do straight and free work. The question, to which those intellectuals from many countries who protested against the Israel resolutions rightly addressed themselves, is whether those resolutions had finally destroyed that balance.

So the regrettable thing about these debates was not that they had a political inspiration; that was unavoidable. It was that they were in themselves distorted, that over the years most speeches had paid insufficient attention to the evidence, and that this was particularly marked after the Middle East oil crisis began.

There had been explicitly political debates in UNESCO before, and this fact was cited so as to question the concern shown about the Israel resolutions. Why were not these earlier resolutions so fiercely charged with damaging UNESCO? The chief instances are resolutions against South Africa and Portugal (under the former régime, of course). But the differences are crucial. The South Africa and Portugal debates were about racism and old-style colonialism, and the charges were fully proved. These issues are within UNESCO's competence because these practices are contrary to those Human Rights which UNESCO's Constitution serves. South Africa and Portugal were thus relevantly censured.

The difference between those and the Israel debates is that the latter—especially the first two of them (the third, or regional, resolution was gratuitous)—were conducted on false premises. The first was ostensibly about 'dangerous' archaeological work and the second about the fate of a culture. Both issues are well within UNESCO's competence. But in neither case were the charges, explicit or implicit, substantially upheld by the evidence. The debates were really about the fact of occupation: a terrible fact, certainly, and within the UN system to be fought at the UN in New York, at the General Assembly and the Security Council. So, a series of explicitly political acts was carried out within UNESCO's Executive Board and General Conference, in the guise of debates on UNESCO-type issues. It is in this light that the objections by intellectuals should be viewed. It is only in this light that one can begin to assess whether damage was done to the Organisation by these resolutions. It is in this light that each member of the Secretariat was required to consider his own position. An international civil servant was bound to try to execute the resolutions fully and objectively. If he found them quite repugnant he could not say so and remain in his post. Nor should he remain in his post and become an apologist for these—or any other—resolutions.

The 1976 Nairobi General Conference brought some relaxation. Two years of careful negotiations brought about an amendment to the rules by which only States within a region could vote on membership within that region. Thus Israel was admitted to Europe. On the Jerusalem and occupied territories issues, there were no gains.

5

THE SECOND CONSTITUENCY
THE INTELLECTUAL COMMUNITIES

Jacques Maritain's address as retiring President of UNESCO at the General Conference in Mexico City in 1947, two years after the Organisation had been founded, shows how soon and how thoroughly some of the endemic tensions began to preoccupy. Like Croce, Niebuhr and some others, Maritain faced the problems directly. Since ideologies divide us, how can we agree on any important worthwhile actions, he asked. Should UNESCO not content itself with collecting statistics, factual data of all kinds; at least that would be more creditable than trying to establish an 'artificial conformity of minds' which would soon collapse. He went on to argue that these were not the only options:

> The solution, I think, must be sought in another direction. Because ... the goal of UNESCO is a practical goal, agreement between minds can be reached spontaneously, not on the basis of common speculative ideas, but on common practical ideas, not on the affirmation of one and the same conception of the world, of man and of knowledge, but upon the affirmation of a single body of beliefs for guidance in action. No doubt this is little enough, but it is the last resort of intellectual agreement. It is, nevertheless, enough to enable a great task to be undertaken, and it would be much to crystallize this body of common practical convictions.

This is a brave effort at making workable distinctions; it settles for advances on a limited front. But exactly what does it mean? 'Common practical ideas ... a single body of beliefs for guidance in action' can certainly get us some way and perhaps quite a long way, whether in archaeological practice or in tackling common environmental problems or in some educational, scientific and other matters. But in the end almost all issues become political; and these include archaeology, environment, population and science. Some are political from the start, such as 'cultural development': we can agree on the general principle that more people should have 'access and participation' (to use a current UNESCO slogan about cultural development); and we can agree on, say, the most useful kits for classes in painting. Beyond such very general or tightly practical points we are in the full political sea. And what about human rights, which lie at the heart of UNESCO's being? As to those, all practical action starts from agreement about the rights of the individual; and that agreement is not forthcoming. Maritain's formulation is interesting and courageous, and all the more so because he was making an early attempt to dam the depredations of insistent ideologies. But by now it simply does not reach far enough, to where the going becomes tricky and the ways divide. It bypasses the need for free, speculative thinking and decisions on matters of human values beyond the simply practical. The later history of the bodies and groups especially charged with upholding UNESCO's intellectual purposes illustrates only too well that such issues are not easily avoided.

i

The UNESCO National Commissions were intended to be the crown, the living expression in each Member State, of UNESCO's commitment to free intellectual life.

Freer even than the Executive Board, they were meant to be composed of highly-qualified and independent individuals who between them would cover within each country the whole spread of UNESCO's interests; they would be able to advise their own governments and UNESCO itself. They would also be able to initiate UNESCO-like activities within their own nations: this was the original idea, and it seemed so exciting in the beginning that Reinhold Niebuhr called the National Commissions 'a genuinely new element in international relations'.

Most Member States now have a Commission; but only a few approach the ideal. Some merely police UNESCO's activities on behalf of their governments instead of impartially scrutinising and, as necessary, supporting or criticising them. Some are explicitly sub-departments of the national Civil Service, a part of the political bureaucracy and hence executors of orders from above. Others, though freer, have no power or influence; they are formal bodies, talking heads, turkeys on a rail. The degree of real freedom each National Commission enjoys varies as widely as the ideologies of different governments. Most Commissions are neither strong enough nor effective enough, and they are often understaffed administratively. They do not work well and their governments do not wish them to do so.

There are a few lively, intelligent and independent-minded Commissions. As likely as not they will be found in countries which are small, prosperous and not too heavily under the influence of one or the other powerful political bloc: for example, Switzerland, the Netherlands, Canada. Other than such as these, there are one or two remarkably lively Asian Commissions, and one or two in the Eastern bloc do far more to live up to the concept of the National Commissions than one would have thought possible.

To be of use, a National Commission must have some genuine autonomy. Of this, the best test is its ability to oppose its own government if need be. The Swiss Commission did this in response to the Resolutions against Israel, and the Netherlands Commission struck out with its own meetings on the same issue; there may be others who made up their own minds. I am not setting these good examples against, say, the National Commissions of some authoritarian or some developing countries (countries in which there is a long way to go before the idea of a Third or Fourth Estate can be accepted). I am comparing them with the Commissions of some other highly-developed and 'democratic', open societies.[1]

1. The UNESCO National Commission of the United Kingdom is administratively and financially ill-nourished. The intellectuals, scientists, scholars who compose it are not tempted to think much about it between one meeting and the next; no doubt they think more about their own international professional bodies. Someone had the bad idea, years ago, that the Minister should be the Chairman of the UK Commission. Even if the Minister were to spend some time every day thinking about UNESCO and wishing it well, this would be a mistaken arrangement. Justice must be seen to be done; the idea must be seen to be at least structurally lived up to; neither applies when the Minister is Chairman. More practically, the Minister is quite simply too busy to lead the Commission properly; and his political rôle prevents him from giving it a free intellectual lead. All he (or she) can really do, no matter how well-intentioned he may be, is to look quickly at the

The development of international non-governmental organisations, or NGOs, was another good idea from UNESCO's early days. Julian Huxley, the first Director General, played a great part in offering subventions to strengthen existing bodies or stimulate the birth of new ones where he saw a clear need. Huxley had a strong and exact sense of the importance to his Organisation of continuous relations with the widest possible range of world intellectual and scientific guilds. By now there are dozens of them representing almost every known major profession, arts, science, skill or interest. Some are very large and have full-time staff on the spot who are regularly in direct touch with the Secretariat; others are heard from only intermittently.

Their relations with UNESCO are meant to run in two directions. They are helped by UNESCO, usually through a basic subvention plus contracts for particular jobs, because they are worthwhile in themselves; after all, the Constitution asserts that it is good for intellectual life to flourish and to circulate freely across the world. Just as important, they help UNESCO and indeed are essential to its proper functioning. I do not mean simply that they carry out under contract a good part of the Programme; it would be possible for the Secretariat to work entirely through individuals. The case for the NGOs is much stronger than that. They should be able to bring to the Organisation's activities the best and most up-to-date knowledge in their fields from anywhere in the world. Secretariat members, no matter how fine their grasp of their specialism may have been when they entered UNESCO, cannot help gradually losing touch. The NGOs must keep a critically alert eye on the very formulation of programmes themselves: is that approach to an environmental question stale? or that model of educational needs narrow? or that paper on some aspect of the relations of science to society badly off-centre? Perhaps most important of all—though this is not a rôle for the NGOs which UNESCO itself greatly likes to stress—they should provide a constant check on governments' behaviour towards the intellectual purposes of the Organisation and should protest loudly if they

---

Chairman's brief shortly before the meeting. The upshot is that the Civil Servants who service the Commission have too much control of its agenda. They are fair-minded, but this is not enough. Hence, intellectuals are even less tempted to give time to the Commission.

believe governments are making it excessively difficult for those purposes to be fulfilled. Finally, being freer than the Secretariat, the NGOs can and should take risks. Sensible Secretariat members, who know a certain job needs doing if a complex branch of the programme is to be carried out adequately and know also that there will be endless political delays and objections if they either do the job themselves or commission it directly from an individual, offer it to a properly-accredited NGO. This is where the two-way process is seen at its best: organisations which might find it difficult to exist without UNESCO's basic subvention can feed back new and experimental approaches which simply could not have emerged in the Place de Fontenoy. It is, all in all, a fine prescription; and sometimes it is fully honoured. The existence of the best NGOs is the clearest continuing indication of the key principles which were thrashed out at UNESCO's birth. In this hardly known and indeed undervalued area of difficult and worth-while intellectual administration, the best full-time officers of the NGOs are brothers of the best international civil servants.

Some other NGOs are not intellectually in the van at all; or are run by petty bureaucracies composed of and kept in position by the old, the proud and the place-keeping in their professions. Still others refuse to recognise that, if they take money from UNESCO, they must also accept the duty to spread their disciplines outside the cosy developed world, that they must give special support to the scholars and scientists who are so often scattered very thinly indeed in the new nations. Some General Secretaries of NGOs have a manifestly ambivalent attitude towards the Secretariat. They are consummate corridor politicians, adept at lobbying, wooing and flattering. At the same time they resent the Secretariat; understandably, since staff members are very much better paid than they are. I have known a part of the Secretariat propose to award its own activities generous allowances for inflation, when drawing up the new Programme and Budget, but tell the NGOs that similar allowances could not be added to their basic subventions. No wonder some NGO officials decide that the Secretariat is more concerned with keeping itself comfortable than with doing justice to bodies without whom its job would be immensely more difficult.

Over the last ten years the wind has blown increasingly cold for the NGOs. Many developing nations think them too Western and resent every dollar they receive in subventions, arguing that the money might better have gone on development aid. Other nations are suspicious of their intellectual freedom, of precisely their *non*-governmental character. Nor do many of the Secretariat like giving a sort of blank cheque—a payment simply to keep them in being rather than for named items of work—to any body. Instead, they argue, let all the money given to the NGOs be in the form of contracts for specific jobs, contracts which would naturally include an element for administrative costs. Then UNESCO would be able to exercise proper control of NGOs and their work, in so far as it was funded by the Organisation's money. I resisted this approach whenever and wherever I met it; but it has now gained much ground. The Programme and Budget for 1977–8 says:

> In the interests of programme execution, the Director
> General, with the approval of the Executive Board, may
> reduce the subventions to these Organisations, and instead
> entrust them, through contractual arrangements, with the
> carrying out of specific activities approved by the General
> Conference.

It is an illiberal move, a blow to the fundamental aims of UNESCO, a pettiness, another instance of the inherent and increasing tendency of UNESCO's governing organs to over-scrutinise every activity. One thing may be said in its favour, though I do not believe its proposers had this in mind: if the NGOs were paid only for contract work instead of receiving a general subvention they would not have to endure, when those subventions are voted every two years, political objections from some Member States. In taking a regular subvention from an inter-governmental agency, an NGO has eaten some of Persephone's pomegranate, forfeited some of its freedom of comment and action. It is up to its members to decide whether the good they can undoubtedly do in various parts of the world by being under UNESCO's aegis outweighs the circumspections they must practise. In my last year International PEN, which has been receiving a regular grant though for specific purposes, was violently attacked by Czechoslovakia because it had run an outspoken conference on current limitations on artistic freedom. The Secretariat resisted the attack strongly; the Czechs insisted on a vote— and lost. Next time round, the objectors may win. If they do, I hope—I speak now as a private individual and a member of PEN—that PEN ends its formal relations with UNESCO. Its purposes centre exactly on freedom of speech; there is hardly any room to trim. I am very sorry indeed to have to conclude this; I know what a valuable air-hole PEN is to writers in, for instance, some East European countries.

The arguments against the contracts-rather-than-subventions position are overwhelming. It will reduce the freedom of manoeuvre of the NGOs at just the point where it is most important. NGOs who spend their energies fulfilling contracts which emanate directly from the Approved Programme of UNESCO will have less energy and inclination to work on programmes which are ahead of UNESCO's present thinking. They will progressively become the intellectual servants of an Organisation which is itself too much under intellectual constraints. Some of them will not mind this, so long as they get the lion's share of contracts through their closeness to the right Secretariat members. But the greatest virtue of a good NGO is that it should be able to go, from time to time, further and faster than UNESCO can.

Early in 1970, I drafted three criteria for UNESCO's regular examination of NGOs: is the NGO at the forefront of its discipline? is it, over the years, making reasonable efforts to spread itself, especially in developing countries? is its proposed programme *complementary* to that of UNESCO? The order and the phrasing were both deliberate, an attempt to respect all at once the intellectual life, the autonomy of the NGOs and the constitutional duties of UNESCO. Above all, the word 'complementary' recognised that the NGOs have a rôle beyond that of helping to fulfil UNESCO's existing programme, that the last word does not come out of any inter-governmental agency. Those criteria were adopted and went on the books; the new position which I quoted above runs directly against them.

In all this, the over-riding principle must be that NGOs have their working-bases secured and that they shall be free to take initiatives. If they were trusted to do that and if more of them showed that they wished to rise to the challenge both they and UNESCO would gain. That would be one of the better ways of countering unnecessary and irrelevant politicisation. But the outlook is bleak: UNESCO is tightening its hold and few NGOs will take a stand on principle.

Beyond the NGOs there is yet another great range of people who both help UNESCO to fulfil its programme of work and can, if they will, provide a further check on whether it is living up to its purposes. These are the thousands of experts and consultants who are individually hired—to visit and advise anywhere in the world, to draft specialist documents, to run a pilot project. The best of them are admirable and invaluable. I remember particularly those who went on UNESCO's behalf into dangerous war-zones so as to report back on the state of monuments and temples; or those elder statesmen of their professions who give much of their spare time to developing the links between scholars and to improving the level of work, right across ideological barriers; or of those who, without pay, will from time to time spend up to fourteen hours a day for several days in UNESCO's basement meeting-rooms so as to produce an agreed statement on world needs in some scientific or educational or cultural matter, a specific statement which proposes lines for action and which therefore can only be hammered out in the face of tremendous political suspicions.

A competent staff member will have a long list of such people, a list which changes as new needs emerge and is well spread geographically. A lazy staff member will have a much smaller list of over-used individuals. There are regulations to prevent such abuses, but they can often be circumvented. It is comforting to employ someone who does not have to be broken in to UNESCO's arcane procedures, who can be relied on to deliver his report on time and who is not likely to cause a fuss if some professional corners are cut because of political considerations. For such people, the Secretariat can become almost permanent patrons; and both sides like that. This most common abuse is often compounded by the giving of too many contracts to people of only a few nationalities. It is easy to understand why so many French experts and consultants are employed: they are handy, numerous and usually very efficient. By contrast, the Eastern European countries tend to be slow, restrictive and bureaucratic in their response to requests for experts. There are exceptions: Hungarian social scientists are reasonably often employed and so are Polish experts on the restoration of ancient monuments; both are excellent. But difficulties such as these, and the problem of distance and so of travel costs, do not account for or justify the grossly distorted distribution of experts and consultants. The last time I made a check over the whole of my Sector I found that, though special efforts to spread contracts had been asked for, Western Europeans had in the previous year received almost 80 per cent of all contracts. Add that the level of fees can be highly erratic, and one sees that the hiring of outside experts has become in too many cases an unpleasant form of small patronage, or of ideological bias.

Not surprisingly, the developing world is deeply resentful about the white faces of so many experts. Their objections are not always reasonable; the developed world does have most of the globe's highly-trained people. But developing countries can reasonably insist on two provisos: that more effort be put into finding suitably qualified people within their own regions; and that experts who establish some sophisticated system in a developing territory always have 'counterparts' at their side, who will be trained to take over at the end of the expert's contract. This second condition is being more and more insisted upon.

There ought to be another group within this range of non-governmental involvements with UNESCO, that of non-specialist world-wide public opinion. It is a firm belief of UNESCO's major governing organs that there is a vast untapped public of 'the common man' which would love and support UNESCO if only it were given more chance to understand its aims and achievements. Hence UNESCO's recurrent attempts, now buttressed by modern 'image building' theory, to make itself known to populations at large.

The idea is muddled. The thousands of millions in the world's population include people of so many different cultures, levels of literacy vary so enormously, access to information is so often limited (whether by economic or geographic forces or by the decisions of rulers) that any campaign which tried to reach the great undifferentiated body of the world's people would resemble pouring a few cups of water into a sandy desert in the cause of irrigation. Any effort which did spread as widely as that would have to drop to such banal and safe sloganising as to defeat its own purposes.

The best general and non-specialist group UNESCO can approach is that of the informed laymen, the 'gate-keepers' of ideas, the opinion formers, teachers and journalists and broadcasters, and workers in relevant voluntary bodies. Of course, in some countries such a group is hardly allowed to exist. In many of those where it does exist, the idea of UNESCO has little force. In others, UNESCO is known and respected; as, for example, the multi-million sales of its illustrated monthly, *Courier*, shows. A crisis can reveal that, though most such people in most countries hardly think of UNESCO from one year's end to the next, they still assume that it has high purposes which should not be betrayed. The widespread and powerful reaction against the 1974 Resolutions about Israel is a striking recent proof of UNESCO's hidden moral capital.

What I have called UNESCO's second constituency has as its prime concern the Organisation's intellectual and ethical purposes and it runs from the great professional associations and the most advanced intellectuals to unknown people who join their local UNA branch or write to the Director General asking him to take action against a particular infringement of human rights. If that second constituency could be made collectively more articulate, the first constituency—the governments—might be persuaded to be less cavalier towards the Constitution they have all agreed to uphold.

ii

Faced with the ambiguities towards its intellectual rôle which I have described, UNESCO has not seen its second constituency become strong and articulate; instead, UNESCO itself has gone soft. From time to time it shows courage; but in general its response to the difficulties of making a decent intellectual showing is to take evasive action. There are four main ways: rôle selection; idea selection; humbug, both verbal and philosophical; and bureaucratic practices so complicated that they end up making procedure dominate substance.

Jean Thomas, an early and particularly brilliant French member of the Secretariat, put his finger on the practice of rôle selection at the precise time it became dominant:

> A humorist might perhaps come to the conclusion that, for want of a speculative or practical philosophy, UNESCO took refuge in action.[2]

2. Jean Thomas, *UNESCO*, Paris, Gallimard, 1962.

He was referring to the most spectacular of UNESCO's selective routines, the over-emphasis on aid to development. As more and more money and attention went into development work, and as intellectual and ethical activities fell further and further behind, the relief all round, Thomas noted, was profound and depressing. It is much easier to be part of a development agency responding to the practical needs of individual Member States than to be awkwardly in the middle of quarrelling States, trying to persuade them to agree on a line of action in a contentious area.

The process had gained ground gradually but gathered immense force after 1960, in both UNESCO and the UN as a whole. Almost all the numerous new sovereign States needed aid badly and meant to keep it in the forefront of UN activities. The developed nations, though they were uneasy about multilateral aid, had been for a decade losing interest in UNESCO's rôle in international intellectual cooperation. So almost all Member States accepted the change of emphasis and did not ask whether it would have a cost.

Certainly the case for UNESCO going heavily into development aid was a strong one, and the Organisation has as a result carried out an enormous number of valuable projects. But it was not an exclusive case, not a matter of doing *either* intellectual work *or* development aid. Nor is development activity necessarily the enemy of UNESCO's other duties. Operational work for development can even improve intellectual and 'ethical' work so long as the two kinds have learnt the right ways to coexist. If they have, operational work can provide a sort of phenomenological roughage, a tethering to reality, a discouragement for UNESCO's congenital tendency to take off into merely verbal gestures. More pragmatically, it provides a ticket of practical respectability which Member States recognise and which can be made use of. It is a foot in the door; if UNESCO has shown that it can effectively set up complex educational institutions, it is more likely to be listened to when it makes proposals for enlarging women's rights in education.

So, when the large development aid contracts began to flow in, it was very sensible not to separate 'Regular Programme' staff (those spending the regular budget) from a specially appointed 'Operational' staff, but rather to let the staff grow as needed and require everyone to be both 'operational' and 'regular'. It can be argued that a special operational staff would have been technically more efficient than a mixed staff. But the argument can run the other way: integrated staff would be less likely to see development projects in a two-dimensional, technocratic way; their sense of the complexity of social and individual costs and benefits should be widened.

Here is the crux. UNESCO was right to go into development, but failed adequately to see that it should do so in a distinctive way. The commitment to educational development, for instance, should have been founded in a more rigorous analysis of aims and purposes, should have been less easily satisfied with hardware-plus-good-intentions, more concerned with cutting through that loose educational rhetoric which can be heard in developing as in developed countries. It should have sought more the bedrock for socially, culturally and psychologically sound action.

Development aid was rarely approached at this level. More often, it became a fairly easy form of functionalism, a let-out from more difficult approaches, a 'retreat into the technical'. So, as we saw earlier, UNESCO's Regular Programme funds are now more than matched by contracts from the United Nations Development Programme and the like; the operationalists increasingly set the pace and tone; the non-integrated specialists increase in number. It will be difficult, if not impossible, to redress the balance. Too much is now committed to UNESCO remaining large, too much in the size of the budget, numbers of personnel, plant and buildings; operations must continue to call the tune and probably to do so increasingly. Add that the power to dispose of a range of development contracts is politically valuable to the Secretariat, a way of mustering blocs of Member States when danger threatens; one then sees that the over-concentration on development will not be easily weakened.

In idea-selection, also, the problem is not that the ideas selected for attention are bad in themselves—far from it—but that they squeeze out other issues. Of this habit, the most striking proof is the emphasis on anti-apartheid activities and the relative neglect of a host of other human rights issues.

The African States virtually demand this. To them there is nothing, no single blot on human rights, so dreadful as this one. It is an affront which is rarely out of the consciousness of an educated African, from whichever part of the continent he may come. They are much preoccupied too with problems of cultural identity and unity; but that has second place to the towering presence of apartheid, of the existence of States on this earth, on their own continent, where they are formally registered as lower forms of human life. The thought sticks like a burr in their minds and inflames them. It is by far the worst survival in a world which has by now got rid of at least most forms of direct colonialism.

It is right that UNESCO should give a great deal of attention to opposing apartheid; it does so with a fair amount of success. But, as with UNESCO's rôle selection, this practice of idea-selection is made to conceal an evasion. Energy and attention given to attacking apartheid cannot be spent on infringements of other human rights, whether in other African States or other parts of the developing or developed world. Much less attention is paid to the political prisoners in jails all round the world, to the widespread and rigid censorship of ideas, to ill-treated minorities, to exiled artists, to the brutal murders of opponents of existing regimes, the lack of freedom to travel, the consistent discrimination against women.

But, then, these things are practised by Member States; South Africa is no longer a Member State of UNESCO. She had become the Wicked Squire and, true to form, marched out in an angry huff after she had been yet again denounced. Out of UNESCO, that is; she stayed in the UN in New York; that is a useful diplomatic listening post and political platform.

We shall have to return to the matter of human rights, in greater detail. Let me only say here that UNESCO's record, though biased so heavily towards anti-apartheid thinking as to be relatively starved elsewhere, is still more effective than the UN's own very much larger Human Rights Commission. In that much more directly political context, the Commission is almost consistently either toothless or grossly biased politically.

Years ago, Lionel Trilling wrote a splendid essay about a much-praised UNESCO exhibition called *The Family of Man,* in which he hit hard and accurately at the futility of apparent agreement on high-sounding sentimentalities, a sort of reductionist pabulum. This is just what Croce had suspected would increasingly emerge and what Niebuhr attacked as easy agreement at the level of 'perfectionist progressivism'. There are many other examples, of which a more recent one is the Faure report on education in the world today. In particular, discussion of 'youth and its problems' brings out the worst in UNESCO, its love of the most recent fashionable attitudes and of the verbal tags which go with them, its uneasy straddling of ponderous establishment positions on one side and of presumed identification with 'the aspirations of the young' on the other. These are all instances of the most pervasive of UNESCO's evasions: humbug of thought and language.

So many projects are forms of pseudo-intellectual action being used as an escape from clear thought pursued to the point where it might disturb. Hence the emptiness and artificiality of some activities. For example, the General Conference decided that the Organisation would celebrate Great Anniversaries of the World. So elaborate routines have had to be devised to draw up a list of 'world personalities', who have each been proposed by their native state as suitable for international homage. Inevitably, the list comprises great personalities and clear nonentities, is riddled with the war of ideologies and much plain log-rolling.

The issue which more than any other brings out humbug in UNESCO is 'Peace'. For some sides the movement towards peace means a slow process of education in mutual understanding; hence UNESCO's early stress on the need to promote greater knowledge between cultures. For others it is a matter of massive verbal injections, simple assertive propaganda. There is no secure evidence that either view is sustainable. The concept of 'Peace' highlights UNESCO's difficulty in arriving at any precise or serious philosophical agreement between its Member States; no other word has generated so much loose speech or vague suggestions for projects. One of its later variants has been the argument that UNESCO should promote a movement towards a 'universal humanism'—which half-echoes the arguments for 'a UNESCO philosophy' in the early days, arguments the Member States rightly rejected though not always for the right reasons.

In fact, 'Peace' splits Member States and provokes some of the more contentious debates. There are two main interpretations. According to one, UNESCO should directly gear most of its programmes to the promotion of peace. For the other, peace is best promoted indirectly, by useful activities which concern all nations and so gradually build up the habit of cooperation and trust: literacy campaigns, joint work on population or environment problems, joint scientific operations (earthquake monitoring, reclamation of the arid zones, preservation of the wetlands, oceanic exploration), and international campaigns on behalf of the world's great threatened monuments.

The main proponent of the direct view is the Soviet Union. Soviet delegates talk endlessly and with passion about the promotion of peace. They do not forget their immense losses in the last war; since they see the UN Agencies as branches of their own and other States' political activities, they expect those Agencies to play as direct a part as possible in extending détente. The papers which their delegates read at conferences always embody the view of communication as a transmission-belt; you put assertions about the need for peace in at one end and the listener at the other end is affected by them. Perhaps where there is no countervailing set of views an apparent conformity of outlook can be produced by this method; whether it gets below the level of repetitive one-way slogans is doubtful.

The work done by UNESCO's Social Science Department on 'Peace' used to have two prongs. One was concerned chiefly with the political causes of war and the promotion of peace within political contexts (support was given to selected Peace Institutes, and projects mounted in conflict resolution). The second prong concerned 'aggression studies', beginning with the origins of aggression in individuals. At each General Conference the Soviet Union attacked this kind of work. Aggressiveness in individuals, its delegation argued, had no relation to the search for peace. An aggressive individual should be in hospital or gaol. The promotion of peace was concerned with the realities of power and politics. It is, of course, possible to hold this view on the basis of research and study. But the Soviet delegates did not argue from evidence; they asserted from fixed prior positions that these were irrelevant bypaths which took UNESCO away from its direct, effective activities for peace.

The argument has been going on since UNESCO began. Julian Huxley argued strongly for the indirect interpretation of UNESCO's commitment to peace. Reinhold Niebuhr noted that the lessening of ignorance about another nation does not automatically increase the disposition towards peaceful settlements but might sharpen dislike. All to little avail. That most inept of philosophising phrases—to understand all is to forgive all—haunts UNESCO like a mismatched wife. Latterly, there has appeared a more technical and modern version: that cooperation between experts in specialist matters lays one foundation for the movement towards peace. Certainly, it may create friendships among individuals and no doubt it increases professional understanding. It does not necessarily affect the experts' attitudes as nationals; nor does it have any necessary relationship to the realities of power. But it is difficult to demur at some of the more optimistic assumptions about hands across the sea without being branded as a war-monger or, at best, being asked regretfully whether one does not after all really believe in peace.

These are the conflicts of attitude which lead the Secretariat into proposing seminars whose terms of reference and composition ensure that they will take off into the safe clouds of empty rhetoric. If they do accidentally come down to earth and threaten to break up in contention, the Secretariat will go into a frenzy of 'diplomatic activity' behind the scenes so as to get them launched again. But in general the Secretariat does its best to honour even foolish briefs, once they are in the book of Conference Resolutions. Some years before I joined UNESCO, the Secretariat were instructed to produce two anthologies in promotion of peace, one on Tolerance, the other on the Horrors of War. The first was at last printed, in 1974, though by an outside publisher. UNESCO itself has not yet put its copies on sale, since some element has still not been 'cleared'. The anthology of the Horrors of War will never appear. After much time, effort and money had been spent, we had a quite unpublishable manuscript. It had been made up of contributions from Member States many of whom thought that the horrors of war were solely what had been done to them in some conflict, long past or recent, by other Member States, and one of them sent photographs to prove its case. It was a dreadful slanging-match, a war through words and pictures, a horror in its own right. Few publications would have been more likely to stir up fresh hatred.

In the basement of the UNESCO building there is a high room, bare except for—at its centre—a huge steel machine which grinds remorselessly. Its job is to shred the mountains of paper which UNESCO produces and discards each week. Lorries wait in the nearby loading bay to take the bales to some paper Valhalla or recycling Heaven. If an atom bomb destroyed UNESCO, that massive machine would be likely to survive. There would be some truth in what it would suggest to the survivors who came upon it: that this building had been a sort of temple to paper, to words; and that here, in this great stark machine, was the godhead. It is not only paper which can be shredded by so vast and conflicting an organism; it is thought itself, ideas, the intellectual life as the most direct of human challenges; the destruction of thought begins with the destruction of language.

UNESCO's taste for a language with no jagged edges to it has one thing which can be said in its favour: that it sometimes reflects effectively the need to arrive at an international public language free of limiting cultural overtones, and so less likely to lead to misunderstanding and affront. For the rest, there is much pretension, fear and woolliness: pretension on the part of delegates, fear on the Secretariat's part, woolliness on both sides. One does not set out to do a piece of work; one 'seeks to implement a project'. UNESCO never says it will do all it can, together with the NGOs; it promises to 'seek to contribute to the consideration of the problem, within UNESCO's fields of competence, in full conjunction with the relevant NGOs'. Very popular words include 'strategies' ('tactics' is rarely used, in spite of all the time spent reacting tactically), 'primary goals', 'objectives' (rarely 'objects'), 'innovation', 'motivation', 'facilitate', 'methodological', 'conceptual', 'appropriate' (techniques, approaches, methodologies, modalities, etc.), 'highly-qualified experts' (it is not that the thought of hiring incompetent experts or irrelevant NGOs crosses anyone's mind; these are simply mild hooray epithets), 'interdisciplinary', 'complementary', 'concrete'. I could have gone unsmilingly to another ADG—when I wanted a talk about cooperation—and proposed that we 'initiate a flexible dialogue at the interface of our two Sectors' areas of concern, having to do with ongoing problems of inter-Sectoral communications with a view to establishing and evaluating variant forward-looking procedures for the medium-term future.'[3]

3. One can see how the Secretariat comes to have almost a vested interest in humbug and obfuscation. To blur the language and obscure the thought, is to avoid explosions. In my time the most striking instance was at the 1970 Venice Conference of Ministers of Culture from all over the world. The Soviet bloc had put down a Resolution roughly to this effect: 'States will ensure that the media of mass communication are not employed to propagate material which is destructive of agreed values, which is subversive, pornographic, etc. . .'. The delegates of some other States pointed out that their governments did not control the mass media in the sense underlying the resolution; so they could not, except within broad limits (libel, slander and obscenity), ensure that these media do this rather than that. Nor did their societies possess 'agreed values' in the sense meant by the Resolution. Indeed, they put

Harold Laski once remarked on the tendency within big institutions for policy to be secreted within the interstices of administrative decisions. That is especially true in cultures such as Britain which mistrust large, general policy statements on any aspect of life. It may be said of UNESCO that, paradoxical as ever, it loves large general statements—and then loses sight of policy in the sheer convolutions of its bureaucratic practices.

These Byzantine procedures reach their apogee in the biennial General Conference itself. Two American scholars, Cox and Jacobson, propose a division between what they call 'forum Organisations' and 'service Organisations' within the UN system.[4] That makes a useful first distinction between the nature of, say, FAO (clearly a service Organisation) and UNESCO (from some angles a forum Organisation). We have seen, though, that UNESCO is also a 'service', or operating body; so the implication that it is merely or chiefly a place for debates is not accurate. But six weeks of the General Conference can leave one feeling that UNESCO really is, above all, a forum or market-place, an elaborate machine contrived to present, on a succession of concurrent stages, almost all the nations of the world addressing each other, at great length, but by procedures which ensure that genuine dialogue is ruled out.

As with all its activities, UNESCO has clear presuppositions about every aspect of conference procedure, sometimes embodied in regulations, sometimes unwritten but accepted as good practice. Yet these rules or customs are infinitely elastic and only a green Chairman would try to enforce them consistently. A Member

4. Robert W. Cox and Harold K. Jacobson, *The Anatomy of Influence: Decision Making in International Organisation*, New Haven, Yale U.P., 1973, pp. 3–4.

emphasis on the freedom of artists and intellectuals, through the mass media as in any other way, to *explore* values openly.

These objections produced a deadlock. No one wanted a vote; the proposers seemed to have no fallback position; nor did one of the more experienced delegates suggest a coffee adjournment so that compromises could be arrived at. At this moment, I was called away by the Director General. When I returned about half an hour later I found the Secretariat relieved; the Resolution was through; a clever delegate had produced an amendment which satisfied a majority. It ran as follows: 'Whilst respecting the freedom of the artists, States will ensure that the media of mass communication are not employed to propagate material which is subversive of agreed values . . . .'.

State which has not paid its dues for years is virtually never prevented from being a full member of the General Conference. Meetings usually start late. There is no effective time limit on speeches. Delegates are frequently told that time is short and the list of speakers long, that unless each speaker restricts himself to fifteen minutes there will have to be a night session; and that even then some people may not be able to speak. All this usually has little effect. Some are under orders to deliver a long approved text word for word; others assume that their speeches, being important and beautifully phrased, are exempt from all such restrictions. Meanwhile, delegates are moving in and out continually, going for coffee, to telephone, to do business in the corridors or simply to stretch their legs.

It is a swirling parade of important people, or of people who were once important, or of people who think they are important. Ministers are likely to attend for a few days only, to require audience with the Director General, to be host at an official meal and to make a speech in Plenary chiefly intended for home consumption. For the remainder of the General Conference, the delegates will be of lower status and greatly overworked. A typical figure is the delegate—his rank not above that of, say, Principal in British Civil Service terms—who leaves the Delegation office at 9 a.m. with a pocketful of briefs and Resolutions to fulfil which requires him to weave in and out of the different Commissions all day, making 'interventions' on topics about most of which he knows nothing. He will pass en route the senior full-time officials of the larger NGOs, making use of their finest opportunity for multiple lobbying. Or he may see, but probably not recognise, one of the grand old men who have been coming to the General Conference since Mexico City in 1947 and have a place in the histories. Through all these move members of the Secretariat of all grades, looking for the ones into whose ears they can drop 'a possibly useful suggestion' about a programme they would like to mount and need support from outside for; or simply about lack of promotion.

By the end of the first week, a routine has emerged in which even the newest official can see the pattern within the confusion. A steady rhythm has established itself, one not likely to be violently disturbed except by a formal walk-out from the Conference Chamber. In the last two or three years, that has as likely as not been inspired by Chile; when their delegates rose to speak, the

bloc, usually led in these instances by Czechoslovakia,
moved out and stayed in the corridor until he had finished. These
are routines everyone understands; at such times the Conference
is a stage for minor symbolic political movements. The most
important idea behind the Constitution, that the Conference can
be host to an 'intellectual and ethical dialogue between States', is
not often fulfilled.

Yet, in spite of all the futilities it is better that the Conference
takes place than that it be made merely a technical and financial
meeting of officials. The debates may usually seem to get nowhere
but, especially when one or two good things are said, can have a
small exemplary importance now and for the future. These great
jamborees of the UN and its Agencies are unique in bringing
together virtually all the States of the world. Something can be
done publicly and a lot more privately on such occasions. Some
delegates are naturally happier with the opportunities for corridor
diplomacy than with the openness of the main debating chambers;
they are true to the instincts of national diplomats. For the
Organisation as a whole, both types of diplomacy are important
and should work in reasonably effective conjunction. These are
new, multi-State, procedures with, by now, their own tones and
styles which are subtly but significantly different from those of
bilateral diplomacy. Dag Hammarskjöld saw this, as he saw so
much else in the strange, complex embroidery of international
procedures:

> The United Nations is not an instrument for so-called
> appeasement from the point of view of either side, but it is
> a platform where a businesslike mutual exploration can go
> beyond what is possible in regular diplomatic forms.[5]

The greatest difficulties arise when one group of Member
States breaks the sustaining rules for this type of debate and, by
manipulating bloc votes, by threats or cajolements, pushes a
decision through the General Conference which affronts many
other States. At such moments the bulk of Conference members
look deeply depressed, and one realises that—no matter how
rarely the idea is invoked—UNESCO meetings are still felt

5. Dag Hammarskjöld: 'The UN and the Major Challenges which
Face the World Community.' *UN Review*, New York, June 1958, 4 (12),
p. 28.

underneath to stand for something better than the usual practices of power politics.

In spite of all such disappointments, there are occasionally moments which remind one dramatically what UNESCO is about. I remember Pablo Neruda, in poor health and only a few months from death, standing before the Plenary Meeting of the General Conference and reminding the delegates about UNESCO's fundamental commitment to the poor and deprived of the world, to them as whole human beings not simply as units who have to be made literate and given more money. It was as if the poor of his native Chile, of all Latin America, of the whole world, walked sadly and in silent reproof through that elegant hall, evoked by Neruda's passion and poetry.

In theory, UNESCO's Executive Board should help provide a counterweight, on behalf of the Constitution itself, to the one-directional pressures of national politics. Hence, the original notion that members of the Board have three simultaneous rôles: to represent their States or regions; to be eminent intelligences in their own right; and to serve the Constitution (as embodied in the General Conference) in itself. That ideal is less and less realised and is, indeed, being step by step formally moved away from.

Like all parts of the Organisation, the Executive Board has experienced a succession of changes. Article V of the Constitution, in its 1977 edition, has a note to paragraph A1, which defines the Board's composition; it runs: 'Paragraph amended by the General Conference at its seventh (1952), eighth (1954), ninth (1956), twelfth (1962), fifteenth (1968), seventeenth (1972) and nineteenth (1976) sessions.' Two main elements have changed: the size of the Board and its members' term in office. The size has gradually crept up as new nations have appeared, and in my time reached forty; it is now forty-five. The term of office used to be six years but is now four. Since Board members are elected by the General Conference, half of them finish their terms and a new half is elected each two years. Members are not immediately eligible for a second term. This is too high a rate of renewal and works against a sense of Board coherence, of collectively sustaining the Constitution.

Back in the beginning, it was possible to argue that the Board would eventually become a sort of world intellectual, scientific and cultural Senate. This proved almost as idealistic a notion as that of a world government. In its characteristically pragmatic way, the United Kingdom suggested right at the start that the Board should be composed of official government representatives. Ascher notes that from the earliest days some Board members used the phrase 'My government believes . . .' and so brushed aside the elegant triple fiction about their roles.[6] As UNESCO itself has been increasingly tied into the normal routines of Foreign Ministries, so the area within which the Board can be seen as more than a body of governmental representatives has shrunk. Sweden, also typically pragmatic, has been a leader in proposals that Board members be simply representatives of their governments (and in some cases, presumably, regions) and that therefore their seats can be occupied at different times by different officials, depending on the issues under discussion. The General Conference has not yet agreed to that major change. As usual it has compromised. In 1976, it resolved to let Board members' resignations be insisted on by members' own governments as well as being decided by Board members themselves. At present Board members are elected by name and in their own right, and can only be replaced by someone they have themselves named to act temporarily for them. So the difference between a country or region having a specific individual on the Board and having a place which it can fill as it will is quite crucial.

There is little doubt that that step will be taken. By now the much-amended Constitution puts the weight first on members' functions on behalf of their governments. It says the Board shall 'consist of forty-five members each of whom shall represent the Government of the State of which he is a national'. The next Article says: 'In electing the members of the Executive Board the General Conference shall endeavour to include persons competent in the arts, the humanities, the sciences, education and the diffusion of ideas'. Finally, the Article on *Functions* smoothly enshrines the paradox: 'Although the members of the Executive Board are representative of their respective Governments they shall exercise the powers delegated to them by the General Conference on behalf of the Conference as a whole'; that is, they will uphold the

6. Charles S. Ascher, 'The Development of UNESCO's Programme', *International Organisation*, Vol. IV–1, February 1950; and *Program Making in UNESCO, 1946–51*, Chicago, Public Administration Service, 1951.

Constitution. So the three concurrent rôles are still evoked, but in such an order and with such differences of stress and such blandness that one is in no doubt which rôle is pre-eminent.

Thus nowadays most Board members are government officials, not particularly interested in issues of intellectual principle and with no such pretensions. One or two others are rather low-level politicians, or old figureheads, and for such people membership of the Board, with its frequent first-class flights to Paris and handsome per diem allowances, is a prized perquisite. In Nixon's Presidency, the USA put on the Board two successive people so ill-equipped that one could only ascribe their nominations to gross ignorance or contempt for the Organisation's purposes. But an odd effect is sometimes wrought in people such as that. After serving for a while, learning something of UNESCO's range of work and hearing so many of the Board's assertions about the power and beauty of its own functions, they often conceive a great institutional pride, an almost religious awe for an organisation of a kind their previous experience never prepared them for. The Board also still contains one or two highly-intelligent people who are not simply government spokesmen. They sometimes irritate the full-time officials on the Board but the Secretariat, especially if they are presenting difficult contentious issues, often have cause to be grateful to them.

The relationship of the Board to the Director-General is always delicate and sensitive. He must have reasonably close and serene working relationships with the Board as a corporate body and know that he can almost always carry it with him in his submissions to the General Conference. But the Board also *represents* the General Conference and must scrutinise his performance on the Conference's behalf. One of the most important balancing acts to which a Director-General is committed, therefore, is this of his ambiguous relationship to the Board.

The Secretariat in general and at many levels is also remarkably sensitive to the Board and some of them spend much time during the six or eight weeks in each year during which the Board is in session in Paris (usually in two longish sessions plus some shorter) strengthening relations with its members. I was once told by a Board member, who wished to be friendly, that some other members thought I was too withdrawn; I should mix more in the coffee-breaks. It was true that I had kept well clear of those mopping-and-mowing interludes. However, I thereafter slipped down to the Executive Board lounge for coffee once or twice. I gave up again when yet another friendly Board member remarked: 'Oh, so *you've* joined the coffee-break lobby now, have you?' Some Board members know how to put such manoeuvres in their place; but too many of them are susceptible to lobbying, either because they hope to get something in return, or because they regard such wheeling-and-dealing as normal practice or because they are flattered. So once again the intellectual pool is muddied.

In a period when the real distinction of Board members has almost gone, when officials are increasingly in position, but when the Board's purposes are still said to be in some ways above those of individual governments, the result is a double one: more and more Board members do their business in the corridors or Delegations; more and more the Board's official main meetings are ponderous and humbug-ridden charades. Yet it is still possible for the Board collectively to rise to its own professed status, within limits and with many saving provisos. It is still impressive to see the Chairman of one of the Board's committees leave the Chair, or a member sit silent, when issues are being discussed in which their official brief conflicts with their own consciences or their sense of the aims of the Constitution. The member's Delegation is likely to put an official in as a substitute on such occasions, with the explanation that the Board member is indisposed. Even such occasional small acts of homage to the idea of intellectual freedom will become less likely as the present trend is confirmed. Still, in late 1977 the Board made public its great concern at Rumania's refusal to respect the rights as an international civil servant of one of its nationals within the Secretariat.

Large institutions evolve internal lives so strong, complex and all-engrossing that their full-time staffs tend to forget from day to day what it is, primarily, that the institution is meant to achieve. UNESCO, for reasons which should be now quite clear, is a supreme example of this process. Another way of evading the challenge of the Constitution is so to complicate procedures that substance is almost wholly submerged. Hence the extraordinary complexity of its Programme management.

Each General Conference evaluates the Programme of the last two years, scrutinises, amends and approves the Programme proposed for the next two years and votes it a budget; the Executive

Board scrutinises progress roughly each six months; the next General Conference comes round, and so it goes on. It sounds reasonably simple but, such are the masses of procedural barnacles which have grown around the process, it is in fact vastly convoluted. The central paradox—once again we come upon a paradox—is that in preparing and executing the Programme the Secretariat is at one and the same time both over-scrutinised and over-free; and the scrutiny is therefore ineffectual, too often merely fussy.

If UNESCO were ever really to assess the time and money which go not into the execution of projects but into political and diplomatic manoeuvres before they are set up, and into the defence of them against attackers from within once they are set up, or into seeking extensions of them when their time is up, the results might shake even the General Conference into remedial action. But it will not happen. Too many vested interests—among Member States, delegates, NGOs and Secretariat members —are against an effective scrutiny. Too many of the projects resist objective assessment, being themselves subjective and 'philosophical'. The result is that a fair number of UNESCO's projects are imitation gold bricks. If someone were to point this out incontrovertibly he would inspire a fierce barrage of rejoinders (heavily reinforced by the Secretariat) admitting what could no longer be denied but arguing that, viewed on that higher ethical level demanded by UNESCO's Constitution, the selling of imitation gold bricks is a considerable contribution to peace and understanding between nations.

The General Conference takes place in the Autumn of each even-numbered year. So to the Secretariat a biennium looks like this. Say, six weeks for the General Conference, plus fourteen weeks of the Executive Board plus four weeks of a sub-committee of the Board; all making a total of twenty-four weeks a biennium or twelve weeks a year of direct scrutiny. To this must be added the weeks spent in directly preparing for the Conference or Board meetings and the weeks spent sorting things out after they have ended. My own rough estimate is that not less than half of a high official's working year is spent, not in carrying out the programme but in preparing for, sitting through and clearing up after these scrutinies.

To this must be added an elaborate pattern of inter-Agency consultation and, in theory, coordination which keeps some members of the Secretariat busy for weeks, sitting in committee rooms in a variety of capital cities. And it would be an unusual General Conference or session of the Executive Board which did not pass a Resolution or two requiring the Director General to report on some new issue in a short time in addition to starting work on the newly approved Programme. So after each such session elaborate analyses have to be made of the implications of the extra and often surprising demands just made on an already creaking machine.

Even all this is only the beginning of the processes which whittle down the time the Secretariat has actually to fulfil the Programme. Above all, there are the massive Conference documents to prepare. They are all identified by the number of the Conference plus their own fixed number. Thus, 18C4 means to any UNESCO habitué the Medium Term Plan prepared for submission to the eighteenth General Conference; and 18C5 means the Programme for the next biennium presented to the same Conference. The C4 document shows better than any other the strengths and weaknesses of the Secretariat. The best statements of medium-term objects and methods are of exceptional intellectual distinction and a tribute to the high quality of some men and women who, because they still believe in international cooperation or because they can't shake off the drug of this kind of life, put up with this bizarre way of working instead of withdrawing to a university. At the other extreme one comes upon plans which are blatant attempts by members of the Secretariat to ensure that their particular parish remains just as it is and has been for years.

Document C5, the biennial programme, has much the same underlying characteristics; it emerges after months of negotiation, manoeuvre, plotting and counter-plotting, compromises and fiats. Then both documents are checked and double-checked by the various services (Budget, Personnel, Publications, Conferences, etc.) until finally the order is given to print both; and yet they are still only drafts for the Executive Board and then the General Conference.

The major document is clearly the C5, since that proposes and costs a Programme for the coming biennium, starting on 1 January of each odd-numbered year, a few weeks after the General Conference. Once approved, as amended, it is reprinted and becomes the bible for that two years. The last such document to which I contributed had 570 pages, each 11¾ inches by 8¼ inches. But even that pales beside the document produced in the course of the immediately next recurrent frenzy: the book called Programme Activity Details, or PADs. Every single aspect of every approved project in the five- or six-hundred-page Programme volume is translated into a separate detailed timetable of precise actions. The result is that, for the part of the programme for which I was responsible and which occupied at my last General Conference ninety-four closely-printed pages in the Approved Programme book, the preparation of the PADs produced another volume of several hundred pages.

Finally, of the regular major documents, there is the Director General's Annual Report which is discussed by the Executive Board at each Spring meeting as well as by the General Conference. It is a monstrous volume. The English version of the last issue to which I contributed ran to 296 closely-printed, double-columned, large pages and listed, small paragraph by small paragraph, virtually every official act the Secretariat had committed over the previous year.[7]

After all this, a Secretariat member in the upper reaches is likely to be left—for paying attention to programme execution in itself—perhaps 20 per cent of the working year. For the rest he is likely to be engrossed in successive, highly-patterned, bouts of frenzied procedural activity, defending, presenting, persuading, amending. Meanwhile, the air rings with the jargon germane to such mad operations, such as: 'deadline', 'viable', 'frontier', 'dynamic', and our old friends 'interface' and 'ongoing' (as in 'ongoing dialogue'). By now, the rituals really have almost swamped the substance. If the Executive Board or, even more, the General Conference, could agree on substantial main lines for the Organisation to follow they would not put up with such excessive elaborations. But they do not and apparently cannot. Hence, programmes of profit to a particular region will be ruthlessly promoted by delegates from that region. Proposals to end such programmes so as to release funds for new initiatives will meet stubborn and, usually, successful resistance. So when budget cuts become inevitable the programmes which are 'deferred' (often a euphemism for killed) include some of the very best, in terms of the Organisation's main international purposes. They are vulnerable because

7. With the issue published in 1977 it became shorter.

they do not represent the interests of particular Member States or groups of States. There are far, far too many sacred cows. It follows that the Programme, so grandly presented as a coherent whole, is forever threatening to fall into little bits and that the Board and the Conference spend far too much time running this way and that after particulars. In this vast and complex wood, virtually everyone can see only a few trees; and nearly everyone has his favourite tree and spends too much time protecting it.

Faced with such complications, the Member States feel squeezed out, unable to alter the programme except in small particulars. The Secretariat always knows more; knows why such and such a proposal is really impracticable and theirs the only feasible one, can usually persuade a friend or compatriot to head off an amendment they do not want. It is not an absolute block: certain changes can be made and are permitted, or else the delegates would feel no more than rubber stamps. They have to be made to feel that their journey and expenditure of time have some justification. But the movement they can make within the proposed Programme is slight. One sometimes feels sorry for them; but not much and not for long. For it is the Member States who lay down in what excessive detail the Secretariat shall prepare the Programme, in what excessive detail it shall be discussed by the Executive Board and the General Conference and so on through all the procedures I have described. The result is inevitably a Programme which has hardly any room for movement left in it. Every project has a booby-trap attached to it, to warn off the inadvertent tamperer. If Member States really want the General Conference to have more command over the proposed Programme, they will have to rethink the whole Programme-preparing procedures from the beginning.

The result is a Programme which contains too many different items, which is both over-detailed and over-grand, and which is inadequately funded for its purposes. It lacks practicality and bites off more than it can chew. It abounds in clotted paragraphs, each asserting what UNESCO will do towards alleviating some vast problem, on budgets of about $20,000. Thus, the aims of this paragraph are fine, the budget paltry:

Equal Access of Women to Literacy Programmes
In accordance with the principal aims of the International Women's Year in 1975 and the recommendations of the

Third International Conference on Adult Education held in Tokyo, particular attention will be given to ensuring women equal access to literacy and post-literacy programmes as a first step to their continued education. Emphasis will be placed in this programme on countries where women are still inhibited from playing their full rôle in society. In addition to fellowships for teachers, administrators, planners and out-of-school educators and assistance to non-governmental organisations active in promoting the access of women to literacy programmes, advisory services will be provided for this purpose upon request from Member States ($18,900).

. . . and this paragraph is both grandiose and, so far as one can understand its drift, underfunded:

The Role of the Arts in Life-Long Education
A contract will be concluded with a National Commission for the organisation of a seminar on the contribution of artists (in the performing, visual and plastic arts), craftsmen and their work to the process of life-long education, including the conditioning of the public by music. The seminar will afford an opportunity for research into the aesthetic dimension of the educational function as a whole and hence of daily life. ($19,400.)

Often such under-funding is justified by the jargon of the profession: that UNESCO's funds are meant to be 'multiplier' money, seed-corn financing, pilot initiatives and so on; and sometimes this is true. More often, one sees Member States ordering the Secretariat to mount projects in difficult areas with far less in funds than they would allot to a national project of that kind; and Secretariat members yield, because they are timid or cynical or muddled. Or Member States use deliberate underfunding so as to corral the Secretariat, because they suspect waste in areas they cannot easily identify. This explains a glaring paradox: that the Budget is costed and recosted, scrutinised and rescrutinised, so that in principle no economies should be possible. Yet at the same time, as we saw earlier, Member States add new projects; but they do not allot extra funds. Face is saved by the use of some such formulation as: 'The General Conference instructs the Director

General to undertake this new project out of economies made in the course of executing the programme.' The real meaning is: 'We know you can gather together some free money in spite of all your protestations that estimates are pared to the bone. Do it and we will ask no more questions.' What Member States do not at all like, and what Directors General seek, is a substantial 'float' of free money which can be used for such extra demands at any time in the biennium. The nineteenth General Conference, in 1976, finally admitted the principle but gave the Director General, predictably, far less than he had asked for.

A yet further paradox is that, though the Programme goes on being fragmented, Member States have from the very earliest days called for it to be concentrated on a few main areas. Julian Huxley welcomed this and fought for it. But even in his short period as the first Director General he saw the principle eroded by just those Member States who were calling for its strengthening; and he saw many in the Secretariat conniving with the process, since it protected their Programme territories.

To sum up, we have a situation in which the level of the Budget is plainly too low for the demands made on the Organisation, a deep reluctance on the part of Member States to increase the Budget to the point at which the programme could live up to its professions; and therefore the strong establishment within the Secretariat of all sorts of bad habits: corner cutting, letting the word stand for the deed, claiming great victories where only a shadow of the promised project has been realised. Shrewd Secretariat members learn to recognise which importunate demands have to be carried out to the letter and which can, after a decent interval, be safely left to die. The Secretariat, formally over-scrutinised, ends by being effectively over-free; and many of them exploit that situation. But not all of them. Some, at all levels, refuse to play tricks, do their best against all the odds to understand and then to execute precisely the instructions given to them. An Assistant Director General, who must ensure that a substantial part of the Programme is prepared properly and must publicly defend it before the Executive Board and the General Conference, learns to rely on such people. They are in a minority; but, as we have noted before, they come from all parts of the world and are the real nucleus of the international civil service.

6

THE SIXTH ESTATE
DAILY LIFE IN THE SECRETARIAT

In UN life, God wot,
No villain need be! Panic spins the plot:
We are betrayed by what is false within.

(after Meredith, *Modern Love*)

i

The internal life of the Secretariat is exceptionally intense and inbred; UNESCO Headquarters is a cocoon, a hothouse, a vast and uneasy hamsters' nest. For many members of staff UNESCO and its internal affairs form a total world, a continuous drama almost wholly concerned with the staff's own common life. This tendency is made more powerful because so many of the Secretariat no longer belong anywhere culturally and this ensures that, in spite of their importance as international officials and the considerable comforts of their lives, many of them feel insecure, isolated units.

It is not easy to live such a life. One hundred nationalities but no common culture; what is the unifying force? If unity is to emerge at a professional level it must come from adherence to a common ideal or working practice rather than from unstated but shared cultural assumptions and attitudes; and the stated ideal is less gripping than the lived-into culture.

Especially for those who come from cultures distant in space and kind from that centred on Paris, the stresses of this sort of isolation are considerable, the psychological tensions complex. Such people are as though cut off from their roots, living in a society which may not cherish some of their major assumptions (about family life, the old, the young, 'face', reverence, deference). Nor can they, and this is of course true also of West Europeans in the Secretariat, belong in the host country. They may like France and enjoy living in it; but they have no organic relation to it. They have no extended family around them, are not working within the French economy (being paid in US dollars, inflation-proofed), and do not have a vote. They may be deeply interested in aspects of French life but still they cannot mesh in with it; they are hanging from the chandelier, looking on. It all makes for a strange and partly attractive sense of unreality, especially if—like us—you regard the whole experience as interim, willingly chosen by you but also with its term defined by you. But those who have that kind of assurance are fortunate.

Still, UNESCO can also be a generous place and hard to leave. A Secretariat member may have been a very important person back home and may regret his lack of equivalent status in UNESCO. But he may well have been paid, as a Minister or senior official in his developing country, only a fraction of what he receives in UNESCO as a professional officer; if he reaches Director level the disparities are even greater. Life at UNESCO may often see the knives being brought out; but he may have been used to that kind of thing in even more intense form back home, and without the protection of Staff Regulations or a Staff Association. The regime in his home country may have changed since he joined UNESCO; perhaps he would not be *persona grata* to the new rulers. His wife may like Paris and, after the first two or three years, have settled in there very happily. His children may by now be more Franco-phone and French in style than Asian or African or Latin Ameri-can (and be unwilling to speak their native tongue, even at home). His capital city or home town may from this perspective seem even more remote, dreary, ill-provided than he had always known it to be. All this makes it difficult for many Secretariat members to think cheerfully about the expiry of their contracts. A wily Director General may therefore give permanent contracts highly selectively and at the price, unspoken but real, of conformity. Most Secretariat members are on fixed-term contracts which expire every three years or so.

Hence the nervous thinness, the extreme tenderness about personalities, the only just-submerged worry which are all endemic to the life of the Secretariat. A harsh superior can easily reduce a middle-aged man to tears or set off a panicky flurry of telephone calls in search of defences. Early in my time at UNESCO a very secure and intelligent Italian Director told me that he tried never to write a harsh memorandum, no matter how much he was provoked; that things put in writing can never be erased, or at least the recipient cannot be sure they are no longer in circulation. Their contents are leaked and they are photocopied out of malice. The recipient, if he is already insecure, will day after day see himself losing face—with his subordinates, his equals, the women in the bar, the commissionaires at the front entrance. It is kinder, the Italian advised, to speak one's criticisms behind closed doors. This is far better general practice than that of the bully; but it doesn't always suffice. The really case-hardened in the Secretariat, if they are criticised orally and privately and invited to cooperate in improving the work, are likely to ignore or misrepresent what was said once they have left the room. I remember also a leathery old Scandinavian Director who said that if he felt the time had come to make a firm criticism and make it unevadable—and whether he was writing upwards or downwards—then it *had* to be in writing. For quite a while I tried to occupy what seemed like good middle-ground between the Italian and Scandinavian positions. If oral discussions in any particular case had gone straight into the sand, I hand-wrote 'strictly personal' notes with no carbon copies. Even so, to such notes I sometimes had no response at all, whether typed or handwritten, public or private. What is not on a file does not exist.

Even more than the other specialised Agencies, UNESCO tends to attract people of high sensitivity, idealism, artistic and intellectual inclinations. So some of its peculiar nervous strains arise from this fact, that it is the Agency most involved with non-technical, philosophic and value-laden issues. Add the strains of cultural uprooting, and the stage is set for a complex register of doubts and uncertainties. Consider only one of many curious phenomena. Where a man is cut off from a culture sharply different from that which surrounds him in UNESCO and Paris, and when such a man enjoys both UNESCO and Paris but still feels obscurely guilty about being separated from his culture, his insistence on the integrity and beauty of his own *lares et penates* becomes all the stronger. He may well stop a staff meeting on the grounds that some particular cultural form to which 'my people' give great force has been flouted. Or he remembers his high status back home and tries to insist on the rights to which he thinks himself therefore entitled, even in Paris. Or he gives as an excuse for bad work a cultural justification meant to still the criticism by sheer spiritual weight: as that in his country they refused to be narrow, one-dimensional time-watchers or habitual desk-occupiers like Western Europeans. There are elaborate, indeed obsessive, procedures to cover all flanks against attack, a subservience to higher ranks which is also felt to pay off in reflected status, fierce internal competitiveness and a sense of the impossibility of losing face so strong in some people that it is unthinkable for them ever to admit an error. At such times, even if the evidence is plain and the atmosphere cooperative rather than punitive, they will stare at the wall ten degrees off centre and deny that two and two do after all make four.

It follows that those Secretariat members who are particularly exposed to such stresses cannot easily resist undue attentions from their governments. More than twenty years ago the International Civil Service Advisory Board noted: 'Governments do not always refrain, as they ought to do, from taking advantage of the presence of one of their nationals in the service by pressing him to assist in the work of national delegations.'[1] In short, and more brutally, they expect loyalty and leaks. The pressures on some Secretariat members can be so constant that they cease to feel like pressures and become an accepted aspect of the job. Many Secretariat members are simply required, by their Delegations, always to have in mind the interests of their countries, to tell all and to act in the way they are told. This totally turns on its head the formal definition of the relationship of a Secretariat member to his own country, as also defined by the Advisory Board: 'Another duty . . . is to give to his compatriots the fullest explanation possible of the work of the international body, especially in connection with decisions which may be unpopular in the country in question.'

On the other hand, some countries seem to leave their nationals fairly well alone. Certainly, the United Kingdom did not try to influence me; the professional distance was well kept on both sides. By contrast, at least one Delegation arranges weekly meetings with its nationals in the Secretariat; one could run into them hurrying along the underground passages which thread below the Place de Fontenoy, at mid-morning on the regular day. The more subtle citizens of such countries are likely to argue that, though— say—Western European countries do not give orders as overtly as

1. *Report on Standards of Conduct in the International Civil Service*, 1954; International Civil Service Advisory Board; para. 24.

their own do, this is because they have no need. Western European influence has been so strong in the Organisation from the beginning, the hold of Western European 'free' persuasion is so all-embracing, that those governments don't need to use the snaffle and the bit. There is something in the argument; only the very rarest people can often step right outside their own cultural assumptions. Yet it is important not to blur such distinctions as can rightly be made; we can't legislate for the almost unconscious. We can distinguish between what may be latent cultural dispositions and the overt pressures through which some nations treat their citizens not even as national civil servants on detachment but fully as continuing national civil servants, which regard all nominations for posts in the Secretariat as wholly governmental matters (most other nations also have by now an over-governmental approach to recruitment; there is simply not enough widespread and non-governmental advertising of posts), or as issues to be settled by nepotism within the ruling groups. Naturally, these attitudes reach their peak in the struggles for ADG posts.

Against this swirling background of constant uncertainties, the writing of any report which may have personal consequences or implications becomes a very tortuous affair. Factual or technical reports are often of a very high standard; but the nearer they approach political issues the vaguer they become. Reports by Secretariat members of their own activities—for example, a report on a mission away from Headquarters by a programme specialist—or reports about other individuals and their work, notably the regular 'performance reports', can be Laocoön-like in their twists and turns. I scarcely remember a mission report which did not present the writer himself in glowing terms. Performance reports, which have to be completed every two years or so, are in most cases inadequate to their purposes and in some cases plainly dishonest. One has to bear in mind that the practice, the very concept, of performance reports is not widespread; and that the more or less frank performance report, with warts at least sketched in, is a thoroughly strange phenomenon to some cultures. Men are got rid of, undoubtedly, but by more circuitous procedures. It follows that the 'confidential reference', meant to be a quite careful weighing of the pros and cons of a candidate's suitability for a particular post, seems odd and disturbing. The UN form of application does ask candidates to list a few persons to whom reference might be made, but that section of the form can only rarely be made good use of. In most instances the government officials whom the candidate cites will be wholly favourable to him. Why should their government make 'X' their candidate if they did not mean to support him unreservedly; and why, by criticising in any way your candidate, should you help another country get their candidate in?

Few Secretariat members find themselves able to write reasonably frank and comprehensive performance reports. For the nationals of some countries, a tender political sense prevents them from criticising the nationals of those other countries with which they have close official ties. But direct ideological opposition can produce much the same effect: I cannot recall a critical remark on a report by an American about a Soviet citizen, or vice versa. So any suggestion of the less than perfect is likely to raise a time-consuming, nervously-wearing series of recriminations and complicated counter-charges. Some people resolve the difficulties by inventing (and French is much more suitable for this than English) more and more elaborate and circumlocutory ways of completing reports. I once asked a Director why, since he had consistently and strongly grumbled about the work of one of his officers, he had now filled the man's performance report with a series of rhetorical arabesques wholly in his favour. His reply went roughly as follows: 'I think—with great respect—that you do not fully see the force and subtlety of the French employed in this report. The English language—which we all so much admire—is extremely direct. But this officer is from a culture which works by indirection and is himself Francophone. What I think you may possibly not have realised is that the placing of that adverb—*there*—before the verb rather than after it in the third clause of the middle sentence in Box 6 of the form is a considerable warning signal to him. Had it been *after* the verb, that would have been praise; but *before* the verb it qualifies and reduces what the rest of the sentence seems to be saying—it introduces an element of critical shading. I assure you he will feel the force of that.'

Or a report may be completed in a wholly laudatory way but steps taken to place elsewhere the person concerned; not outside the Organisation, unless he has no friends or national officials to call to his defence, but sideways to another Division. There is a small sad army of such people, at several levels, who are thus shifted every few years. They are known; there is sometimes resistance to accepting them; but a deal is usually struck. They are deeply unhappy people underneath the carapace of contempt for the Organisation and its ways with which they have usually provided themselves.

The Organisation does its best to improve assessment by introducing ever more complex pro-formas, types of question which make lying and bluffing more difficult. But the old hands, like experts cracking a code, soon find ways round those too and the bad habits substantially continue. Behind it all is a sort of galley-slaves' mutual protectiveness: 'don't rock the boat' elevated to a fine art. Hence it is extremely difficult to ensure that someone who is unwilling, no matter how poor his work may be, will actually leave the Organisation on the expiry of his contract. Most have enough diplomatic and political connections to protect themselves. The hardened cases, recognising the weakness of their positions when a performance report looms and seeing signs of their superiors' wish for a change, will spend hours at the photocopier preparing material for defence and counter-attack. The procedures for contesting an adverse performance report are, rightly, elaborate and weighted in favour of the staff member. But the complexities are now so extreme that not even the Director General, no matter how convinced he may be that an official should go, can be sure that that will happen if the official concerned uses the full apparatus of official and unofficial appeals— from the Staff Association and his Delegation, to his Foreign Ministry or the UN Administrative Tribunal. Where there is a shadow of doubt—and even in the worst cases that can usually be invoked—'equity', a moral commitment to someone who has served for, say, five years, requires that they be at least given a further three years' trial. The next time round equity demands that someone who has given eight years' service to the Organisation be not cast out. Only a few in my Sector were plainly not at all fit for the jobs they held. Some left; others remain. The only periods when such people show sustained energy and negotiating skill is when they are mounting their recurrent defences of their own positions.

In UNESCO especially, these Secretariat problems are compounded by the difficulty of getting a right balance between specialists and generalists. Self-evidently, the case for staffing the programme departments with high-grade intellectuals, artists and scientists is strong. But such people are not always good administrators; and specialists, though they may be at the forefront of their disciplines when they enter UNESCO, become rusty from sitting at an executive's desk. Yet UNESCO must be responsive to new intellectual and scientific movements. It is not easy for any of us to admit that we have fallen behind, even though at the backs of our minds we know that re-entry to our old university or research institution would be painful. Nor can the Non-Governmental Organisations wholly make up for intellectual out-of-datedness within the Secretariat. Hence the Secretariat's tendency to resist change, to insist on writing the programme much as it was before, to keep the semi-private allotments much as they have been for years.

At the extreme, Secretariat members can become like the intellectual equivalents of ageing prima donnas, more and more strongly speaking for their art, their specialism, as their hold on that art or specialism becomes increasingly blurred. If modifications are finally forced upon them, they quickly learn the latest jargon and take credit for the new look; and they more and more join the demand for time off for retraining. That is not bad in itself, but the scale of the demands—especially in the light of the generous leave already allowed—has become excessive.

The solution, I am by now convinced, is to place at the heart of the Organisation a solid core of generalists, people who are willing to learn how to be good international executives but know an idea when they see one and can pick qualified people for carrying out the bulk of the programme under contract. They may well have entered the Organisation as specialists but have come to recognise that they can carry out UNESCO's difficult work with enjoyment, can be competent and also remain sufficiently aware of developments within their disciplines. Around them, whether for periods of three to five years within the full-time Secretariat or as short-term consultants, should be a large range of thoroughly up-to-date specialists. This basic structure would do more than any other single innovation to reduce the worst dog-in-the-manger habits within the Secretariat. It would take years to effect and would be resisted step-by-step by some in the Secretariat and some Member States.

It will be clear from all I have said that the assuming of normal legitimate authority can be difficult in organisations such as UNESCO. Charles Winchmore finds this feature so central and limiting that he says: 'Cooperation depends rather on persistent recourse to the arts of persuasion than on continuous exercise of the power of command.'[2] During my time at UNESCO the Director General employed more often than not a monolithic authority, so I have a more than usual sympathy with Winchmore's position. But it only takes you two-thirds of the way; for the rest, persuasion in these circumstances is a rubber weapon; some one person simply has to decide and take the consequences.

It will also be clear that a Secretariat member is likely to be on much firmer and happier ground if he has some stay against the shifting, cosmopolitan, nervously stretched sweep of his day-by-day professional life. So much the better if he has a firm and supporting family background. I do not know if the incidence of broken marriages is higher here than in other professions; it often seems so. So much the better, too, if he has a sense of professional security, has not been forced into the position of regarding his job at UNESCO as the only raft on a hostile sea, since he fears to go home and does not know whether France would give him diplomatic asylum. Most of all, such a person needs to feel in touch with his own roots and his own psyche. He will be a better civil servant if he knows or has known what a 'home', what 'belonging', is. With that basis he can move around and make some contacts which are real, not anxious movements in a void.

ii

' . . . the worst
Are full of passionate intensity.'

For reasons which will now be clear, the bad practices within the Secretariat are very bad indeed; it is not pleasant to write directly about them since they may well darken the total picture more than would be justified. But they cannot be passed over with a few

2. See *The U.N.: Accomplishments and Prospects*, p. 624, op. cit.

general comments; undeniably, they have a nasty exemplary importance.

The worst habits are extensively and habitually practised by only a few. But they affect to some extent the tone of the whole place, and only the rarest individuals can avoid picking up one unpleasant trick or another when they are under special pressure. Many members of the Secretariat are skilled at pendulum swings between excessive timidity—say, yielding to Permanent Delegates even on important matters of principle—and excessive arrogance, in defence of their programmes. In all this coming and going, the substance of the programme itself, the substantial questions about whether it is well-conceived, due for renewing or dropping, receive very little attention. Such staff members will unashamedly lobby anyone who seems likely to be useful, in or out of the Secretariat, in Paris or back in their home countries. They will alter drafts and workplans after they have been approved by their superior officers, who are then responsible for something they did not agree to. They will persuade conference delegates to present resolutions (which the Secretariat members have provided already drafted) designed to move the programme or more funds in their directions.

These are only a few of the many kinds of professional derelictions quite frequently practised by some people; they amount to a refusal to accept even the basic norms of civil service behaviour. The records show that this is not a new situation in UNESCO. The early Directors General, weary after months of negotiation in advance of the General Conference so as to reach internal agreement on the best ways of apportioning the funds, sometimes found their plans undermined by quite senior staff members who had subsequently gone to work with the delegates of their own States or with friends in the non-governmental organisations. Such betrayals are always hard to expose categorically and are always denied; but everyone knows they happen and who initiated them.

That is the most spectacular form of deceit: bringing about amendments to the proposed programme and budget after it has been agreed with the Director General and other colleagues. Day by day many others are practised, less important in themselves but all contributing to an atmosphere too much shot through with petty or large dishonesties. Some people habitually steer contracts towards friends, relatives, members of their own nations, anyone who might possibly be useful in the future. Or they make internal trade-offs between departments; or they are adept at passing nasty problems on to the next man's desk; or they break the regulations by sending letters on matters of business privately from the post office across the Place de Fontenoy, letters which do not exist on the files but have their effect in moving matters the way the writer wants.

In all this, a *locus classicus* is the handling of 'visas'. Visas are initials on documents which signify that officers at all the right levels appropriate to the importance of a particular document have seen and approved its contents. Almost all Secretariat members, and especially those at the lower professional levels, are loud in their contempt for the 'bureaucratic nonsense' of the visa system. But they know it has to exist; there is not a sufficient basis of trust in working relationships to allow moderate interpretations of policy or the disposal of even modest sums of money to be settled below senior levels. Many junior members of staff are, privately, grateful for the protection a higher visa gives. Senior officials may and sometimes do try to delegate responsibility for the issuing of visas; but they know this can only be done un-officially; if a visa is misused below their level on a document they should have initialled, then the fault is theirs. The book of Secretariat Regulations or manual of practice lays down all this in precise detail. Meanwhile, visa malpractices flourish. The most common is that of holding a number of important documents for visa until shortly before the diplomatic bag is due to leave and then rushing in with a request for immediate visas, on the grounds that the recipient governments are going to be angry if the documents do not arrive by the next pouch.

Then there are leap-frogging telephone calls both inside and outside what is known as The House, calls which bypass a superior but get a promise of intervention from an ambassador or Permanent Delegate which he will subsequently find hard to retract; so the immediate superior is put on the spot. But this is miserable stuff; best to move on—after giving the *Report on Standards*, which I have quoted earlier—another, and as always measured, word: 'It is thus inexcusable for an official to lobby with governmental representatives or members of legislative bodies in order to secure support for improvements in his personal situation or that of another staff member, or for blocking or reversing unfavourable decisions regarding his status.'

Such people, and I had best stress again that they are a minority —though a substantial minority and one whose style to some extent affects almost everyone from time to time—are likely also to be alternately bullies and cajolers with their own subordinates. Those subordinates are given to understand that, whatever fiddles they see practised, they must keep quiet or expect sharp retribution. In my last General Conference one competent and decent junior officer prepared the text of a very important Resolution. The case had been much fought over, so this version had to express accurately the finally agreed position of Member States. I discovered by chance some time later that the printed text contained a small but significant alteration. The young official had been ordered by his Director to make the change *after* the document was returned, initialled, from my office and take it directly to the printing department. The official was embarrassed and ashamed; but, after all, I was soon to leave and his Director would stay.

We had occasional discussions within the Sector for staff of all levels, with no restrictions on the issues raised. For the first few meetings they revealed a strange paradox: the themes which most concerned people were bad relations and bad practices within their units; but the grumbles generally had an ineffectual, generalised air. It was as though there was an invisible but strong barrier between the point at which they insisted that serious human problems abounded and their own ability to be precise and concrete about them. After a few weeks, by which time a degree of trust had been built up, a group of them told me directly that if they were to voice identifiable complaints the consequences for them would be extremely unpleasant.

Idleness can be found in any place of work, large or small. But in some people at UNESCO it can reach such heights that one needs a more poetic word to describe it, such as 'sloth'. Apart from those for whom it is a natural predisposition, Secretariat members who are national civil servants from authoritarian countries on fixed-term leave of absence tend to be most prone to slackness. To them, unless they are people of more than usual imagination, it is difficult for UNESCO and its problems to seem real. They tend to live still within the cauls of their national delegations, to spend their spare time at their national family

clubs, to have virtually no informal links with their working colleagues, to see Paris as a backdrop, to know that their few years
there will quite probably put them a rung or so up the promotion
ladder when they get back home to real life . . . and to be immensely keen on missions to all corners of the world. Their time
at UNESCO will be the only period in their lives when such
constant and wide-ranging foreign travel is possible. The most
amiably shiftless of this type of official whom I encountered once
missed a most important programme planning meeting, in the
middle of a midweek morning, because there was a birthday party
over in the Delegation offices for the Deputy Permanent Delegate.
We were almost sorry when they finally recalled him, out of embarrassment; he was a once-born innocent, not a plotter or
schemer.

No wonder dispiritedness can settle in at all levels, from the
best and most willing secretaries to Directors themselves. If your
boss is lazy and leaves you regularly to handle documents which are
clearly his responsibility, if he overloads you for that reason or
because he wants to make you crack so that you are more vulnerable to criticism and threats, if he absolutely refuses to cooperate
with anyone outside his own unit or even within that unit—sometimes to the point of leaving orders that no decision, however
minute, shall be taken in his absence on leave or mission . . . if you
are subject to this, at bottom paralysingly frightened, behaviour
then you will sooner or later lose heart; and many good people
have.

Above all and overall, there is the endless, many-layered, intense
gossip. Harrod makes the interesting point that gossip in such
institutions tends to be defined by national personalities. I would
want to add that there are recognisable gossip-clusters and of two
main forms. First, the national or group clusters by which gossip
is directed at 'That African caucus' or 'that Soviet bloc in the
Secretariat' or 'that Western European gang'; plus 'mafias'
ascribed to many lands and regions. Then there is the more common type of personal and personalised gossip chiefly running
upwards all the way through the hierarchy. Hardly anyone escapes
except, for a short time, the newest and lowest-ranking member of
staff, since for the present no one depends on him or her and so has
grounds for feeling threatened. Let me give one instance, quite an
intricate one, of how this practice works.

A professional officer is very anxious to be appointed to a vacancy just above his present grade. His immediate superior, with complete disregard of the size and strength of the field and quite disingenuously, will promise warm support for what he calls his subordinate's first-rate candidature. After all the complex and careful appointing procedures have been gone through the job goes to someone else. Thereupon the disappointed candidate goes to see his superior officer again. His boss hints that he is himself as disappointed as the candidate and that, were he not such a discreet official, he could reveal much. A few minutes later discretion melts and he reveals, 'in the strictest confidence' that, in spite of all he had himself done to make sure his subordinate got the job, the case proved to be lost from the start since the Director immediately above him or the ADG or the DG simply disliked the candidate now being consoled. Thus the superior has done two things in one: he has escaped the blame for having said too much in the first place, and he has struck another blow in the endless war of gossip he carries on about all his superiors.

In such a world every act, no matter how trivial it may seem to an outsider, is seen as a political act and its meanings obsessively enquired into. A sinister explanation can usually be found for even the most apparently simple matter. Recurrent phrases are of this type: 'What does he mean by that?' 'How is this likely to affect my programme, my Division, my promotion prospects?' 'He sounds convincing and obviously has the ear of the Director, but where's the trap?' Hardly any offer can be taken at face-value and all have to be subjected to close tactical scrutiny. One of the most recurrent of all expressions is: 'You do realise, I hope, that what he *really* meant by that was . . .' That road leads to an endless maze of imputed motives, counter-actions, misreadings, floated denials or new rumours, and misrepresentations. To me it seemed on balance not greatly damaging and certainly it was more economical in time to take everything at face value unless its duplicity stared me in the face, or unless I knew that such and such an official was congenitally incapable of telling things straight. Inevitably, to some people this quite deliberately practised lack of defensive devices was worrying and seemed against nature; they were happier once they had decided that it was, after all, only another instance of the consummate low-key cunning of the British.

I have argued that the most important tap-root of Secretariat unease is cultural displacement; that is the larger perspective. To the internal life of the Secretariat itself the most common cause of unhappiness is promotion-sickness. The phrase is not excessive. For some people the desire for promotion really does have the effect of a kind of illness, which drives the more extreme cases to tranquillisers, bouts of frenetic marginal activity or long hours of simply staring over their desks working things out inside their heads. The most important single urge is to 'make P5'. A P5 carries a number of diplomatic privileges, notably a CD plate for one's car. A good number of Secretariat members feel underneath, and so do their wives, that they will only be able to retire happily if they have that plate for their last few working years. After a few years at P5 the urge to become a Director begins to grow like a cancer too. Sometimes friends try to help such a desperately promotion-sick man by altering the description of a vacant post so that it fits his qualifications; but that is too sophisticated a device to be employed by any other than very experienced and highly-institutionalised staff members.

It is important, before turning away from this pathetic record, to stress again that the more striking of the bad habits practised within the Secretariat are important less for themselves, since crooks and fiddlers can be found in any organisation, but because they are the more obvious manifestations of a malaise which runs virtually throughout the place and so affects almost everybody. It sometimes feels as though the human texture of the place, like brittle elastic, has dried out. One incident more than any other brought home to me how, when that texture, that blood and muscle of assumed relationships, has lost its power and virtue you are left in a wasteland.

We were once mounting an important conference in the capital of a Member State. A handful of us arrived a few days early to make final preparations. Then, at about ten o'clock in the evening of the day before the conference, the DG was due to arrive. Two senior officials, both Europeans who belonged to the staff of the DG's private office, were going to meet him together with the Foreign Minister and Head of Protocol of the host country. I didn't seem needed and said so, but the DG's staff officers told me with considerable insistence that I certainly should attend since I was the highest-ranking Secretariat member on the spot.

At the airport there was the usual flurry of official and unofficial greetings and we then set off to the cars. At that point I noticed that the Spanish Permanent Delegate who had arrived on the same plane from Paris as the DG was struggling with his luggage. I gave him a hand and we arrived, more slowly than the rest, at the terminal entrance where his embassy car was waiting. I turned to get into the UNESCO car and found it had gone; it was already disappearing into the darkness towards the capital fifteen miles away. I got a lift in the nick of time from the Permanent Delegate.

The next day I spoke to the two officials who had so strongly urged that I go to the airport. How could they drive off without an apparent thought for a colleague, whoever that colleague was? They were genuinely astonished and embarrassed. They are both gentle and kindly men and certainly had not acted out of conscious carelessness. Of course, this kind of thing might happen anywhere (though in most such cases the car would have turned back before it was far down the road). But, in UNESCO, what those officials were displaying is all too common a quality. When they are in attendance on the Director General or on some other very senior person even men who are helpful and well-meaning in normal relations can lose that awareness we usually have in a reasonably relaxed situation of other people with whom we are in human not hierarchic contact and who, like us, have needs, obligations, dues. They lose it because their whole conscious being is screwed up to, focussed upon, seeing that 'nothing goes wrong'; otherwise, who knows what bolts will be hurled from heaven. So they become as it were temporarily lobotomised from the ordinary give-and-take of communal life. In such a state, some men would leave their wives and children on airport steps.

iii

Between the very bad members of the Secretariat and the very good, whom we will come to later, there lies the vast middle range, many of whom are more-or-less-decently disillusioned. Some long-serving members, quiet and devoted family men, settle for cultivating their domestic gardens, do their jobs quite

effectively but no longer with enthusiasm and in general tend to
have that rather attractive air of not expecting too much, of being
amiably sardonic but still steering fairly straight. Neither damned
nor blessed, they sit in the middle-circle, not demanding overmuch
of themselves, or of anyone else or of any idea of principle. 'A
plague on both or all your houses' is one of their guiding rules,
together with the assurance that virtually everything comes down
finally to politics or self-seeking. The best among these hurt nobody;
the worst have become self-destroyingly cynical because they have
defined their own general level of work by the worst habits of
others. They see—among their colleagues, in the Delegations, in
the non-governmental organisations—fiddling, laziness, improper
pressures; and they ask, in that favourite UNESCO expression
I have quoted before, 'Why should I be more royalist than the
King?'

On the whole these are not bad men and women and in some
ways they can be relied on. So long as it is someone else who is
taking a stand, they will sometimes carry the ammunition. Nor
would they dream of indulging in the rhetoric commonly adopted
by representatives of Member States during the public business
of UNESCO. There is at least no contradiction within them
between stated principles and action. For them, to paraphrase
George Eliot, everything is below the level of rhetoric; it is also
below the level of willed commitment to a principle. I once heard a
delegate from a highly authoritarian Member State criticise some
members of the Secretariat for showing too much 'initiative' and
'imagination'. I thought the remark both funny and ghastly, but
few other members of the Secretariat who were present seemed to
think it either significant or curious. One wonders sometimes if
there is any limit to what some of them will take. They seem so
worldly-wise, so much more at ease in being unexpectantly knowing than in being open and vulnerable, so much older than the
rocks on which they sit, so Tiresias-like, that one begins to
wonder whether, if they found themselves being eaten alive by
mad rabbits, they would say: 'Ah well, we always knew that's the
way the world goes at bottom.'

For another group, bafflement before the enormity of the
Organisation's paradoxes has led them to make that great 'retreat
into the technical' which I mentioned much earlier. They would
rather not know about political implications, no matter how glaring

some of them may be. This is most noticeable where UNESCO is providing help in framing specific national policies; say, a national communications policy or cultural development policy. In each case, as in others like them, you can have official policies which help develop freedom or which restrict it. Secretariat members who do not wish to face these implications will claim that what Member States do with UNESCO's practical advice is their affair; they try to restrict themselves to a tight servicing role, the provision of hardware and verbal technicalities.

It will be seen how widespread is the uneasiness about introducing ethical considerations into the work, how strong the desire to operate at the level of the factual and pragmatic. That might be supportable were it not for the fact that UNESCO lives on the assumption, to use one of its own favourite public phrases, that there is 'an ethical dimension to international intellectual cooperation'. If that is consistently shrugged off, in the name of hard-headed effectiveness, then pragmatism gradually becomes expediency and all considerations of a moral kind are lost in the blur of relativism. Whatever happens, is the unspoken agreement, let us not raise the ghost of either the Constitution or of our oath as international servants. In the particular challenge which, more than any other during my own five years there (the Israel Resolutions of 1974), most called on officials to face directly their own places and purposes, one of the most common reactions was this deep uneasiness and unwillingness to face the fact that the issue presented them with a moral problem at all. What they did, therefore, was enter into elaborate and complexly-argued explanations of the situation in purely political-pragmatic terms.

These are sad but not actively wicked types of behaviour, and the people who practise them are often quiet and kindly people. Indeed, UNESCO can be, for all its very bad habits, an extremely friendly community and show gentleness and care in relations between colleagues as strongly as anywhere else. Perhaps just because they are so often under pressure to do shoddy work, Secretariat members will honour with great warmth someone who seems to have managed to keep clear of such entanglements. I remember a great crowd of staff members of all grades—possibly a thousand of them—coming together one evening in the huge seventh floor restaurant, to wish godspeed to a colleague who was retiring after almost thirty years' service. He was a middle-range technician and therefore known to all types and levels of Secretariat member. He was greatly respected for the consistently high quality and fairness of the service he gave. It was intriguing and touching to realise how much this record was admired, even by people whom one knew to be exponents of some of the worst Secretariat practices. Probably such a man would be likely to be more respected than an equally honest and competent person in a different kind of post: his work did not raise divisive political issues, nor was he in a position to make or mar anyone else's promotion. Institutions choose their own small secular saints, Billy Budds, surrogates, M.B.E.s. Then one reflected further that even the undoubted niceness of some Secretariat members towards one another has the slightly desperate air of the occupants of a well-equipped but rudderless and threatened ship, of castaways on a comfortable but remote and volcanic island. They are, such people, holding on decently rather than nastily; they have their pride. And others, their blood brothers, are less gentle but still highly-skilled, hard-working, hard-drinking, rather contemptuous of Member States but always sure to deliver the goods on time.

Nevertheless, all such attitudes ensure that the Secretariat yields too much, too often and too soon to improper pressures. Where all is a matter of contingency, where the notion of 'patience' is so often used as to have become an evasion, almost any compromise is finally resorted to so as to avoid a confrontation. From time to time this may be good diplomatic practice; just as often it is founded in woolliness or fear. Almost any outrageous act by any Member State can somehow be made to seem acceptable; and 'we reached a good consensus' can actually mean that the lowest common denominator of positions was settled for.

Hence the Secretariat's tendency to over-interpret Member States' likely positions and then over-react. Faced with admittedly difficult and politically sensitive issues, staff members will often worry so much in advance about what this State or that bloc may do about them, are so anxious to anticipate criticism, that they extend possible reactions to some exaggeratedly gloomy distant point and then set about taking pre-emptive action against these imagined reactions by cutting out any reference in their basic documents to this or that issue (important though it may be) or by editing a consultant's paper until it is disembowelled. From many such incidents I especially remember a good internal discussion—unusually good in that at the beginning we thought we might actually take the step—on the proposal that Bishop Helder Camara be nominated for a certain Peace Prize. In the end it was decided that there was no point in 'unnecessarily' antagonising Brazil. 'Why should we be holier . . .'; so we were left again with the response of the fearful courtier.

Thus the Secretariat now finds itself in an excessively weak and exposed position when the programme meets, as it must from time to time, tough political issues. They have yielded too often, too soon and on both big and small issues; they have little ground left to stand on when a stand is needed. For instance, their records and statistics in some major fields are not now complete because over the years they have yielded to the insistence that, since State X does not recognise the existence of State Y (and State Y is not a member of the Organisation), the statistics on this or that educational, scientific or cultural issue shall not include those of State Y; in fact, they are no longer comprehensive world statistics.

The worst such case I met concerned a proposed conference on torture throughout the world, sponsored not by UNESCO itself but by Amnesty International which is an NGO affiliated to UNESCO. They had obtained the use of UNESCO's premises. Just before the conference they issued a document which recorded the widespread governmental use of torture today. The following morning a good number of Permanent Delegates waited upon the Acting Director General on the fifth floor to express their governments' deep displeasure over the document and to demand that the conference be refused the use of UNESCO's halls. There were a few very troubled hours whilst the Secretariat tried to sort everything out for the best; but in the end the organisers were asked to take their meeting elsewhere.

It would be fair but futile to dilate on the bad behaviour of the governments concerned. It would be easy to say—and some Secretariat members said it all the more forcefully because they had been forced into an uncomfortable moral impasse by the issue —that Amnesty International should have known better, should have recognised the restraints inseparable from working with inter-governmental agencies or have found an elegant way of circumventing them. But these are not the most important considerations. The heart of the matter is that, when those numerous Permanent Delegates went along to the Acting Director

General, they did so as people who assumed that their demands would be acceded to. With no embarrassment, with all the assurance of landlords demanding the rent, they made their stipulations; and they would have been extremely surprised if they had not been able thereafter to cable home that those demands had been met. That is the rub: the clear expectation that the Secretariat would yield on an important issue of principle. In this case, I know that the Secretariat was in serious distress and tried hard to find an honourable solution; but I do not think the outcome was ever seriously in doubt. The UN Agency with a special commitment to the protection and development of human rights, and to free speech, has progressively become more timid, mealy-mouthed and yielding. If it had been bolder over the years those Permanent Delegates would have thought twice before laying their protests. At what point does 'accommodation'—no matter if always made with the best of intentions—amount to a fatal letting-go of the fundamental aims of the institution?

One of the major principles of survival for big organisations is that no matter how much the organisation may deviate from its original purposes, the survivors—so long as those purposes remain publicly the same—will claim that the organisation is fulfilling them better than ever. Whatever is, is right. Almost any organisation with intellectual and ethical aims will find itself trimming from time to time, if only so as to stay alive and able to continue doing some good. The point of danger comes when its staff are trimming simply so as to stay in business, when survival is the pre-eminent though implicit aim, when all justifications are made, though again implicitly, not in furtherance of the organisation's basic purposes but so that the organisation shall merely continue to exist, when the cost of repeated compromise has become a hollowness at the heart.

In view of all I have said so far, it might be thought that the Secretariat's most apt epigraph should be: 'the best lack all conviction'. It would be more accurate to say that a great many lack conviction and that the best certainly don't wear their convictions on their sleeves. But the best do have, and on occasions clearly show, convictions. When Trygve Lie was calculatedly frozen out by the Soviet Union (so that eventually his position as Secretary General became untenable) some UN Secretariat members went to no USSR social functions for the remainder of his term of office. Trygve Lie also noted that no delegates of Member States made the same decision.[3] I do not think many staff members of UNESCO today would make such a clear stand; but I hope and think that a few would.

For the most part the best Secretariat members hide their convictions, and on occasions their distaste, behind a restrained politeness to Member States' delegates. They are no longer starry-eyed, whatever the depth of idealism with which they entered the Organisation. No one intelligent enough to do the work competently could remain naïvely optimistic. But this core of, usually, quite long-serving officers is not wholly disenchanted. They still retain a sense of what the UN is about and of its possible value. To have this confidence in the face of the disappointments they meet weekly argues great patience, a very long breath indeed. To continue in the belief that the work is at bottom worthwhile, rather than to settle for simply doing what you have been told to do without questioning its value, means that you are committed professionally to living in a state of constant tension.

Good behaviour isn't as dramatic as bad, so the practices of the best staff members are harder to describe than those of the bad hats. There is a much-used remark in UNESCO that if about forty people were taken out of the Organisation, not forty from the top but forty hand-picked from all levels, the place would collapse. The figure is probably on the small side but the point is a good one. This is a small group and, interestingly, they are known to most members of the Secretariat, even to those who try to dismiss their achievements. They assume that they will have to work extremely hard day after day; they have considerable executive ability; they operate under conditions so insecure and so consistently in crisis that many national civil servants in developed societies would be shocked to think of working month after month in such circumstances. At their very peak, they are magnificent: highly intelligent, of great probity, precisely and relevantly effective in carrying out extremely difficult assignments. To see such a senior official, faced in the morning with a cable which announces some disaster in a far corner of the world, one which calls for aid from all parts of the UN system—say, a landslide or flood which has destroyed homes, hospitals, roads, schools and all major public services—to

3. Trygve Lie, *In The Cause of Peace*, London, Macmillan, 1954, pp. 408–9.

see such a person move into action on a global scale is to be given an enlarged view of the definition of work itself. He can set in motion within a couple of hours decision-making across a range of governments, the release of funds from the right agencies, the movements of men and materials and in particular of experts and specialists towards the stricken area, a whole range of discussions at different levels (political, logistic, technical). He will stay with that problem for however long is needed to make sure that every thing it is possible to do in this first phase has been done, so that he can now snatch a few hours' sleep before the next phase begins. These qualities, powered by devotion to the task, high intelligence and the willingness to subordinate private life for as long as is needed to do the job properly, are not solely the preserve of the professional officers. Members of the clerical staff can show them just as strongly; at such times the work is essentially team work and this, in the best offices, binds all levels together.

As a group, such people are not much given to speculation; indeed, they tend to shrug off general considerations and to be happiest when they can—like surgeons on a difficult case—get down to the intricate logistics. This unease may lie partly within their natures; perhaps people of this disposition are attracted to international executive and operational work because it offers opportunities for their urge to make complex things work more smoothly. The inhibition may also be increased precisely because they did join the Organisation out of idealism, have seen that idealism take many knocks and so are now—though they remain serious and committed—disinclined to talk about high purposes.

It may be as well to underline, though I briefly made the point earlier, that these pillars of the institution are by no means only Western European or from other parts of the developed world. To assume that would be to confuse form—a style, a certain way of being a civil servant—with substance. When you work with people from many different cultures you are being invited all the time to recognise that there are many more and subtler ways of being a good worker than you had ever realised. Insights from other cultures repeatedly throw a critical light on much you have always taken for granted. Then you realise how easily you have been tempted to settle for a routine exemplification of your own, hitherto apparently secure and unquestionable, cultural styles. I guess this may be something of what Karen Blixen had in mind when she said, speaking of Africans and their response to Europeans:

> I sometimes thought that what, at the bottom of their hearts, they feared from us was pedantry. In the hands of a pedant they die of grief.[4]

Most of the older, strong Secretariat members entered the Organisation between 1946 and the early 'fifties; so those who are still serving are likely to be at least in their own early fifties. At the other end of the time-scale are some remarkably good officials now in their late twenties or early thirties. These are often found among the 'stagiaires' or specially-chosen trainees from countries at present under-represented in the Secretariat. This seems to me an admirable and in large measure successful scheme, one which attracts a good number of people who look like becoming first-rate international civil servants. A useful rule-of-thumb for recognising the most promising is that you find yourself, after a few months, no longer consciously aware of what country or region such an officer comes from.

Given these two stronger ends of the Secretariat—the older and the quite new—one tends to think that the staff structure sags in the middle; and then to wonder how it will be when the older men go. But of course there are some good people at all ages. Still, the middle years of life in the Organisation are hardest to bear. It is among those middle years that one most notices that range of attitudes which runs from the hurt and tired to the bored and cynical. Cynicism is no doubt sometimes a front. Manning reminds us that jobs such as this call out in some people, unless they are to be worn down, a 'game' element, that therefore wry and ironic and disillusioned styles do not necessarily indicate continuous depression or cynical conviction that the work is useless.[5] All such styles may be, he argues, a 'skilled and successful playing'. In these circumstances, he continues, 'it is best to be dependent on those who know it for a game and themselves for players'. In other words, teach us to care and not to care; to go on going on, with a touch of dry humour.

4. Karen Blixen, *Out of Africa*, Putnam 1937. Cape paperback ed. of 1964, p. 26.
5. C. A. W. Manning, *The Nature of International Society*, London, Bell, 1962, p. 164.

7

THE DIRECTOR GENERAL

The Director General deserves a chapter to himself because he is a force unto himself. The nature of his job shows in high, operatic relief most of the good and bad possibilities within UNESCO. Almost the whole of my service was passed under one DG, René Maheu. By the time he resigned, in late 1974, he had been in charge of the place for thirteen of its twenty-eight years. He died a year after retirement; not, I think, because he found life insupportable with his great occupation gone; he knew he had not long to live. Rather, one could say that he would have died some years before if he had been willing to succumb to his dreadful illness. He beat it by sheer determination to see out his term of office.

For one who worked closely with this pugnacious, driven, irascible character it is almost impossible to separate the nature of the job of DG in itself from Maheu's own personality; and I shall not strain to separate the two. I will say more towards the end of the chapter about Maheu the man. In this first part, in which I discuss the general terms of the job, I shall let him and his personality move in and out of the analysis. There is a justification for this procedure: the possibilities of the job, for good and ill, went with the grain of Maheu's personality: he capitalised on those terms and extended them. They drew out the larger-than-life qualities which must have been incipient in him but only found the right ground for expression as he moved up the career grades in UNESCO; he was the first career DG. The challenge of the job developed and also distorted his personality; in turn, his personality defined and, again, distorted the role of the DG to a degree which was not true of any of his predecessors but which will affect all who follow him.

Maheu was the fifth DG. In the autumn of 1971, at the celebrations for the Organisation's twenty-fifth anniversary, it was still possible to assemble all five for a group photograph—with Maheu, in the middle of his second six-year term, looking immensely attentive to his predecessors, relaxed but dominant. He was always deeply respectful to the other four but quite assured that no one of them could have run a ship of that size with such intellectual and executive skill. Two of the group died soon afterwards, Julian Huxley from illness and Torres Bodet by his own hand. He had cancer behind the eyes and was in great pain.

It is easy to list those characteristics of Julian Huxley which made him unsuitable as a DG; for example, administration bored him and the Executive Board bored him extremely. But in some important ways he was an excellent choice for a first DG. He had foresight: over thirty years ago he recognised the emerging import-ance of environmental and population questions, and even saw forward to the likely costs of mass tourism. He was inventive: one still comes across activities set off by good ideas of his, whether to do with non-governmental organisations or cultural initiatives or much else. He had great courage; he argued directly that respect for human dignity and for the individual should be more important for UNESCO than the idea of the State. Reading his early speeches one is struck by how many fundamental matters he got right, whether about emerging major issues or about the best way to tackle a potentially vast programme on a tiny budget. Sooner than almost anyone else he was talking about the need to concentrate the programme. He was less perceptive in proposing that the Organisation propound a sort of world philosophy, a new humanism; that could never have been adopted. But in general he kept up the flow of good ideas throughout the two years of his tenure, and his speech to his last General Conference is still not only useful but exciting reading. He gave UNESCO an intellectual head of steam and a restless sense of enquiry at its start.

I knew Huxley slightly but never met his successor, Torres Bodet. I particularly regret this since Bodet was clearly a man of great imagination, dignity and courage. He had been Mexico's Minister of Education, so knew the political and diplomatic world well; he was also a distinguished writer. It is generally believed that his idealism could not endure the fact that, within two years of the Organisation's coming into being and throughout his own term of office, many Member States were spending more time arguing about economies than about what needed to be done to promote education, science and culture in a world still in many respects crippled by the war. After a hard-fought battle he resigned, since the General Conference refused the budget he had asked for.

The third Director General, Luther Evans of the USA, is usually credited with giving the institution more effective administrative practices. He was certainly experienced in high-level academic administration. Less strong was his sense of the fundamental challenge being presented in his day, the high water mark of McCarthyism, to the difficult balance between the intellectual life and politics. UNESCO suffered from his failure to stand up to McCarthyism. The fearfulness which lies behind so many Secretariat practices, even today, seems to me a hangover from that period; like someone badly burned in childhood, the Secretariat has ever since shrunk too quickly from political challenges.

Evans's successor, the Italian Vittorio Veronese, had and has a fine reputation as a diplomat and negotiator. When last I met him he was President of the Banco di Roma and still voluntarily very active on behalf of UNESCO's causes. But actually running the Organisation damaged his health, was quite simply too much for him, and he had to resign. One does need to be extremely tough, physically and nervously, to run UNESCO. Maheu, who succeeded Veronese, had all the toughness needed and some to spare.

i

The most useful brief way to set about analysing the job and its peculiar isolation is to say that the Director General has at one and the same time too much power—vastly too much power—and too little power, so little that for some main aspects of his rôle he is rendered ineffective.

The Director General, as the only elected member of the Secretariat, himself appoints everyone else. In fact, the word 'elected' is a misnomer. The Executive Board, after much negotiation, submits one name to the General Conference. The 'election' of the present DG, Maheu's immediate successor M'Bow, was paradigmatic. The African states had made it plain that they wanted a black African as Head of a major Specialised Agency. The bulk of other nations decided, severally or in groups, that the wish could be acceded to; UNESCO's Director Generalship became vacant at about the right time. As the line became clear, Member States began to say more and more that M'Bow was indisputably the best man who could be found for the job; which was an insupportable claim, since his candidature had not been seriously tested against any others. M'Bow was appointed with the usual acclamation by the General Conference.

Being 'elected', the Director General starts with a special place in the hearts of the main governing organs, the Board and the General Conference; he has to live up to the trust they have put in him. They want, as corporate bodies, to continue thinking they have made a splendid choice. But since those bodies are themselves riven with differences, some of them profound, he has to perform a continuous balancing act so as to maintain the suffrage of the chief groups within each of them and of the corporate organs themselves—especially if he hopes for a renewal of his term. It seems and is an ambiguous position; that ambiguity is also the source of the Director General's remarkable powers.

He is called upon to serve a single entity—the Constitution— by governing bodies whose commitment to that entity is spasmodic and who have hardly any sense of common purpose. They come together only once each two years, as the General Conference; and the Executive Board meets each six months. The Permanent Delegations are on hand all the time but have not yet found an effective role, except in isolated cases; nor do they have even the beginnings of a collective role. The Director General has much room for manoeuvre among these wide spaces and contrary winds.

What complicates his position further, and increases his opportunities, is the fact that the Director General is not—as one might have assumed on a quick assessment—a kind of Permanent Secretary to a large quasi-Ministry with world-wide commitments, the top civil servant in an international Secretariat. In one sense, he has duties similar to those of a Permanent Secretary. But he has no Minister, no one to be publicly answerable for the work of the institution and no one to shield him from attacks by his equivalent of a Parliament or from public opinion. One might argue that his 'Parliament' is the General Conference, but then one recalls the incoherence of that congregation and the analogy fails. One might say that the Executive Board is roughly his 'Minister': he carries out their orders as they have received them from the General Conference; they oversee him; and they to some extent report on his work and may also shield him at General Conference. But the Executive Board, too, is divided within itself and its corporate spirit goes into recession when a major political issue appears. Members of the Board are at such times just as likely to be criticising the DG directly on behalf of their governments as simply checking whether he is faithfully carrying out the mandate given him by the General Conference.

Hence the Director General has far greater powers, powers indeed of interpretation, than could be allowed to a Permanent Secretary. The execution of the many tasks assigned to him at each General Conference often brings him up against serious political snags, and to a large extent he must decide for himself how best to surmount them (though he may in some cases, and as a protection to himself, consult the Chairman of the Executive Board). He is constantly making political decisions, knowing that a few months later, after they have been noted and discussed in Foreign Ministries, they may return to plague him at the Executive Board or the General Conference. Given the insanely rigid recurrent timetable and the often inhibiting divisions among Member States he must have and must exercise wide discretionary powers. If we need analogies, it would be reasonable to call him something between both a Permanent Secretary and a Minister.

This ambivalent, suspended position can be exploited. He can shuttle between groups, and play them against each other so as to get what he wants. If he chooses his topic and his time carefully he may play the developing countries against the developed. He can, for example, propose a budget increase far higher than the developed nations want; but this gives him good credit with the poor nations. He must be ready to trim, since he knows that to stick hard to his first figure would greatly anger the developed nations, and he does not want them to harbour a grudge against him. Yet the developing nations are demanding a large increase. In the end, if his moves and counter-moves are well played, so that he taps the unwillingness of the developed nations to have a serious clash over the budget with the developing, he will end with a budget considerably higher than the developed nations really want and one which even looks respectable to the rest.

The increasing direct politicisation of UNESCO in the last few years has had the complementary effect of expanding still further the Director General's powers. When the whole institution seems even more likely to fall apart than it has always done, he is seen more and more, and sees himself, as the one main stay against centrifugal disaster. He must find forms of words, formulae to paper over cracks, means of getting together a respectable budget. It is an ambiguous, nervously exhausting and lonely situation. Yet shouldn't the six or seven senior colleagues who make up his top Board of Management give him strong, continuous and reliable support? In theory, yes; in practice, they do so only marginally; and in some respects they simply cannot do so. There can be no collective Cabinet responsibility; the decisions have to be his. He should listen and assess how far advice is disinterested and sound, or how far—though not at all disinterested—it gives him a clue as to what an important Member State or group thinks on a particular matter, or how far the advice is merely parish-protecting. Directors General seem almost to forget from one month to the next that they have a Direction Générale; and when it does meet the atmosphere is odd and awkward, the procedures jerky through lack of use. The conditions favour, and generally produce, a monologue by the DG rather than a discussion. There is no basis for general trust or a serious devolution of powers. The Director General cannot identify himself too closely with any one group of Member States; nor, given the composition of his staff even at the very top, can he share power.

Yet that last statement is too unqualified. It would be difficult and risky to share power, and the kind of man who is likely to become a Director General is not likely to take that risk often. If a DG were willing to do so, he could act more collectively; but he would all the time be afraid that he had given hostages to fortune, left some flank unprotected. For those members of the Direction Générale who would like to be responsible international civil servants this is the most depressing single fact of their professional lives. That, in all public matters, the DG is like a great and glowing sun to their small and watery moons matters not at all. What they do mind is working in a situation where trust is lacking and where every member of the staff, no matter how great his effort at probity, tends to be treated as though he planned to run away with the Organisation's political and ideological cutlery.

Hence, enormous deference is accorded the Director General inside the Organisation and, when he is on official business, outside. Within the building, words such as 'deference' itself, or 'loyalty' and 'discipline' are commonly in play; second-order words such as those are far more common than first-order words about values. Any large organisation, even one with an intellectual brief, will evolve internally a language of operational style rather than one about fundamental purposes—those may be assumed to have been settled before the institution was set up; even more, to discuss them when one is actually trying to make the place work seems embarrassingly self-conscious and pious. Nevertheless, UNESCO's weak internal consideration of intellectual implications and the very high incidence of purely operational, ship's crew language go far beyond what might have been expected.

A similar sense of deference governs the accepted conventions as to which members of the Secretariat can speak to which governing organs. Normally, the Director General himself will sit at the side of the President of the General Conference in Plenary session; if very pressing reasons take him away, the Deputy Director General will sit there; on the very rare occasions when neither can be available, one of the ADG's may ascend the rostrum temporarily. Lower than that, I never saw the representation on such occasions fall. In presentations to the Executive Board, the convention in my time was that the Deputy Director General sat to the right of the President throughout except for major debates, when the DG appeared (and the DDG stayed). The relevant Assistant Director General, sitting one further to the right, would probably make the actual presentation and withdraw to the rear when his item was completed. That practice began to ease in the early Seventies, so that nowadays Principal Directors or even, quite exceptionally, a simple Director might speak to the Board, once permission had been obtained by the DG or DDG.

In visits to Member States the Director General may well wish to be treated as a Head of State or at least as a First or Prime Minister. Many Member States will humour him here, especially the new, smaller and poorer countries; others are likely to be more cavalier about his status. Still, in many countries he may assume that a large limousine will be at the aircraft steps, with the UN's blue and white pennant fluttering at the wing and a few motorcycle outriders ready to do what is called a 'sweep' out in front.

One of the many preoccupations of the DG's personal staff is to ensure that the protocol officers of the host country give him the fullest respect due to his office. If protocol habits differ, there may be a major incident. The state opening of one Ministerial level conference in Indonesia might have seen a walkout by Maheu himself and his immediate staff if we had not noticed in time that he had not been placed in the front row for the ceremony, close to President Suharto. It was not easy to persuade the local officials to make a change, since the meeting was in Jokjakarta and the protocol rules in force were those of the court of the Sultan of that province; and by those rules no full-time paid official—as distinct from a person of high birth or a statesman—could sit at the front. There were many members of the local aristocracy present, closely watching where everybody else was placed. The situation was saved by an Indonesian ex-member of the Secretariat who luckily happened to be in attendance on Suharto himself; he used all his national and international diplomatic skills to find a form of words which allowed the protocol officers to put Maheu's chair in the front row. Ostensibly, at least; I had the feeling it was still a couple of inches behind those of the others in that row. If Maheu had walked out, and I have little doubt that would have happened if the original placing had remained, he would have made the statement which is standard practice when protocol has done less than justice to the honour someone believes is due to him: 'It's not for myself, of course. But I represent my country/organisation, and will not have it demoted.'

In one sense it is right and inevitable that the DG should himself finally decide on all major issues. He cannot be a collector of majority opinions from below, without reducing the Organisation to impotence and being even more open to attack himself. He is given great honour by Member States, but will not be spared if things go wrong; he has to be willing to trust his own judgment. But that inescapable fact has led to an excessive centralisation in virtually every matter where a decision is needed. One is altogether too aware of the Director General, day-by-day and job-by-job. He signs too many things, too many documents go out in his name, too much directly flows from him, too much patronage depends on him.

This process finds its natural peak in the making of appointments. In my time—and today the decisions are even more extensively in the hands of the DG—all appointments down to and including the level of P5 were made by the DG himself. This covered the Deputy Director General, the ADG's, the Principal Directors (D2), the Directors (D1), and the top rank in the Professional grade (P5). The Director General took advice, certainly, and for Directorships and above was required to consult the Executive Board, orally or in writing. But the decisions were his. If he had consistently gone against the clearly expressed majority view of the Board, the question might well have arisen as to whether there was a sufficient basis of mutual understanding between him and it. Before that point is reached, an astute DG will yield a few positions and so retain his extensive freedom of action largely untouched.

At the next grade down, P4, appointments were made by the Deputy Director General; it was only at that relatively low level that the DG did not intervene directly. So far, it will be noted, the Assistant Directors General who between them carried out the programme and who each therefore had under their authority some Principal Directors and plain Directors as well as a great many P5's, P4's, P3's, P2's and P1's, had no powers of decision on appointments at all. Here is where the procedures became even more outlandish: all appointments at P3 and below were made, in my day, not by the programme ADG concerned but by the ADG in charge of Administration.

There is this to be said in justification of the procedure: the ADG for Administration, since he has house-wide responsibilities and is directly responsible for the Office of Personnel, can keep the needs of fair geographic spread habitually in mind when considering appointments. Programme ADG's might be careless of them or biased towards one region, though I think they would soon learn better ways. But reaching agreement with the programme ADG's is quite different from deciding over their heads. The ADG for Administration had final powers to appoint to posts at P3 or below, even though he could have little understanding of what makes a good specialist in all the many disciplines involved. It is as though the Bursar of a University were to have final say over all appointments up to lecturer level, whatever the subject, on the grounds that only he could ensure that some non-academic factor was properly taken care of.

The ADG for Administration in the early seventies was a Soviet citizen and this meant that, if we put up a candidate who was both the best qualified and also of a suitable nationality, this ADG was still quite likely to dig from the bottom of the pile of applications that of an East European not necessarily well-qualified for the post. I would protest to the Deputy DG and the DG, and sometimes the protest was upheld; not all could be upheld, since that would have caused the Soviet ADG to lose too much face.

Far too many items go from Member States direct to the DG, and from him—probably with a note indicating the general line to be taken in response—to Sectors, Departments and Divisions and then back to him for signature. The whole process reduces even further the sense of personal initiative, gives the lazy and fearful something to hide under and produces a sense of dispiriting blockage in others. One knows that what will finally be done is what the man at the top chooses, often after inadequate discussion since he cannot possibly brief himself thoroughly on all that flows over his desk and the pressures of his job make him unable or unwilling to listen for long to others. Similarly, the politics of his rôle make him increasingly suspicious of all changes within Secretariat practice which have not been initiated by himself. That jealousy extends to the other Specialised Agencies, except when they are collectively threatened by outsiders; then, they band together firmly.

A Director General begins to see spies everywhere; he constantly fears conspiracies. If a senior official is attracting unusual loyalty he is likely to be accused of running 'a Latin American mafia' or 'an Anglo-Saxon clique' or something similar. Quite early in his term of office, a Director General will establish his own unofficial spy-ring. What they say may stick and rankle and thereafter some poor unfortunate suffers, is posted to a very distant place or his contract is not renewed. It is only too easy to see how this state of affairs comes about. The Director General feels driven, unable to trust, surrounded by time-servers, politically-fixed men or the purely floating; he becomes more and more suspicious and more and more convinced that in the last resort he is quite alone. He is right: in spite of all the overt deference and indeed subservience, he is constantly being watched for weaknesses, is the favourite subject of partial and often malicious gossip. He knows most of the flattery is false, that he must watch for hidden traps being sprung, learn how to recognise poisoned cups, and detect all significant changes of tone, all new and unusual groupings among subordinates.

For, in spite of all I have said about his importance, a Director General has in some respects very circumscribed powers. Precisely because he has been 'elected' by a series of accommodations between groups who do not often see eye to eye, his head is always quite near the block. Because he often has to help the representatives of Member States out of tight corners, especially when their conflicting national briefs prevent them from going straight for a sensible solution, he can build up the kind of resentment reserved for anyone who gets us out of impasses created by our own folly. If things go badly astray in the public negotiations of the Organisation then, no matter what awful follies and disagreements their own debates may have shown, Member States will regard it as his job to get matters back on to an even keel. If the Executive Board finds itself in the full flood of a debate which cannot fail to reveal deep and violent disagreements they will blame the Director General for letting the debate get on to the agenda, and will save themselves from overt mutual recriminations by turning on him. Maheu was a past master at handling the Board and usually enjoyed it; but when once again he had pulled off a remarkable feat of giving them at least a narrow ground on which to stand together and also saved himself from excoriation, he would be likely to turn to a senior colleague whom he knew would share his sense of the occasion and give a twisted, strained but cocky grin—he had come through again. I never forget, he told me once, that when a major issue is being debated the Executive Board is a corrida and I am the bull.

There are moments when it seems as though the DG simply has to be humiliated, as a purgative act for the internal workings of the governing organs. No Director General will admit this publicly and some of them, one has the impression, would not have admitted it even to themselves. But it tells on them all, as they spend more and more time making tactical moves to protect themselves. The quite extraordinary isolation of the job pushes them that way. Zimmern noted this as a characteristic of the life of high-level international civil servants forty years ago; it is still quite particularly a feature of UNESCO and its Directors General; they are:

Suspended in mid-air . . . permanent officials without a
Minister to supervise their activities or to cover their
blunders or to defend them from unjust attacks.[1].

Surrounded by man-made pitfalls, unable to trust many of his
colleagues whatever their rank or formal duty towards him, a DG
seeks, internally, not so much a power-base as a support-base, a
fixed base if possible even if a small one. He needs at least a few
people whom he can trust almost absolutely and who will be his
eyes and ears. Though he cannot afford to practise collective or
Cabinet responsibility he can even less afford to be totally un-
connected; that would be a form of suicide. If he is to retain
majority support within the General Conference he must be sure
of having reliable political reports at the end of each day's business
there. Having adjusted his own position as necessary, he must then
be able to issue modified orders, ranging from changes in texts to
instructions that such and such a delegate is to be won over by
argument or flattery or the promise of reward; and he must be
able to rely on these things being done to the letter and in the
spirit in which he has ordered them.

He must learn to practise that strange love-hate relationship to
the Executive Board, to exploit that image of the 'Club of the Good,
the True and the Beautiful' which the Board likes to weave around
itself, accepting their great respect towards him whilst recognising
that it is given only on the understanding that in the last resort he
is expected to remember that they appointed him and that he can
only continue comfortably so long as he has, fairly consistently,
their majority support. To see an experienced Director General
such as Maheu making notes throughout a Board meeting, de-
tecting a swing and adjusting on the run the draft of his own
subsequent speech, no matter how carefully it has been prepared, is
an encapsulated education in the internal realities of international
intellectual life. And below the Board are the Permanent Delegates,
always on hand and certainly not to be antagonised habitually;
but to them or most of them the DG can be directly fierce on some
occasions or relaxedly hail-fellow-well-met on others; they are the
Second Division.

1. Sir Alfred Zimmern: *The League of Nations and the Rule of Law*
1918-35, London, Macmillan, 1936 (2nd revised edition of 1939)
p. 484.

It follows that in all these shifting sands a DG quickly seeks to provide himself with an inner office staff he can trust. They should begin with his chauffeur from whom anything other than total, almost dog-like, devotion would seem against nature; they move in rank right up to his chef de cabinet, the very senior official in charge of his personal office and all its staff. Taken together, they become a wholly loyal small court. They are also sometimes toadies; and sometimes their advice is simply bad; they tend to have in view not the larger aims of the Organisation but the need to keep their man in power. And so they begin to play back to him his prejudices, his preconceptions, his fears. They comfort him and protect him and he builds up a strong protectiveness towards them. But in the end they insulate him from reality; they have too much power. We have seen that it would be very much harder and more dangerous to take advice and information more widely, to trust more people more; and I see no sign that that risk is being taken. If an exceptionally brave Director General did expose himself so much he would certainly be battle-scarred; but he might also be a model to the Secretariat and to Member States.

ii

During his long Director Generalship, René Maheu enormously extended the powers of the post; at his peak he *was* UNESCO.[2] He became larger than life in his relationship to the governing organs and to the Secretariat. Like any large-scale magnification, this showed up strengths and faults in both the setting and the subject. His personality hovered over the place like an outstretched great bird, even when he was absent. His style was that of a little Napoleon. As his car drove up to the front entrance the porters would stand deferentially with the glass doors open; another porter would be scurrying across the length of the main hall to the special lift so that its doors could be open by the time the DG reached it.

2. M. Jacques Havet, of UNESCO, has written a superb memoir of Maheu, three times the length of mine, and based on longer and closer acquaintance.

If he was feeling angry he was liable to stride quickly through, his eyes baleful and tail lashing; if he felt easy he could show such casual charm to a porter, a passing typist or anyone else he happened to run into, that they passed the day basking in the glow. For those who worked closely with him—his personal office and the senior people throughout the buildings—the temperature altered according to whether he was in Paris or not. If he was, a telephone call was possible at any minute asking for some major job within an almost impossible deadline. When he was away on mission there was a discernible drop in the emotional temperature. 'And kings crept out again to feel the sun': those who habitually suffered his wrath at any slight malfunctioning of the organisational machine (what were known as the Headquarters Services as distinct from the Programme Departments) breathed a sigh of relief and either extended their lunchtime intervals at the bar or got on with their work in a steady, uninterrupted way, free from the threat of sudden dislocation. Very many people disliked him intensely because he could be harsh and unjust. But when he was around they all felt at least that they were living dramatically; he charged the air electrically. One very senior British official told me that, sitting one day next to Maheu in the Executive Board when he had angrily rejected some criticism and then gone on in a long speech to win them all over, he felt sure he could feel heat building up and radiating from the man's body.

He was the son of the schoolmaster of a village in the South West. Brilliance took him to the École Normale Supérieure, in the Rue d'Ulm. He was a contemporary and friend of Sartre and Simone de Beauvoir and his subject, too, was philosophy. As is traditional, he spent some time teaching in a lycée, then some time as a Cultural Attaché in London. He joined UNESCO in the early days, appointed by Huxley. From then on he climbed with utter determination for about fifteen years until he reached the summit. He was one of those medium-size men whose personality so blazes from their eyes and the set of their bodies that they look much bigger than they are. In his prime he would stand at the rostrum during the Plenary meetings of the General Conference and dominate the packed Hall with a two- or three-hour survey of what had been done in the preceding two years and what would be done in the next two; he seemed then about six foot tall and broad with it. In his later years, when the leukaemia which finally killed him had begun to take hold, his body shrank and his suits hung on him loosely; but his eyes blazed more than ever as if out of two pits.

From the time he settled into being Director General for his first term of six years he seemed intent on merging his own identity with that of UNESCO, and vice versa. It was a case of both 'I *am* the state' and 'Madame Bovary, c'est moi'. He loved the politics of the job and could be adroit at playing them. But one sometimes felt that the purpose of it all had become the expansion of the Organisation he had made grow under his hands rather than the aims it had been set up to serve. The pressures on him were unending and far greater than those on any of his predecessors; but he never lacked courage or devotion or passion in meeting them. He was very typical of one kind of French intellectual; he felt he knew what the intellectual life and culture meant, but defined them in the high bourgeois, traditional Normalien sense. He loved Britain but knew in his bones that the centre of European civilisation was Paris, and that it was in the care of a few highly-trained Frenchmen. He was quite capable, on a plane journey, of initiating a discussion on definitions of Truth and Beauty, with ample references to Plato and others all the way through to Boileau. For he did care about the life of the mind; ideas excited him.

He had a dream, similar to one of Huxley's, that UNESCO and he—he and UNESCO—could help forge for the world a New Humanism, a sort of elevated, non-political ethic which would inspire and unite men. At first I was puzzled as to how one so hard-headed and realistic, professionally, could believe that kind of thing. Then I realised that it was the necessary foil to his day-by-day practical ruthlessness, the dream which justified the remorseless and often cruel drive he put into getting his own way for the Organisation. But when he was touched by the international idea he could become gentle and as if transformed. We once—he, my wife, I and some others—stood looking at that most beautiful Buddhist temple Borobodur, in Southern Java. UNESCO was heavily involved in collecting funds and resources so as to preserve it. That was very dear to Maheu's heart, the preservation of the world's greatest cultural treasures, and he put his fullest energies into promoting the work. My wife remarked on how lucky the two of us felt in having seen Borobodur twice, set into its soft hills with all the smells and sounds of that lush but humanised landscape around it. Maheu turned to her with tears in his eyes and said: 'Yes. But as for me I now feel an added pleasure and poignancy. I look at all such things as if I may be seeing each of them for the last time.' He knew the leukaemia would not give him much longer and that there was very much still to do in Paris, so missions could not be long or numerous; but he spoke without self-pity or histrionics. It was a dramatic statement, certainly, but he had a right to make it, and he made it with a depth of true feeling which ensured that the tone was appropriate.

I also remember watching him, in Tunis in 1972, engage in a dialogue of exceptional frankness and bite, about politics and society, with a group of intellectuals forty or fifty years younger than he was and not willing to make any special allowance for age. Nor did he ask that. His courage in pursuit of his own intellectual principles never faltered.

He had great panache and could be exceptionally charming— especially to women. His fondness for a beautiful face and a fine figure were, it goes without saying, a source of continuous gossip in UNESCO and he never denied them. The French tradition did not require him to disguise his sexual interests or adopt, no matter how tongues wagged, the circumspection in such things habitually practised by the British.

He could be charming to men, too, on occasion; and in particular just after he had been brutal. At such times his voice acquired a Chevalier-like music. Like most people who alternately use brutality or charm, he recognised instinctively those on whom the device would not work.

He and I did not become friends, and we did not always like each other. We were too French and too English for real friendship to develop. When we came into conflict—and that had to happen with Maheu if you worked close to him or he would, as one who had suffered said to me in my early days there, 'despise you and eat you alive'—when these conflicts occurred each of us became like a caricature of our national styles, he venting a violent anger and trying to destroy my position by a relentless 'logic of reality' which, he gave me to understand, he hardly expected an Englishman to appreciate; me arguing that, for instance, the human costs of what he proposed were being underestimated or that the political gains would be bought at too great an intellectual price. Eventually, and after two spectacular disagreements, he decided that I was not after all an agent of the British government nor under anyone else's thumb. I might be difficult and sometimes in his eyes plainly stupid in not seeing matters in the clear way he did; but this was the native inadequacy and wilfulness of a British provincial academic. So, though we could never become close, we ended with some respect for each other and this now and again came to the surface, particularly in his latter days.

At his best, he braced the Organisation, asked it to address itself to its fundamental purposes, made the Executive Board and the General Conference face the Constitution they had signed, tightened up Secretariat practice so that it approximated more to the best in French civil service practice and lost some of its self-indulgent amateurishness. So much of all this was for the good of the place that one regretted all the more his capacity to spoil months of good work by a single wilful act. For he could be a quite dreadful autocrat. At the height of his régime, bossing and bullying had become part of the normal order within UNESCO. He could fly into violent rages with senior men, threaten to send them home the moment their present contracts expired, demand immediate improvements and leave them literally shaking with the violence of his assault and fear for their own futures. So they went back to their offices and either wept or set about bullying their own subordinates, or both. The first year of my time there marked the low water-mark in his relations with the Secretariat. There was a strong smell of mutiny in the air and an enquiry into working conditions had to be set up. He survived it with much of his power-base and authority intact, but things were never quite as bad again. He could still, though, mercilessly dress down a Director in front of that man's own junior and senior colleagues whilst the latter, usually, kept silent and let him endure it. He did that once to one of my own staff, in a large meeting in late 1970; I stopped him and told him to attack me if he wanted to criticise the work of my Sector. He was furious and hinted to an aide that it might be better if I left the Organisation since 'he apparently cannot work with me'. He sent me a fierce letter warning me to rein in my tendency to see myself as 'a systematic defender of the Secretariat'. But his temper cooled and our relations were the better for the incident. I do not recount this out of pride. It took no particular courage for me to speak up. Whatever the inadequacies of British professional practice, we do not usually indulge in or tolerate public scorn and sarcasm towards subordinates. And I was a free man, ready and able to go back to my home country at any time.

So, in spite of his considerable intelligence, his unremitting hard work, his devotion to the Organisation and his moral courage, Maheu never seemed to recognise that a person at the top of a large institution is emulated much more for his bad acts than for his good, even if the time devoted to good acts far outweighs that given to bad. Wilful actions give all the latitude they need to the lazy and unscrupulous and become excuses for bad work on their part far more than good work is taken as an example. One single, perverse, self-regarding act destroys the effect of months of impressive other work. Maheu's wilfulness showed itself most in his appointments or promotions of favourites or friends. He would hear of a candidate at a dinner, from some Minister or high official, and the word would go out that that candidate had to be specially favoured; he would override the recommendations of the Interviewing Boards and give promotions to some who had worked closely and loyally with him, or to someone who appealed to his snobbery before French titles. Rightly, he was not forced to appoint the person recommended by a Board; we all like to back our own hunches and some of his could be excellent. But he did make nakedly interested appointments too, acts of unjustifiable patronage in the low sense of that word. In such acts he could be wanton and take notice of no one, in spite of the elaborate games of 'consultations with colleagues' which he played.

Some of these were poor appointments and the worst were of people who proved to be appallingly inefficient, but who could not be moved or indeed hardly criticised by anyone except the very hardy, for fear that they would make a phone call to the Director General's office complaining that they were being ill-treated because of their friendship with him. Then the Heavens fell on the official who had been complained of. The situation of such appointees within the Secretariat may easily be imagined. Obsequiously or at least circumspectly treated on the surface, disliked underneath, they lived the lives of Quislings. That was to be expected in a situation where Gulliver might be expected to lean over any minute and crush some small creature whose only crime was that he had frightened a favourite.

I have said that Maheu had a strong political sense which he enjoyed exercising. In a way he enjoyed it too much, and this at certain moments led him into his second major fault: overplaying politics to the point at which some more important consideration—intellectual objectivity, the rights of the international civil service itself, the just dues of a human being—suffered. My own worst experience of this habit concerned a Czech member of my Sector who had been appointed in Dubcek's day. With the new régime the handful of Czech staff members came under considerable pressure of several kinds, especially pressure to go back to Czechoslovakia. Theoretically, Maheu had total power to keep any staff member. I imagine he decided that, if he did not himself let one or two Czechs go—chosen by him—he might find himself losing some he really wanted to keep. He set in motion a complicated set of movements to that end. As to the Czech member of my own staff, it was made plain that a recommendation for non-renewal was expected when, as was shortly to happen, the man's contract expired. Matters were not handled as blatantly as that, of course; I believe Maheu came to convince himself, partly on the basis of gossip and because he was looking for faults (and who would escape some criticism under such attentions), that the man was not sufficiently competent. For some months complaints came down about the man's work, complaints I had to rebut; his work was up to the average and better than that of some who enjoyed Maheu's favour in that part of the Organisation. The Sector's performance report recommended renewal and was sent back angrily as inaccurate and incompetent. And so the matter went backwards and forwards for some time; clearly, the intention was that I provide the knife to do the deed. When that was not forthcoming, Maheu himself finally refused renewal.

The man concerned challenged the decision before the internal Board of Enquiry which can be invoked in such cases; the Board upheld the Director General's decision. The man then went to the final form of arbitration, the UN Administrative Tribunal at Geneva. He won his case and a good indemnity. I gave evidence on his behalf, not in criticism of Maheu's practice nor against his right to make his own mind up, but simply on the appellant's professional competence. The Tribunal concluded that the documents covering the months in which the matter had gone back and forth showed that Maheu had acted wilfully, had played politics at the expense of more important considerations.

When I try to decide whether I think Maheu's reign did the

Organisation more good than harm, I find myself deciding differently according to which memories come to the front of my mind at any particular moment. I more often than not come down to thinking, though, that the loss was greater than the gain. He found a small organisation and made it a big one; he vastly developed its operational work for developing countries; he greatly extended its activities in saving some of the world's finest cultural monuments and sites; he helped quite a number of people to develop a precise and well-honed professionalism; he occasionally made delegates and politicians from Member States feel ashamed and challenged before his own high sense of the institution's calling. But overall he left an Organisation too centrally run, too much urged on by fear, internally, and by political manoeuvrings in its external relations. He left an Organisation far too short on inner courage, and so all the more open to the even greater politicisation which now threatens it.

I have two late memories of him which come into my mind more than any others. When the time for him to go drew near, there were a succession of rumours about the enormous farewell party which was to be held in the seventh-floor restaurant. It did not take place. Instead, I received a brief note inviting me to drink a farewell glass of wine with him. So did my secretary, who was greatly surprised. He knew her because at two major Ministerial conferences, one in Helsinki, the other in Jokjakarta, she had served both him and me. The other girls were afraid of him and his tantrums; my secretary, being herself of very tough French high bourgeois stock, could match him in explosiveness. So we went upstairs that evening and found less than forty people there, out of the two or three thousand who worked in the building. Not even all the members of the Direction Générale had been invited. After a while Maheu silenced the slight hum and, with a diabolically amused grin, told us that we were there because we were the hand-picked few he respected; he had of course fought us all; what was more important, we had all fought him back. As for the rest . . . and he dismissed them with a gesture of his hands. It was one of his last professional acts and it encapsulated that arrogance, that candour and that cavalier sense of his own life as a special drama which never left him, except at the very end.

The weekend before we finally came back to England, I telephoned his flat and asked if he was able to receive visitors. He was

and would be pleased to see me, I was told. We sat on the balcony
of the flat overlooking the circular structure which used to be
ORTF Headquarters, he in his dressing-gown and slippers since
he was just recovering from a bad dip in his health. He had by then
been six months out of office and so, since there were no actual
decisions for us to discuss and perhaps argue about, we were able
to talk about the basic nature of the Organisation, about its
possible future rôle, and especially about the likely results of the
recent Israel resolutions. It was the closest we ever got to any
depth of mutual understanding. I saw in his eyes, which no longer
blazed but still looked firmly out of the emaciated face, and I heard
in his voice, which had lost its Draconian bark and become
musing, something of the idealist who thirty years before had
sought a job at UNESCO because the international idea fired his
aggressive intelligence.

iii

Clearly, all is not well with the post of Director General, no
matter which particular individual occupies it at any one time. It is
inescapably a very taxing job indeed; but for a great variety of
reasons it is now more taxing than it need be. Member States put
too much work on to the Director General and show no sign of
learning better. As we have seen, when they cannot agree and fear
that further discussion between them might highlight the rifts,
they tend to hand the problem to the DG. In the UN at New York
this used to be known as the 'Leave it to Dag' habit. It probably
occurs in all the Agencies and further enhances the Chief Executives' tendencies towards grandiosity. UNESCO's Director
General nowadays has hardly any time or energy left for thinking
about where the Organisation is going and what it might best do.
The conveyor-belt existence to which so much of his job has been
reduced takes away almost all the opportunities for thinking about
anything other than tactics, diplomacy and survival. Member
States should think much more about how to save the DG from
himself, by reducing the number of matters for which he is directly

called to account, by encouraging him to practise delegation safely and sensibly, without having to devolve according to some rigid geographic or ideological pattern (which would leave him feeling constantly threatened). His isolation and the burden of having almost everything pushed at him need to be lessened. Then the strain and the incipient megalomania which seem to hang over UNESCO may go away.

All such proposals for reform will meet the usual rejoinder: that the 'realities' of political life do not allow for substantial changes. But if the assumed realities of political life are always the base from which we start, they come to have the appearance of natural phenomena and so are self-validating; then the Organisation and its Constitution seem like a rag in the winds of the politics of the moment. Political realities are not to be denied or ignored; they have an important and relevant place in UNESCO; but informal conventions and formal agreements can be established on various kinds of good practice which would discourage politics from spreading ever further into all the interstices of the institution.

An ideal Director General would have three main kinds of quality: great intellectual distinction, great diplomatic abilities and high competence in complex administration. He needs the first so as to be accepted by and able to stand up to what I called earlier UNESCO's second constituency (world intellectual and scientific opinion); he needs the second so as to be able to work with the first constituency (the Member States): he needs the third quality because, if he cannot steer such a large and complicated machine, its work will come to nothing. The best-meant programmes will disappear into the sand as the bad habits I described earlier riot unchecked. UNESCO is not, nowadays, likely to acquire a Director General who combines all three qualities at a high level. I entered the Organisation with the assumption that, whatever qualities a particular DG might lack, all Directors General ought above all to be of great intellectual distinction. At my lower moments during my time there, I used to think that the best DG for the next ten years would be one who, though his intellectual and diplomatic claims were not outstanding, nevertheless had a highly-developed sense of organisational probity. Such a man would have a grasp on the Constitution which, showing neither the penetration of a profound thinker nor the empty rhetoric UNESCO so loves, nevertheless expressed itself day-by-day in just and firm actions; so that Member States knew that here was a bench-mark.

It is a pity Directors General are so often led into the traps I have described, since the post offers so many better possibilities, possibilities for useful political and intellectual action rather than for playing politics at the risk of intellectual purposes. Langrod put these possibilities very clearly:

> There are two possible lines of action for the Director
> General in the political questions following out of the
> competence of the Organisation. The Director General
> may interpret his constitutionally objective position in such a
> way as to refuse to take a stand in emerging conflicts, in
> order thus to preserve the neutrality of the office. He may,
> however, also accord himself the right to take a stand in
> these conflicts to the extent that such a stand can be firmly
> based on the Charter and its principles, and thus express
> what may be called the independent judgment of the
> Organisation.[3]

That is the heart of the matter, and we shall be looking at such possibilities as they offer themselves not only to the Director General but to the Secretariat as a whole, in the next chapter. They are the great hope for UNESCO, and that hope is not yet altogether vain. For the Director General himself, the role Langrod is postulating is rightly much more than a balancing-out by seeking compromise positions. That can soon become a cancelling-out of the possibility of worthwhile action. A Director General may hope that he will be able to bring Member States to a larger measure of agreement than they have been able to reach through the usual diplomatic processes. He must know when to go ahead on such a line, and how far he can go at any particular time; and so how to retreat gracefully if he looks likely to over-extend his credit and incur some risk for the Organisation. And sometimes he must be willing to push out beyond his established base, leaving himself exposed and risking serious unpopularity among important Member States, in the hope of making a change to which he is deeply committed.

3. Georges Langrod, *The International Civil Service, Its Origins, Its Nature, Its Evolution*, A. W. Sythoff, Leyden, Oceana Pubs. Inc., Dobbs Ferry, N.Y., 1963, Trans. F. G. Berthoud, p. 286.

In such circumstances, he is quite clearly not an 'impartial' civil servant but an actively political figure. But that kind of thing must be able to happen; he must exercise from time to time what Hammarskjöld called his 'right to take a stand'. I remember Maheu, towards the end of his time, doing just that in an Executive Board which was ostensibly about human rights but was in fact narrowly political. The Czechs, as spokesmen for the Eastern European bloc, were castigating Pinochet's Chile. Maheu listened with a typical sardonic pleasure and then, having accepted instructions calling on him to intervene in defence of human rights in Chile, reminded the Czech spokesman and his supporters that— and he loved English idioms—what's sauce for the goose today can be sauce for the gander tomorrow. Maheu's enemies remarked at once that he would only have said such a thing near the end of his time, when there was nothing to be gained by sitting silent under such political pettinesses. Maybe; but he did say it in the end. Within the Secretariat, only a DG can make a rejoinder without having it dismissed as unprofessional backchat and being rebuked. It is right that a DG should say such things; for him to do less on some occasions would be to fall down on the job. Between the politics of individual Member States and the claims of the Constitution there is, as we have noted so many times, all too often a vacuum: it is sometimes inescapably the job of the Director General to fill it.

8

SHOULD UNESCO SURVIVE?

UNESCO cannot be re-formed. Born after small reflection, it
has so far had a fairly scattered and stunted growth. It is therefore necessary to take courage and want it to be dissolved. If
it is dissolved by returning its mandate in spontaneous homage
to that world of liberty whose needs it was intended to interpret,
then its death will be a voluntary and a fine one, an example
which will remain. It will therefore give proof that our
Western world of liberty knows how to correct its errors.[1]
Those who advocate world government and this or that
special form of world federalism often present challenging
theories and ideas; but we, like our ancestors, can only press
against the receding wall which hides the future. It is by
such efforts, pursued to the best of our ability, more than
by the construction of ideal patterns to be imposed upon
society, that we lay the basis and pave the way for the
society of the future.[2]

Quite early in this book I recorded the obviously useful things
UNESCO can do. They make an impressive list. But it is obvious
also that the world does not need an organisation with a high-
minded Constitution such as UNESCO's to carry out these
straightforward activities in technical cooperation. Now that we
have seen, in the last few chapters, how much is at fault
in UNESCO the question arises directly: is UNESCO worth
saving?

My own answer is that UNESCO is worth saving precisely
because it has a Constitution which calls it to activities beyond
technical cooperation. Because it is a driven and divided Organisa-

1. Benedetto Croce, quoted in 'Should UNESCO die?' *Manchester
Guardian*, 19 July 1950.
2. Dag Hammarskjöld. 'The Development of a Constitutional Frame-
work for International Cooperation.' University of Chicago Law
School; 1 May 1960, cit. Brian Urquhart, Hammarskjöld, Bodley Head,
London, 1973.

tion it falls well short of its constitutional aims. But it does not altogether fail, and if those who are associated with it look again at its purposes and possibilities and try to live up to them better it could have a new and valuable lease of life.

We have to go back to the old, enormous phrasing: UNESCO has operational, intellectual and ethical rôles and will have to be judged on all three terms. A convinced cynic would say that the operations are hardly ever well-done, the intellectual work at far too low a level and the ethical rôle a total failure. For all my criticisms of the institution, I do not dismiss it in that way. After the initial post-war hopes there was bound to be a trough; and the fifties were a bad period for UNESCO, for reasons largely outside its own control. When 'operations for development' came in, with the new nations in the sixties, UNESCO had an immense accession of strength and apparent importance. We can see now, in the late seventies, that that physical strength was bought at the cost of a drop in intellectual force. In the period when the Organisation is under increasing political pressure, its intellectual weakness is inescapably revealed. With insecure intellectual anchorage, UNESCO is like a barge adrift and caught in powerful political cross-currents.

So the question of whether the institution is worth retaining— the question Croce answered with an unambiguous 'no' thirty years ago—is still fully on the agenda. It is worth saying, before examining whether justifications for a continued life can be found, that—useful or not—UNESCO is likely to survive. It is in no nation's interest actually to propose its dismemberment. To do so would be to incur disfavour from others and lose the vote anyway. As we have seen, it is a useful world platform for the developing countries, it dispenses some reasonably inexpensive development aid, it can from time to time be made into an ideological platform (and is particularly so used by the Eastern Europeans and, at the present time, the Arab nations). The big developed nations will not propose its winding-up; they will express their sense of its limited usefulness by restricting its budget so far as they can.

Hence the crucial question is not 'will UNESCO survive?' but 'can it be made to survive valuably?' In seeking an answer we should put aside first the common simplifications which see the UN and its agencies as part of an 'emerging world community', a slow but steady movement towards world government. For as long as any of us now living can foresee, there will be no substantial voluntary yielding of sovereignty by individual States. This is the reality Dag Hammarskjöld recognised in the passage quoted at the head of this chapter. Niebuhr wrote sharply and effectively against such myths, too; he saw especially clearly the force of those distinctive cultural roots which do so much to sustain nationalisms.

At first glance, the functionalist case seems a more realistic way of approaching the question of how states may gradually arrive at agreed ways of living together and of yielding sovereign rights. That 'the multilevel interpenetration of governments' in tackling practical tasks will lead to coherent and sustained non-aggressive cooperation between them, that they will gradually learn to live together more harmoniously because they have learned to work together harmoniously, is an attractive idea: but it is not convincing. There are already all kinds of 'multilevel interpenetrations' and will be more. But since they do not operate at the level at which major political decisions are made, they are cut off from serious political impact by a technical *cordon sanitaire*. Technical cooperation has had so far virtually no effect on foreign policies; as we noted earlier, it works below the levels of power and does not necessarily have links with those levels. In any event, even if functionalism could work in the way the most optimistic hope, one would not need a UNESCO to develop it. UNESCO cannot thus escape all the burdens of its intellectual/ethical/political Constitution.

Inis L. Claude turns on its head the case made by those who would like to see the UN system as a first sketch for a World Government. The job of the UN, he argues, is not to 'put States out of business' but to contribute to 'the capacity of States to stay in business'.[3] That is to say, the UN is best occupied not in trying to stand for an emerging supra-nationalism but in helping to make the multiple and diverse nationalisms better informed, in giving them fuller perspectives. At a time when regionalism is coming up strongly to reinforce individual nationalisms, that is a good practical starting point.

3. Inis L. Claude, Jr., *Swords into Plowshares : Problems and Progress of International Organisation*, New York, Random House, 1964, 3rd ed., p. 17.

Given the particular difficulties UNESCO faces in fulfilling its peculiar Constitution, perhaps it would be better, then, to settle for Conor Cruse O'Brien's game theory? He applied it to the UN as a whole; it would fit UNESCO best of all. According to this view, there is no 'substantial work for the UN. Its whole purpose is not substantial but rhetorical, aesthetic, artistic, symbolic. The UN and its Agencies provide an arena where a necessary (and in its own terms useful) form of 'play' between nations is acted out; the arena for a long-running 'sacred drama'.[4] This view also, which is as far removed as is possible from functionalist theory, has its attractions and illuminates something in the character of the UN and its arcane procedures. But it is not enough; the UN and its Agencies can do more and be more. One cannot adequately justify UNESCO, in particular, in any of the above ways. In different respects they are all too easy, and reduce UNESCO's potentialities; as one of UNESCO's earliest supporters said: 'The possible is worth more than that.'

i

UNESCO is a privileged place in that it brings together in an international context governments—those who make decisions—and people who are at the fore-front of the study of contemporary problems. Few if any organisations or individual governments can mount conferences which contain so wide a range of top officials with an equally wide range of scientists and experts, to discuss major problems which affect the developed world no less than the developing. Similarly, the recurrent large 'policy' conferences at Ministerial level (on scientific, educational, cultural or communications policies and much else) can, if they are objectively prepared by the Secretariat, improve thinking in some nations, and do so more rapidly than any other means.

The important point, and it has greatly increased in importance during UNESCO's lifetime, is that most of the major issues before

4. Conor Cruse O'Brien & Feliks Topolski: *The United Nations: Sacred Drama.* Hutchinson, London, 1968.

the world today are in their nature 'intergovernmental' and require joint and complementary action. If, for example, nations do not get together to work at environmental problems they will not move far towards a solution. They are interacting with each other environmentally all the time, via shared water-systems, large-scale atmospheric pollution and much else.

It will be said that by now there are UN agencies specifically designed to address themselves to most of the world's recognised 'problem areas'. So what part can UNESCO play? The justification is delicate and risks sounding arrogant on UNESCO's behalf. But I have seen it borne out from time to time. UNESCO's special function is to remind the rest of the UN system as well as its Member States that most major problems (of population, environment, development itself) have a more than economic dimension; that they involve more than one part of human experience, that value-implications, the social and individual costs of programmes, are to be put in the balance.

To use UNESCO's old and now oddly-sounding phrase, as it is usually translated from the French: UNESCO must try to 'give the ethical dimension' to issues when the thrust of modern societies tends to ignore that dimension. In all such matters, UNESCO must not only 'expose the options' before States; it must also try to expose the human implications, so that national policies can be decided in the light of—or consciously against—those implications. UNESCO has to try to give greater precision and depth to all those big words so much bandied about by administrators and planners today.

The history of the debates on the population question within UNESCO show that, once again, almost any question to which UNESCO turns quickly reveals a political character, and also that some progress can be made if pressure is kept up. Attention to population issues within UNESCO's programme was proposed very early, notably by Julian Huxley who was a convinced and powerful spokesman on the dangers of uncontrolled population growth. But for many years it was difficult to insert the subject in the programme effectively; indeed, for some time it was difficult to have it within the programme at all. When it was at last included, UNESCO's treatment was for some time restricted to the offering of limited information and educational services, and then only in response to direct requests by Member States. Even as late as

1970, when I arrived, the population issue roused the fiercest debates in the General Conference. Certain Latin-American countries, notably Brazil, opposed any extension of UNESCO's population programme beyond its existing simple base. Many of the new nations are likely to interpret all population programmes as forms of neo-colonialism, attempts by the developed world still to control them by keeping them numerically small, even though their territories may be large. Or the developed world's promptings in favour of population restriction are regarded as self-justifications, attempts to attribute the poverty of the developing world to rampant population growth rather than to the West's economic stranglehold.

Within all these contrasting stresses it has been difficult for UNESCO to advance work which badly needs doing. Nor has advance been made easier by the fact that many of the developed world's 'action programmes' in Family Planning are over-simply activist. They ride over the cultural complexities of the nations they hope to influence. They thus rouse understandable and serious doubts in the minds of people in those developing countries who are inspired not by the desire to make political capital out of the issues but by concern for the social costs of such programmes. Hence there appeared in the middle seventies, in many developing countries, what the population experts called the 'backlash' against their policies. Some have been tempted to dismiss the backlash as the folly of young intellectuals or the regressive nostalgia of artists and writers. They are unwilling to recognise that the backlash raised important questions about dominant approaches to population issues.

The backlash is fed by the suspicion that many of the planners lack an adequate model of human life and of the varied realities, the integrities, of different cultures. Many of those who argue for family limitation on behalf of economic growth sound as though they are willing to see the importance of family or the love of children eroded for the sake of developing a society of high-level consumption. In most societies fertility in itself has for centuries been regarded as good, in very complex psychological and cultural ways; it has been part of the sustaining fabric of community, family and individual life. On a very large scale, the population experts are asking people to change that deep-seated set of attitudes and to do so very quickly. An immensely important inner shift is being asked for, a shift which cannot fail to cause great disturbances in the cultures it affects. The thrust and tone of many population programmes is largely operational, manipulative, designed to encourage people to behave in new, non-traditional ways, as soon as ever possible. Success is measured by a rise in the use of fertility control devices and a drop in the number of children per family. I have myself no doubt that extensive population limitation is needed in most countries of the world if famine, malnutrition and other scourges are to be defeated. The backlash is not necessarily denying this. It is, though, a sign of an organism protecting itself against too sudden, too massive and too ill-considered an assault on its old cultural balances. In these matters, the anthropologists, and above all the poets, are better guides than the technicians of 'delivery systems' or of mass persuasion. A society's poems and songs illuminate better than anything else the meanings for that society of the idea of the family, married love, the pride of parenthood, the respect due to old age. What is needed, therefore, is more and better social and psychological research around population problems. This is a clear responsibility towards people whose attitudes we seek to change, a responsibility to them as whole human beings, living in societies which may be technically underdeveloped but nevertheless often have considerable coherence. Research of this kind will be difficult and slow, will not always have in mind an immediate, population-policy target and will be as much concerned with the cultural and individual implications of population policies as with the policies themselves.

These are matters which go well beyond any brief or budget UNESCO is likely to be given. But UNESCO has its contribution to make, and is trying to make it. Its brief has widened and improved. Today it can talk about the social costs and benefits of different kinds of population change, about the relations of demographic movements to environmental issues and to economic growth, and above all about the relations between population issues and human rights. There has been a real gain.

Population issues are usually regarded as integral parts of the larger issue of 'development' and so lead naturally into questions about the definition of development itself. Here again, assumptions have traditionally tended to be too narrowly economics-based. But the demand for a wider definition is gaining ground and once more it is UNESCO's duty to be at the front of that demand within the UN system. Fortunately the call in this instance can now be found among the developing nations themselves, in some of the main funding agencies (the World Bank, after being strongly committed to narrowly measurable criteria of development, has recently led the way in questioning the adequacy of those criteria) and in the UN's own Agencies. As with the population 'backlash', the demand is that all projects should be founded in a better understanding of the needs—the rights—of the local community, the small group, the family and the individual. One has to add that sometimes the hardest-nosed and narrowest interpretations of development come from the developing countries. A single country or region may produce some of the finest statements on the nature of cultural change, statements more subtle than those one commonly hears from statesmen or executives in the developed world; the same country or region may well also contain a powerful number of Western-trained planners who insist, in the name of sovereign powers and economic growth, on their countries' inalienable right to rush into just that sort of urban squalor and environmental pollution to which the developed world committed itself decades ago, and which it is now painfully trying to undo.

There are many other instances of such belated questioning. One of the most striking, and most relevant to UNESCO, is about the pros and cons of tourism and especially (since this has been one of UNESCO's favourite initiatives) of 'cultural tourism'. The story of 'cultural tourism' neatly arches a decade of changing attitudes. In the early sixties UNESCO, hampered by the difficulty of acquiring extra-budgetary funds for the preservation of ancient monuments, first made an economic case for so doing. It pointed out that if money is provided to preserve some ancient but decaying monument in an underdeveloped part of the world and to provide the 'infrastructure for the tourism' which would follow (airstrips, roads, hotels, etc.) this would make a substantial contribution to economic growth. It is possible to say how much money per day each such tourist might be assumed to bring into a country. People would have to be trained to man the hotels, to service the planes and buses; several industries and professions would begin to be created.

The argument was found persuasive and so it gradually became easier to persuade the major funding agencies to give money to cultural tourism projects. That kind of work goes on, but now those concerned have begun to ask more difficult questions. What really are the effects of sudden tourism on societies which have been traditionally 'non-progressive', and very far removed from the manners and styles of the developed world? Does tourism encourage in those societies assumptions about the relationships between people quite different from those habitually held—relationships based on buying and selling, on *using* other people, on seeing other people as objects from which one gets something, a whole way of seeing life as a matter of getting and spending and tasting and passing on?

Even more important, the internal rhythms and styles of such a people, which may have been part of a complete and organic pattern of life, can themselves become under tourism—even cultural tourism—something offered for sale; and in that process they change. Think of that kind of Asian dance which is contemplative, intensely religious, which has no need of nor recognition of the concept of an 'audience' in the Western sense. People have always watched it, it is true; but they are part of the ceremony (which is more like a celebration of mass than a 'performance') and observe intensely but silently. A response from them is not needed because nothing is, in the Western sense, being given to them. This is not an audience-with-actors relationship as the West knows it.

But tourists want to see such things and tourism promoters in the countries concerned want to offer them; so shows are organised. A few rows of seats are put in for the tourists; prices are charged; the locals stand at the back outside a roughly-made compound. What happens to the dance itself? To begin with—as a Minister of Culture pointed out to me once—it becomes in some ways 'better', more expert and 'finished' than it was before. A competition sets in between villages to provide an even 'finer' spectacle. It also becomes finished in another sense, because it is now no longer a contemplative ritual; it is a performance for an audience. It is turned outwards towards the people in those rows of chairs, who click their cameras steadily and—this comes with an extraordinarily shocking (in the exact sense of the word) effect— who clap at the end. The dance has become an offering to tourists, not a shared rite.

The most important test of UNESCO's ability to cope adequately with such subtle and complex problems as these will be its involvement over the next ten years with plans for the Kathmandu valley. The valley is still one of the most harmonious and beautifully integrated combinations of the natural and the man-made in the whole world. The wild and the cultivated landscapes, the string of townships with their superbly-carved wooden buildings, the great variety of richly-ornamented temples ... all this and much else is a living demonstration of how man can live with nature, do it no violence nor yet be dwarfed by it. The scale in the towns is intensely human, their relationships to the landscape exact and just. Nevertheless, the standard of living is very low and disease rife. Industrial development is on the way and also massive tourism; concrete cubes of hotels have already begun to spring up. They will eventually bring with them a much-needed running water supply and sanitation. They may also destroy the meaning of the valley itself; reduce to a simulacrum of itself the phenomenon the tourists have come to see. The task for UNESCO is to bring to bear all the international knowledge and understanding it can on helping the Valley to gain the manifest advantages of twentieth-century technology without having its balance destroyed and without it letting itself become a museum piece for photographers and cultural-tourist voyeurs.

In recent years the demand for UNESCO's aid in cultural development has grown beyond all expectations. So therefore has the need for analysis of what that demand means and how best UNESCO might meet it within the terms of its Constitution. For almost all Member States this is an intellectual/ethical area of great and growing importance. So far UNESCO has on the whole contented itself with meeting demands for information and help within terms pre-defined by Member States; it has not sufficiently enquired into the human implications.

Twenty years ago only a few countries had a Minister of Culture; today almost all do. Some still balk at that exact title and find another form of words, such as the British 'Minister with Special Responsibility for the Arts'. But the general drive is the same: more and more money is being given to this general area called 'cultural development'. A British Minister will characteristically open his speech to an international conference with the disclaimer: 'I will let you into a secret—in my country we have no clear idea what culture means.' But no one believes him; and he doesn't really believe his own words. Meanwhile, the budgets increase by leaps and bounds.

The countries of the world show, on the whole, three different main interpretations of the phrase 'cultural development' (there are, of course, a number of sub-divisions and variants). The first is based on the idea of culture as the acquiring of individual virtue and is widespread in the developed capitalist world. After the vote and literacy and with the coming of prosperity, one should seek to promote cultural development widely. The urge is partly defensive, defensive towards a feared mass of incipiently dissident and now powerful workers with their ubiquitous transistors and second-hand cars. 'We must educate our masters' gives way to 'We must cultivate . . . embourgeoisify . . . our masters'. On this view cultural development is usually assumed to be almost synonymous with certain traditional high bourgeois art-forms, their creation and appreciation. The process itself of cultural development is seen, centrally, as one of transmission, of passing the appreciation of these objects down to those masses so that they shall become, individually, more refined and well-behaved. One can easily be snide about this complex of attitudes; but it shows a kind of respect for people; it is a version of Matthew Arnold's outlook, watered down for twentieth-century governmental purposes in capitalist democracies.

The second interpretation of cultural development sees it as ideological underpinning. On this view the rôle of the artist is to reflect, embody, celebrate and justify the status quo. Thus Mme. Furtseva of the Soviet Union, speaking at the International Culture Conference (Venice 1970) where the British Minister, Lord Eccles, made the disclaimer quoted above, asserted:

> The art of socialist realism truthfully reflects in its various
> forms the exploits of the people in building the new society,
> disseminates among the peoples the noble ideas of revolution-
> ary humanism and internationalism, calls upon them to
> struggle actively for peace and friendship among peoples,
> and educates in them a feeling of patriotism and a deep
> sense of civic duty.

Truth, it is believed by one who makes such a statement, is objectively known and is outside—not related to—the actual processes of art. Artists must reflect it; they have a fixed rôle. Art forms are channels for known truths, not answers provisionally arrived at after exploration and experiment. The assurance is considerable because the categories are fixed:

> Alongside the development of painting, graphic art, sculpture and decorative-applied art, monumental art glorifying the historical exploits of our people has, owing to the care lavished on it by the state, made particularly spectacular progress in recent years.

The artist works in known forms and utters known truths. He does not have any kind of privileged relationship to the exploring of experience; in any event, individual views are of no particular interest. The notion of the artist as both inside—sharing, and outside—interpreting, his culture is, almost strictly, inconceivable. The artist is the spokesman or celebrant, through a particular set of forms, of unchallengeable truths, decided elsewhere and by other processes.

We once, in UNESCO, agreed to tell Mme Furtseva's Ministry that a very famous Western European musician had been so shocked by what he thought a harsh Soviet act towards one of its own musicians that he proposed to cancel a projected visit to Moscow. The hope that the Soviets might think again about their treatment of their own citizen was wholly unfounded. When the matter was put to them they were even more shocked than the Western artist. They were shocked with a kind of harsh purity; it seemed inconceivable to them that any *individual* should have thought his personal view could have any weight in a governmental matter. The notion that Western artists tend to see their artistic and moral integrity as interconnected seems a bizarre deviationism.

The last of the main interpretations of cultural development among UNESCO's Member States relates this kind of development directly to the search of national identity and so national unity; and this is a more intense drive than the other two. The Minister of Culture for a new nation will say, typically: 'we can never hope to build a nation if we are not united by a common culture.' Another such Minister will say: 'our culture is our identity card in the community of nations.'

Not surprisingly, this impulse is strongest in nations which think their former sense of themselves has been subverted or destroyed by Western colonialism. They aim to get back to what they were, or think they were, before a deep ditch was cut between them and their traditional cultures by the colonisers. They want to get back to their past, to reconnect with their roots so that the good sap flows again.

The complications are enormous, especially since so many in the ruling groups have only a vestigial memory of their own traditional cultures. They have stronger memories of the Sorbonne, LSE, Cal.Tech. or the Harvard Law School. So the strain is all the greater:

> . . . when we come to speak of our own values, we find
> ourselves following patterns derived from our imported
> cultural requirements. Thus we are always, or almost always,
> somewhat apart from the mass of our people, since nothing
> in our intellectual and cultural background predisposes us
> to have an insight into their concerns or to understand their
> deep-seated aspirations.
> It is therefore time for us to turn to the people to hear the
> message of our cultures, handed down by word of mouth
> from generation to generation, so that we can adapt them to
> our present-day life without allowing ourselves to be dis-
> concerted by their diversity. What we have to do instead
> is to lay hold on the similarities . . . a sustained effort to
> adapt and to return to the fountainhead . . . since we, the
> intellectual élites, have been nurtured by foreign cultures
> rather than by the realities of our native African soil.

It would be easy to make fun of the earnestness of such a passage. But how many politicians in developed nations could show so thorough and serious an attempt to come to grips with their own cultural situation as this, which is by a young Francophone African Minister? And behind all such speeches is the difficult truth that oral cultures do have some good qualities which are not so evident in the West today, especially qualities of communal life.

The present rulers are driven by immense purposes, and time is short. They govern newly-created societies, many of which have never before been unified. Even their boundaries, often drawn by the departing colonial powers, may cross natural geographic, linguistic, trading or ethnic lines. They are therefore always in danger of disintegrating, subject to the centrifugal pulls of tribes or ethnic groups who have not been used to living together except under the quite different umbrella provided by their European rulers. So the search is not for a lost, unitary, national identity; one may never have existed; it is for a new and unique unity in a very divisive situation. W. Arthur Lewis has pointed to the democratic impulses which may also lie behind this urge for unity among African leaders:

> They are for the most part revolutionaries, in the sense that they wish to break the power of tribal chiefs, and to advance the status of the common man as against the old family oligarchies.[5]

This reveals a paradox at the heart of their efforts. They are trying to start afresh; but they cannot afford to and do not want to ignore all previous cultural experiences. They must have a history, a language, a common past. But which history, which language, which past? To say that the elements chosen are usually those of the culture of the President or ruling group is true, but to think of this search as merely a cynical political manoeuvre is to under-estimate the concern which can go into it. The importance of the Minister of Culture in such a country is clear; he must help to identify, must give credence to and gain assent for, the chosen and defined culture of the new nation.

It will be seen that all three main strands of the huge new official interest in culture across the world share these qualities: they assume some and probably a great deal of responsibility by the state for cultural development; they seek some greater social harmony or cohesion; and they assume that cultural development is both a serious and a political matter. After that, they differ, with only the Western version giving pride of place to the rôle of the free, judging individual as distinct from the needs of the community.

5. W. Arthur Lewis, 'The Tension of Inequality: The Emergence of West Africa', in *The Promise of World Tensions*, ed. Harlan Cleveland, New York, Macmillan, 1961.

ii

I described much earlier the three main types of agreement employed in UNESCO's standard-setting or 'normative' activities, and listed some from the great range of such agreements. Those I named then were in relatively uncontentious areas. The real test of UNESCO's authority is its ability to gain assent to agreements which make good sense and are more than rhetorical, in contentious ideological and political areas. At these points the Organisation comes head-on against that jealousy about sovereignty we have met so often; it is deliberately trying to push further what one optimist called the 'slow spread of voluntary limitations on sovereignty'.

The movement towards effective agreements on such issues as the uses of the mass media or racial prejudice—past the points at which drafts have been so distorted by one group that they are quite unacceptable to others—is a long way from its term. Some other agreements, though still highly political, have found a more or less satisfactory working form. Of these, the one which most directly concerned me was what became popularly known as The Hague Convention. Its proper title was The Convention for the Protection of Cultural Property in the Event of Armed Conflict (1952). It is not, strictly speaking, a UNESCO legal instrument; but UNESCO looks after its operation. Its aim is to keep to a minimum damage to monuments, temples and the like in territories occupied by acts of war. Signatory nations have to allow Hague Commissioners into territory they occupy so as to check on reported desecrations or other damage. This is not simply so that the world's cultural heritage shall be protected: at least as importantly, it is inspired by the knowledge that the seeds of the next conflict are often sown during an occupation, and that particularly virulent strains are sown where the religious or cultural heritage of the occupied people has been desecrated. The fact that such alleged incidents can be examined helps discourage their occurrence; more, a Commissioner's visit in response to a rumour of some terrible depredation may reveal that the rumour is false and so discourage unfounded gossip, which can be as damaging as the well-founded.

Throughout my time at UNESCO the Convention was chiefly,

and regularly, invoked in the Middle East. The Commissioners tended to be retired senior officers from the armed forces of 'safe' nations such as the Netherlands or Switzerland. One telephoned them when a complaint was received and very soon they would be as likely as not bumping over the desert in a jeep. Some time later a cable would reach Paris, either substantiating the charges (in which case the next difficult diplomatic steps were up to us) or providing evidence that the allegations were ill-founded. In such instances we tried to make sure that that information, with all the force of a neutral Commissioner's report, reached the accusing power as quickly as possible and was made as public as possible. There is much else in the Hague Convention, having to do with the correct behaviour of occupying troops towards religious and cultural monuments, the labelling of buildings and sites, and so on. But I have said enough to indicate the Convention's uniqueness and value; it is a sort of Red Cross Convention for the world's religious and cultural heritage and a most useful damper on the forest fires of rumour.

The Hague Convention substantially works, chiefly because it has a well-defined area within which one can keep ideological and political differences under some control; and by now there have been more than twenty years in which difficulties in operation could be ironed out. In all my own activities at UNESCO few things were more rewarding to be involved with. The fiercest invocation of the Convention which I recall arose on the accusation that Israeli occupying troops were violating the ancient monastery of Saint Catherine in the Sinai desert and had caused a fire which had seriously damaged one wing. Our elderly Dutch Commissioner made the difficult journey out there, and soon reported back. There had been a nasty fire, certainly; but the monks did not blame the Israeli soldiers. In fact, they found them well-behaved and very useful as guards against thefts by visitors. The fire had been caused by a monk who had fallen asleep in bed whilst smoking.

So I do *just* believe in the growth of that 'collective legitimisation' to which I briefly referred much earlier. The phrase is by Inis L. Claude, Jr.; as is its obverse, 'delegitimisation'. One is very, very slowly helping on the appearance of a body of case-law; and nations can be surprisingly sensitive to that. The very existence of the debates, and of the subsequent documents, can sometimes have a slight deterrent effect and usually sets off a welter of self-justification. In my experience the anger behind complaints that sovereignty has been impugned tends to be in direct proportion to the justice of the accusations made against the complaining state. For very complex reasons, most Member States would rather not flout, or at least not be seen to flout, an international instrument. The existence of a body of instruments makes it a little harder for some States to ignore recognised good practice; they begin to look over their shoulders more. This may be the hypocritical tribute which vice pays to virtue, but it has some force. It is all part of what Sir Alfred Zimmern, discussing the role of international organisations, calls 'the organisation of the hue-and-cry—nothing more'.[6]

One could hardly describe the process as a steady building-up; it is more like a slow sidling-up, a getting into the habit of professing—and even slightly practising—more virtue than usual, a bit-by-bit coming nearer the high professions of this intellectual-ethical Organisation to which these States belong. Perhaps, like Max Beerbohm's Happy Hypocrite, some States will find that the mask gradually affects their physiognomies. That would argue for a new definition of 'functionalism', one tailored to UNESCO's special rôle. Even that least binding of international instruments, a Declaration, can provide this sort of moral massage: even the Declaration on Human Rights, battered though it is, has something of that power. UNESCO's 1966 Declaration on the Principles of International Cultural Cooperation, because it asserts the distinctiveness and equal value of all cultures, might make the blatant oppression of minorities rather more difficult to practise, might give these minorities grounds for taking their cases to the international agencies and raising a public storm about them.

Wilfred Jenks, the Englishman we have referred to before and who ended his career as Director-General of the International Labour Organisation, never seemed to lose his intense and serious faith in the slow but sure growth of international law. He even floated the idea of an international Ombudsman who would deal with accusations that Member States were breaking the instruments they had formally adhered to. That such an institution might be established seems almost impossible; that it would, even

6. Sir Alfred Zimmern, *The League of Nations and The Rule of Law*, 1918–35, London: Macmillan, 1936.

if established as a troika, be allowed to be effective is even less likely. It would be easy to laugh at Jenks's idea. But he was clear-headed; I imagine he knew that one way of pushing international codes further was by keeping up the pressure, urging Member States to go further than seems reasonably likely at any given moment, in the hope that they will settle for an advance which, though less than that being called for, is nevertheless ahead of what States had originally intended.

Such assertions, like the instruments themselves, are important for a further reason: that world public opinion (and I believe that, in spite of all the difficulties of definition and communication, such an entity can be seen from time to time to exist) does expect a lead from the UN system, feels it right to push forward the growth of internationally-agreed good conduct and to apply such instruments fairly rather than through one-sided pressures from one group of States or another. I have in mind here the anger at the gross misapplications of, especially, the Declaration on Human Rights in recent years. These instruments are at their best flags, markers, rallying points; it would be an unimaginative mistake to undervalue them, in spite of their obvious current limitations.

The field of human rights shows at its most difficult this strange process by which States may edge into virtue. Hass summed up the problem more than a decade ago:

> Generalised agreement on values among national élites is
> probably the most elusive way of conceiving consensus,
> especially if the rights of the individual are selected as a
> focus: the claims upon clashing ideologies, social structures
> and conflicting policies are gargantuan.[7]

Nevertheless, UNESCO does have special responsibilities towards the development of human rights of several kinds, whether those of women or children or oppressed groups of many sorts. In present conditions, those responsibilities are only patchily fulfilled. Far more States than most of us realise do not recognise the individual's claim to any rights other than those the States themselves, their particular sovereign States, decide they shall have: the concept of rights which transcend the régime is not accepted. Or, to put the matter another way: such States tend to recognise social rights, not political. They may well grant the

7. Hass, E. B., *Beyond the Nation State*, 1964, p. 41.

individual the right to work, to social security, to equal opportunity; but they will not recognise the right to free expression. In
some of those new States whose energy is heavily invested in
arriving at a sense of national unity and at economic viability, the
idea of individual human rights is bound to take a low place.
That some of the more powerful States whose own record in
human rights is known to be appalling make on occasion the greatest noise in favour of those rights, so as to attack another nation
which has been caught publicly in the act, is only another instance
—though among the more striking—of the humbug which
characterises so much UN debating.

If the main provisions of the Declaration are set against the
names of the nations which have officially agreed to those provisions, even a hardened observer of international life marvels at
the starveling state of truth. The free movement of persons? Of
ideas? Equality before the law, and equal protection of the law?
Freedom from arbitrary arrest? And from torture? Innocence
until proved guilty? Freedom of association? I once saw Mme
Furtseva demanding, with all the force of a long-standing Soviet
Minister, that a British delegate to a conference on Cultural
Development be forthwith sent home by his Minister and Delegation leader. The offending delegate had suggested that, whilst
most people recognised the considerable advances in library
provision throughout the Soviet Union (which had just been
recorded at length), they would be glad to see rather more freedom
of publication. To Madame Furtseva this could only be an
officially prompted insult rather than one man's statement of
opinion; she was outraged and threatened to withdraw the Soviet
delegation. The Britisher stayed; and that night we all went to a
concert of superb Russian music. At the close we passed Madame
Furtseva again; she was literally crying with joy and pride at the
music of her country.

Since the individual can get no purchase on the matter at an
international level—Western European Regional provisions give
him more scope—the development of human rights is a question
for States as States. No State likes to complain about the practice
of another, unless there is some particular political advantage in it
and some group consensus to criticise in this way. This has happened, with varying degrees of reasonableness, apropos South
Africa (which, as we saw earlier, left UNESCO as a result of

attacks on her racialist policies), Israel and Chile. One or two recent events have begun to weaken the no-interference convention. The agreement which came out of the Helsinki conference on European Security linked greater freedom for people and ideas within Eastern Europe with economic and technical cooperation. President Carter's early criticisms of Eastern European practice are the other major shift and produced the inevitable criticisms in the Western world that they are unwise, premature, ill-judged, ill-phrased. They may have all those faults, but the fact is that for some people in authority in the West any cross-national statement on human rights, made at any time and no matter how carefully worded, will call out doubts about whether it should have been made at all. In general, States keep off each other's grass; sovereignty is too sensitive an issue, and no government wishes to be led into an escalating series of disputes about its own and others' human rights practices. In the main, criticism, evidence, pressures will have to come from other kinds of body.

Hence the various ways by which human rights activities within UNESCO are corralled. There is, first, a philosophical argument: that the achieving of peace must be prior to the extension of human rights. What good will human rights be, it is asked, if we are at war? As we have already noted, this is a bad argument. Work for peace which is not at one and the same time work for human rights will result, if it ever succeeds, only in the peace of the grave. Nations may not then be at war; a tight balance of power between them may have been found. But behind the absence of overt war the people of certain nations might be almost wholly without crucial human rights. Human rights are integral with Peace, not postponable; and in the last resort they are more important than peace. Men fight and are ready to be killed for their rights as humans.

One of the areas of human rights which receives a great deal of attention in UNESCO is especially promoted by the new nations, and concerns the 'right of self-determination' of peoples. It is an important right and inspired, obviously, by the existence of remnants of colonialism in various parts of the world. Within that overall title attention is heavily focused on attacking racism, and in particular apartheid as practised by South Africa. Again, this is easily understandable. But there can be an evasion at the heart of all this activity. One sometimes feels that, given the difficulty of doing anything effective about human rights within the UN as a whole, given the immediate cries that sovereignty has been breached if the slightest criticism of any nation is made, South Africa has become a convenient wicked Squire. The energy spent on fighting apartheid has become a useful way of diverting energy from other matters: political prisoners, exiled artists, enslaved minorities. Anti-apartheid work needs doing, and UNESCO can fairly claim that it does good work here. But it is over-concentrated on this aspect.

More and more, the thrust of human rights work within UNESCO reflects, not a considered judgment on where those rights are most seriously infringed and how best matters might be step by step improved; it reflects rather the immediate preoccupations of this or that group of Member States. UNESCO may and does produce enormous Resolutions on Peace and Human Rights. These Resolutions include everything but the kitchen sink: charges of submerged colonialism, economic misdeeds by the ex-colonialist powers and the multi-national corporations, cultural neo-imperialism, the misuse of modern mass communications for the international spread of pornography and other 'undesirable material'—all this without one word about the violations of human rights practised within the nations which take the lead in promoting such portmanteau resolutions. For those nations, in particular, the overriding emphasis on neo-colonialism is a convenient lightning conductor. It is, in its central form—apartheid—very precise, since it concerns whites denying human rights to blacks. It has little other resonance, and so is not likely to spill over into or prompt more difficult debates on less dramatically-defined malpractices.

Once again, Croce put his finger on the general dilemma, this time in UNESCO's involvement with human rights issues. Almost thirty years later, his analysis has not lost force:

> Representatives of all currents, especially the two most
> directly opposed . . . cannot possibly proclaim in the form
> of a declaration of rights, a declaration of common political
> action, an agreement which has no existence, but which
> must, on the contrary, be the ultimate outcome of opposed
> and convergent efforts . . . nor do I ever see how it would
> be possible to formulate any half-way or compromise

declaration which would not prove either empty or arbitrary.[8]

The Secretariat can do little to improve this situation. Yet it could have done more over the years. It has too often and too consistently looked the other way when States have skated on very thin ice in their relations to the Organisation and its Constitution. If States had been more often told that they were asking too much, bending the rules, distorting the Organisation's purposes, UNESCO's human rights activities would be in better shape now. But, as we have abundantly seen, the Secretariat has too often preferred to hedge and compromise, to settle for the muddled and muffled so as to avoid coming sharply up against the distinctions that divide.

I see one slight gleam of hope in all this, in the very gradual extension of the principle of UNESCO missions of enquiry into sovereign or occupied territories. For UNESCO to be involved in examinations on the ground gives it powerful opportunities. I have in mind, for example, Professor Lemaire's scrupulous visits to Jerusalem during the first half of the seventies, designed to allow him to report back to the Director General on the extent and nature of Israeli archaeological work there. There was, in the same period, the agreement—after tortuous diplomatic negotiations—to allow a UNESCO mission into Cyprus after the Turkish invasion, so as to check on accusations and counter-accusations about damage to cultural property. There was, too, the mission to Israeli-occupied territories to report on the state of Arab education and culture there. A couple of years earlier, again after difficult negotiations, we had managed to get a French expert into Angkor Wat to assess alleged depredations. Latest of all, in late 1977, Israel agreed to receive another UNESCO mission.

What may be the most significant of these missions, because it could in no way be connected with the necessarily limited scope of the Hague Convention, was the mission to Chile which I mentioned in the last chapter, whose brief was to enquire into allegations of violations of human rights. The irony was that the nations who called for that mission—chiefly the Eastern

8. B. Croce, 'The Rights of Man and the Present Historical Situation', in *Human Rights: Comments and Interpretations*, a symposium edited by UNESCO, intro. J. Maritain, London, Wingate, 1949, p. 94.

Europeans—were those who most readily invoke, when they are themselves challenged on human rights questions, Article 1-3 of the Constitution, which prohibits UNESCO from interfering with States' domestic affairs.

UNESCO will not at present be proposing to send missions of enquiry about human rights practices to countries other than those whom a predominant voting bloc has an interest in attacking. Still, an important point has been conceded—a principle of intervention—and in the long run that may make life more uncomfortable for those who use the brute force of the bloc vote to accuse others of crimes which they themselves regularly commit. At the least, they have given their critics a stick with which they can be beaten; and we have seen that they tend to be sensitive to being pilloried. That is why, to revert to a point mentioned earlier, I do not think 'Basket Three' in the Helsinki agreement is only a mockery. Perhaps some of those who signed it had no intention of taking seriously its main elements—freedom of movement for people and ideas. But they have committed themselves publicly to honouring a principle which up to the present they have not even recognised. From now on they are in that respect more vulnerable and accountable. Such situations have a habit of growing stronger, very slowly and quietly, like plants in the cracks of a wall. That is to be almost wildly optimistic: but it has some point; better that as a working hope than flat unexpectancy.

iii

It is now possible to see more exactly the rôle members of the Secretariat can play as good servants of the Constitution. They are, it should be remembered, one of the six prime organs of UNESCO, a main constituent element meant to have a life and force of its own. That, at least, was the intention of the founders.

Twenty years ago, a Joint Disciplinary Committee tried to define the duty of the UN Secretariat:

The Committee thinks it particularly important that the staffs assigned to the Secretariats of political bodies, operating either at HQ or in the field, should not only subordinate their personal views to the decisions of their responsible superiors in the Secretariat, but also understand and accept the overriding authority in all matters of substance of the bodies themselves.[9]

The intention is clear: to discourage Secretariat members from taking orders from their own countries. But the formulation falls into a different trap. It misses the complexity of both the formal and the on-the-ground situations of UN personnel. Given its dates it is, I suppose, still hung over by McCarthy-induced fears. It is of the same order as statements that a civil servant's duty is simply 'to execute orders', which wholly begs the question of professional and personal ethics and their interrelations. To complete it by saying too soon—though there is a point where this may be the right thing to say—'You can always resign if you cannot tolerate a particular order', crudely short-circuits the problem and ignores its most interesting feature: that even in executing orders there are margins for movement, margins with political and ethical characteristics.

Roughly speaking, there emerged quite early two distinct conceptions of the ideal international civil service. We can call them for convenience, the Drummond and the Thomas views. As first Secretary-General of the League of Nations, Sir Eric Drummond tried to create a force which was hard-working, competent and self-effacing. He hardly ever spoke in official meetings (though he gradually acquired more and more power behind the scenes, as a very fair-minded and discreet adviser). The Frenchman Albert Thomas, the first executive head of the International Labour Office, had a different idea of his rôle. He did not believe that an international civil servant could or should be as self-effacingly in the background as national civil servants are—in some countries—theoretically expected to be. As we have seen, he cannot simply serve a Minister, since he has no Minister; he has to serve the Constitution, especially when the members of the Organisation risk damaging it through quarrels between themselves; he has to hold the boat steady until squalls have passed; he has to find usable common ground.

9. Joint Disciplinary Committee of four Senior Secretariat Members, 1958, quoted Hazzard, S. *Defeat of an Ideal: The Self-Destruction of the U.N.*, London, Macmillan, 1973, p. 134.

All this was true for Albert Thomas, but was still not enough. He believed his job required him all the time to think about possible new directions for the Organisation to take, to seek those which promised to have great international significance; that his duty then was to offer these ideas with all the persuasiveness he could to his governing councils. After all, none of the members of those councils were occupied full-time with the work of the Organisation; the top full-time official ought to be thinking ahead in a way and with an intensity no one else could afford.

Most interpretations of the international civil service have admirable sides, but Thomas's is plainly more active and interventionist than Drummond's. Thomas's regular reports to the ILO governing body show this as well as anything; they were deliberate political acts, carefully planned and phrased efforts to contribute to the continuing debate on ILO's aims and purposes. Dag Hammarskjöld respected both approaches, and it is not self-evident to which side he leaned the more; but I would guess to Thomas's. He certainly made use of the celebrated Article 99 of the UN Charter ('The Secretary-General may bring to the attention of the Security Council any matter which in his opinion may threaten the maintenance of international peace and security') so as to extend and intensify the Security Council's own rôle. He saw the dilemmas early and well, and insisted that the Secretariat was not an anonymous sub-structure but a main constitutional organ, executing programmes whose execution in itself carried enormous and difficult political implications, and therefore called upon them to find workable ways of taking initiatives which representatives of Member States—though privately many of them might agree the moves were necessary—would find difficult to take.

So there we have another of those endless contrasts: this time between the patient and the promotional approaches, the view of Secretariat members as instruments or actors. Most books on the international civil service assume the former rôle and so stress the art of diplomacy, of helping compromises to emerge, of the value of limited gains, scaled-down agreements, the constant careful recognition of national jealousy about autonomy. Most writers stress the importance of consensus-seeking rather than of initiative-taking.

My own general position is nearer Thomas's than Drummond's. I believe we are forced to become actors from time to time, whatever our wills, if we are to do what is required of us. We have to learn at what point, whilst still trying to be objective, and indeed just because we insist on trying to be objective, we need to stop being self-effacing; we have to recognise at what point the Constitution looks like being compromised. No acceptable professional code requires a man to do as he is told in all circumstances without question or argument. The Secretariat sometimes shows itself at its best when it bends its skills to forcing a creative solution out of the restraints of its working conditions. As well as having the duty to 'hold the line' in stormy periods, it has also—from time to time —to become positively the 'conscience of the Organisation', the keeper of the institution's better purposes; it has to practise a creative neutrality.

Auden has an interesting passage on historians which can be amended to fit the dilemma of international civil servants at such times of crisis:

> The characteristic virtue of the [international civil servant], his impartiality, which refrains from intruding his own moral values upon events, leaving that duty to the [Member States], then becomes meaningless, for moral judgments can only be passed on personal deeds and in the world he [is asked to inhabit professionally] men are incapable of deeds and only exhibit social behaviour.[10]

To break from this impasse requires the members of the Secretariat to recognise as fully as possible the harsher facts of political life; and, having done that, not to be bothered by them to the point of becoming exhausted, depressed, suspicious and ineffective—to recognise them, in short, so as to act more effectively. They need to be able to retain an uncynical sense of the value of the institution itself. The old International Institute for Intellectual Cooperation could not have effectively survived in such a harsh world. As we have seen again and again, an inter-governmental agency with intellectual and ethical purposes has a hard job of surviving and is always in danger of becoming bogus. One of the jobs of all those who care about it—one of the jobs, pre-eminently, of the Secretariat—is to keep the corporate body well pressed up against that bed of nails, the Constitution; in other words, they

10. W. H. Auden, *Secondary Worlds*, London, Faber and Faber, 1968, p. 83.

have to encourage Member States to cash when absolutely needed those high-minded cheques they issued on joining, and which some of them continue to issue when they think themselves free from any danger of having their bluffs called.

As so often, Dag Hammarskjöld put the issue cogently:

> In the last analysis, this is a question of integrity, and if integrity in the sense of respect for law and respect for truth were to drive him into positions of conflict with this or that interest, then that conflict is a sign of his neutrality and not of his failure to observe neutrality—then it is in line, not in conflict, with his duties as an international civil servant.[11]

Creative neutrality or positive objectivity can be expressed in several main ways, all of them risky. Overwhelmingly the most important is the insistence by the Secretariat that in all the work it is given to execute it will insist on the greatest possible honesty and depth, that there will be no compromises for the sake of a quiet life. I do not mean that Secretariat members have to go out to seek trouble. I mean that if, for example, Member States ask for advice on various kinds of policies, it is the duty of the Secretariat to expose the options as fully as possible, and that those options should include the social and human costs of any given line (even though it may be known in advance that a particular government is contemplating that line, and will not like the analysis). Whatever policy that government subsequently pursues, it cannot argue that this has been on the advice of the UN agency. Where a government has not already made up its mind, it may take a better measure of the implications of its choices. This standpoint means also that, if the Secretariat is asked to produce a statement about—say—the mass media and racism, or the mass media and peace, or the mass media and obscenity, it produces a precise document which faces the limited amount of firm knowledge in this field and lays things out as they are, not as the sponsors of the enabling resolutions might wish them to be. This approach also means that there should be no holy cows among subjects under examination, that all the preambular humbug, the vague definitions of projects, the jargon and the rest will be cut. It means keeping to a minimum the bogus symposia on big issues in which the stage army of the officially Good from each country face each other for the umpteenth time. It means taking the fluff and contradictions out of draft resolutions, pointing out to Member States that such resolutions will make the Organisation a joke. It means that Secretariat members should not edit reports so as to make them safe but should remove bias from them when, as often happens, bias has crept in as draft succeeds draft. It means, in short, aiming all the time at honest consensus-building; that process, though slow, is the only good basis for UNESCO's work.

The Secretariat's second main rôle is more circumspect; it is the practice of private diplomacy. I have already said a little about the degree to which the Director General is asked to exercise this function. The most difficult cases concern individuals—intellectuals, writers, politicians—who have fallen foul of their governments. The Director General's scope for initiative is limited but clear. He must first, if he possibly can, establish the exact facts. He must act quickly; but he must not look like Don Quixote, going into battle with his shirt-flaps hanging out. He is, as so often, on a knife-edge. Concessions exacted from Member States are assumed to have their price, and regular concessions may exact a high price. A nation which habitually flouts human rights can now and again be persuaded, as if magnanimously, to release some well-known figure whose case has come to world attention. For the Member States, such small, point-by-point concessions can build up a fair hedge against the risk that the Chief Executive may some day be tempted to take such a problem publicly to the governing bodies of the Organisation. As we have seen, that last resort has to be taken sometimes and may make for greater sensitivity in future; or it may make for greater controls against leaks: 'stone-dead hath no fellow'.

In all this area, the Secretariat's duty, though difficult and sometimes dangerous, is not in doubt: they have to try to honour the spirit of the Constitution. We need only recall that Resolution which accused Chile—rightly—of denying human rights. Suppose some individual or group somewhere in the world, seeing that Resolution on the record, now writes asking: if Chile's record in human rights is to be examined today, why not Indonesia's or Brazil's or the Soviet Union's tomorrow? If such a correspondent encloses detailed allegations against any of these or other countries, it is not the duty of the Secretariat to send a soothing answer and file the letter. The Secretariat's responsibility is to let their ruling bodies know that their own decisions are having these natural consequences and to ask them how they propose, in the name of the Constitution, to respond.

Sometimes the Secretariat does act thus. It may be remembered that the third Israel Resolution at the 1974 General Conference required the Director General to 'withhold all assistance' from Israel until she had mended her ways. As was noted earlier, an extremely limited interpretation of the phrase was possible and—this was the critical moment—was publicly adopted by the Secretariat. The representative of the Director General, after asking for the floor on 'a technical point', announced that the Secretariat would take the narrowest possible meaning of the phrase. He told them there and then, so that they could object if they wished; and it was a bold act. Surely, one felt, the sponsors could not have intended their brandishingly polysyllabic phrase to end in such a feeble slap at Israel? But there was no reaction from the floor.

My own most striking experience of Secretariat 'active neutrality' arose when the Organisation was asked by a UN Resolution to produce a 'teachers' kit' on the evils of apartheid. We knew that such a kit already existed, prepared privately, and that it was this particular kit we were expected to publish. So we sent for the typescript. On reading it, we realised that some time would be needed before it was publishable by UNESCO. It had been produced by voluntary helpers. There were very important omissions; one part, being past history, was far too long; others were too small; the quality of the writing differed markedly. There were pedagogic problems, especially about the text's suitability for a world-wide audience; the age of the children for whom it seemed designed differed from chapter to chapter; there were local references which would have made the kit unintelligible outside its country of origin.

More important, the manuscript contained passages which would have given great offence to some Member States. These States' commercial links with South Africa were identified. If we had printed it as received, there would have been, on the day of publication, a queue of Permanent Delegates at the Director General's suite demanding, with every expectation of success, that the book be withdrawn. But the book needed to be published. So the Secretariat set about improving its quality and effectiveness. It was tried out in a number of schools. At Headquarters we set out to find ways of making the same important criticisms of some Member States without giving those castigated a foothold for complaining under the Constitution. In such matters most Member States tend to be more concerned about the exact letter of the law (the naming of names) than about less obvious but still identifiable phrasings. We finally produced a manuscript which had force but against which it was difficult for even the most sensitive Member State to lodge a specific complaint.

In all this, we were not helped by the Executive Board. Some members were watching the kit's progress very carefully, in case their own countries or regions were to be criticised. One delegate told me categorically that if his State were adversely named, he would ensure that the book remained in UNESCO's cellars. On the other hand, some of the African states were very anxious that the kit should see the light of day. I formed the impression that they did not greatly mind what appeared, even if it was unbalanced propaganda, so long as it attacked apartheid. One or two began to think that the delay in publication was due to the Secretariat's fear of offending Western European Member States. They had to drop that suspicion when they heard that some of the States most sharply criticised were black African nations who do business with South Africa.

All in all, the Secretariat had in this instance done a job with which it could be quite pleased. It had steered clear of those articles in the Constitution which might have been used to sink the project; it had produced a text with at least as much strength as the original, and had done it on its own initiative. This is the kind of operation which builds up a proper status for the Secretariat within the Organisation and nourishes its self-respect.

I am not, it should hardly need saying, arguing that the Secretariat is more important than the other organs of the institution; I am saying that it has a particular rôle which goes beyond the simple 'obeying of orders'. Nor am I saying that only the Secretariat can remember the Constitution and assert it against other interests; individual Member States sometimes do, and so do from time to time the General Conference, the Executive Board and some Permanent Delegates. I *am* saying, however, that the Secretariat's wholly compatible double loyalty—to the Constitution and to the idea of an international civil service—is not sufficiently borne in mind by many staff members today. There is scope for more courage, and courage of that sort will be well received by some Member States; their representatives recognise that, if it wills, the Secretariat is in one sense freer than they are. If in following this line things go badly wrong, if major principles continue to be eroded in activity after activity, there remains always the right to resign. But that step should not be taken because one is simply fed up or put out, or because one has been pushed by others (as a nuisance to be got rid of), or out of the desire to make a dramatic gesture.

iv

> The value of public diplomacy in the United Nations will
> depend to a decisive extent on how far the responsible
> spokesmen find it possible to rise above a narrow tactical
> approach to the politics of international life, and to speak as
> men for aspirations and hopes which are those of all
> mankind.[12]

A paramount need today is for the developed Western democracies to revise their own attitudes towards UNESCO, and give it something of the attention it receives from most other groups of States. Since these 'open' States officially uphold within their own territories the cardinal principles of the Organisation—freedom of thought and its free circulation—they should recognise a special relationship between them and UNESCO. By 'States' I mean in this instance more than governments and their civil services; I mean also the National Commissions of those countries and their intellectuals, scientists, artists, writers, journalists, broadcasters.

It is not difficult to see reasons for the West's decreasing interest in UNESCO over the last two decades. They feel resentful at the

12. Dag Hammarskjöld: 'The UN and the Major Challenges which Face the World Community', *U.N. Review*, 4:12; New York, June 1958.

demands, often querulously made and accompanied by calls for past misdeeds to be expiated, of some of the new nations. They dislike the political misuses of the Organisation by some nations and blocs. They have less and less heart for giving UNESCO the time and effort needed to put it on a better road.

For several reasons, this is a mistaken policy—or lack of policy. If these countries continue to linger morosely on the sidelines, only recalling at intervals that they are paying a large part of the budget, they will cause the new nations more and more to make common cause with those authoritarian developed nations who care little about UNESCO's Constitutional principles but a lot about the political capital to be gained from operating within the institution. One can see this process in the two main debates with which UNESCO will be involved for the next few years, that on the use of mass communications and that, the larger debate, on the New International Economic Order. We shall turn directly to them a little later. Nor does the prevailing attitude in the West do justice to the increasing number of responsible politicians and officials in the developing countries who do not wish to choose the way of authoritarianism but find insufficient sympathy in the West for their difficulties. The Western nations should remind themselves more often that UNESCO's extraordinary Constitution is a Western invention, founded on Western intellectual values; and that these values are not easily lived up to. It is odd that the nations which assert them find it so easy to neglect the one international body which is centrally committed to them. If the West did once again become more involved in these ways she would certainly arouse some resentment; but the move would be generally welcomed. Even some nations which do not practise these principles themselves often have a sneaking respect for the traditions of objectivity, tolerance, fairmindedness and openness. In short, if any nations were to choose to recall the uniqueness of the Constitution, to press for a more effective General Conference, to remind the Executive Board of its triple mandate, to give the right autonomy to their own National Commissions and persuade its best people to sit on them . . . if any nations were to reassert these needs today, they should be the Western democracies.

To make such changes would require a big effort of the imagination. Above all, it has to be recognised much more that the Third World is now at the centre of the stage, its problems at the head of the agenda; and that they will not go away simply by being ignored. The two main issues I mentioned in the last paragraph show this dramatically. I am not qualified to offer detailed, technical proposals on how the West might better approach these debates. What I can say, because I have had experience of observing it, is that in general the developed world has not been sufficiently willing to take the full force of what the developing world is saying. Improvements are not going to be easy to bring about; but they are more likely to be found if we listen more carefully.

Take, for example, the negotiations about the Law of the Sea, which are one branch of the larger demand for a New International Economic Order. Briefly, the developing world wishes the international sea-bed to be under UN surveillance. If something such as that does not come about the technologically-advanced nations will, they fear, raid the sea-bed for its riches, as a century ago they raided Africa and elsewhere. I once tried to discuss this with the senior maritime adviser to one of the major Western delegations to the Law of the Sea conference. I expected an account of the great technical and political problems, set against a perspective which at least recognised the force and indeed legitimacy of the new nations' concern. What he said was, almost in these words: 'the claim is preposterous. Because they are themselves scientifically backward they want us to mark time for fifty years so that they can catch up. But you can't stop progress. Of course, we will not agree to letting the UN have surveillance.' That is fairly typical of an all-too-common type of official thinking. The UN and its Agencies can be left alone so long as they continue to know their place. But let other nations try to give the system the teeth its Charter meant it to have and the rich nations come to life, brusquely. Some time later I described the above encounter to an even more senior official, the Ambassador to the UN itself of another major European power. He smiled at the maritime adviser's simplified statement of the issue. 'Still,' he went on to muse, 'none of us in the advanced world is in fact likely to agree to UN surveillance. We will sort it out between ourselves.' I believe the tide of feeling elsewhere, and to some extent in the advanced countries also, is running more and more against these still dominant official attitudes; but it will be a long time before the tide in actual decision-making changes much. Meanwhile, no one who has worked within the UN, even and

perhaps especially one from a developed Western state, can funda-
mentally regret—in spite of all the difficulties they have brought—
the greater political plurality and the greater cultural openness
which the last thirty years have seen emerge in those institutions.

The call for a New International Economic Order is a call for
greater distributive justice. In a world in which 70 per cent of the
population receive 20 per cent of the wealth, in which millions lack
bare necessities—adequate food, medical care, employment—in
which the rich, mesmerised by the imperative that their already
high standard of living should steadily improve, get richer and the
poor poorer, it is no wonder that the statesmen of the poorer
nations are alarmed and angry. As one American observer has
said, the demand now is for equality not charity. The developed
countries are, it is true, doing more to assist development than they
used to, but the increase in slow and inadequate. They have not
at all convinced the developing world of their seriousness of purpose. Their general attitude still looks too much like the habitual
taking-things-for-granted, including the distress of others. These
are often-repeated accusations and simply to make them does not
make the appalling problems of redistribution any easier to solve.
But, as with problems of the Law of the Sea, they will be even
further from being solved if the developed world does not make
more effort to grasp imaginatively what is being said to them and
asked of them. Once, not long after I left UNESCO, I was asked
to speak about the Third World to a large group of high-level
Western European civil servants, business men, executives of
various kinds and diplomats. I found myself virtually alone; almost
to a man they assumed that people at their level were right to be
annoyed by and dismissive of Third World attitudes. It was as
though they had moved from military colonialism to technological neo-colonialism without a thought beyond the purely
practical and profitable. They seemed to have no perspective, no
point of entry into Third World concerns. At that moment I felt
an almost filial gratitude to UNESCO, poor battered UNESCO
which is nevertheless in a more real world than that distinguished
Western European gathering.

UNESCO's role in the whole New International Economic
Order debate is necessarily small. But it has a part to play; and for
UNESCO itself such a debate could hardly be more relevant.
UNESCO was founded on the idea of an appeal to the sense of a

common suffering mankind, exhausted and reduced by a long war and determined to build a fairer world. In its origins it has more in common with the universe of King Lear than with that of Machiavelli, and should not be allowed to forget it.

The debate about mass communications, which will take place more in UNESCO than in any other part of the UN system, will be the second most important issue of the next few years. Here the West, if it wills, could quite soon make an important and unique contribution. The debate concentrates on the imbalance in media resources and output as between the developed and the developing world. Most of the equipment for broadcasting and other modern communications is made in the developed world, of course; so are most of the programmes which fill the television screens of the world; most books are published there; and the great information agencies such as Reuter's are overwhelmingly American or British. All this has been well documented by UNESCO and elsewhere; the flow of material and opinions is massively one-way. Not surprisingly, the developing nations want more share in the process. On the whole, the West has not responded sensitively to these disquiets. By contrast the Soviet Union has been very active indeed. She has joined with the new nations in accusing the West of substituting for colonialism maintained by force the neo-colonialism of mass-media saturation with 'degrading' commercial material. About satellites, the Soviet Union is particularly nervous since satellites are difficult to jam. Hence the Soviet stress on the need, in any convention on the use of satellites, for provisions to ensure they will not be used to beam 'undesirable materials' into countries other than the originators. In short, the pressure is increasingly for greater government control of the mass media. In the Eastern bloc that is an act of policy; in the new nations it is proposed as a means of combating neo-colonialism. Some politicians in the new nations will not be averse to the move; governmental control, no matter how it is justified, suits them. Others recognise the risks and do not wish to be led down that road.

For their part, the Arab States have been using this debate as an element in their campaign against Israel. These activities came to a head at a meeting in UNESCO in December 1975, during the drafting of a Declaration by a group of government-appointed experts on the principles governing the operation of the mass media. The meeting endorsed Resolution 3379 of the UN General

Assembly, which had been passed a month before in New York, and defined Zionism as a form of racism. Galvanised at last, a dozen Western countries walked out in protest. But that gave the Third World and Communist majority the opportunity to prepare a draft Declaration containing stringent limitations on the free flow of information. This left UNESCO with a problem at least as great as that posed by the original anti-Israel Resolution of 1974: the most powerful Western nations were scandalised and the continuance of their contributions was in doubt. At the Nairobi General Conference in the Autumn of 1976, the mass media issue was postponed for two years. The Western nations stayed, and time had been bought. It is time which the West should use to the best possible advantage; to begin with, by helping the work of the new body UNESCO established in 1977: The International Commission on the Problems of Communication in Modern Society.

The mass media debate is at the heart of UNESCO's whole meaning and purposes. If the debate continues to go in the direction the Soviets want, the victims will be the principles of free thought and its circulation, those ideas which the West itself embedded in the Constitution. For the new media to be used in ways which deny these freedoms, by new nations led in this direction by the conviction that the West is above all selfishly profit-seeking in its international promotion of the media, for this to happen whilst the West neglects to enter the debate seriously, is a huge compound irony. Without being self-righteous, the West has to remind itself that the best it can offer the world is not, after all, technical know-how but less ponderable things, certain social concepts: the rule of law, the freedom of the individual, democratic process, free exchanges of people and ideas, at least intermittent critical honesty before the weaknesses of one's own society. These are all still worth exporting.

The West should therefore work out a plan for the mass media, one careful and honest enough to convince the new nations that they recognise the scope of the problem and are willing to help resolve it. It can be done if the right agreements are proposed, if there are some voluntary restrictions by the West, and much practical help by them also. As I write, there are signs that some Western nations have taken the message. The calls being made on experts to help draft proposals regarding the best use of the mass media are at a level some UNESCO National Commissions have not seen for many years.

It would be a serious mistake to think of this or any similar process as that by which a highly-sophisticated West teaches the poor and benighted nations how to live in the twentieth century. The West too is under stress and on trial; whatever is done will have to be in partnership. The criticisms made of the West by its own writers as well as by writers from the developing world are forceful and run in similar directions. Fanon, Illich, Freire and the rest are contributors to a common critique, but one almost wholly ignored by those in authority in the West. So they find it difficult to believe that, in any consideration of what sort of life is best worth working for in this threatened and puzzled world, the cultures of the Third World have anything to offer.

In all such enquiries UNESCO has a central part to play. To recapitulate finally: its best contributions will always be over the long term. Governments will not quickly learn to think and act collectively before common problems. UNESCO itself will always live in a state of paradox and tension. It will continue to be both excessively wide-open and excessively turned in upon itself. It will always be seeking a balance between trimming and effective compromises, always in danger of falling into a meaningless total relativism. Its ideals are exceptionally high and only rarely lived up to. It has no formal power but can sometimes exercise moral force. But bit by bit the case law is established, and the frontiers move slightly. After thirty years, it is still not working anything like as well as its founders or its later supporters hoped. But its death would be a great loss; the world would be poorer in expressed and—occasionally—achieved ideals if UNESCO collapsed, its sight that much shorter. Some parts of our common life—some aspects of peace-keeping, some elements in human rights, some kinds of Development—are a little better than they would have been if UNESCO had not existed. In spite of all its fantastic, baroque, bewildering failings, UNESCO remains one of the more hopeful institutions created in this ambiguous century.

EPILOGUE

I went to UNESCO for three years but, in my second year, was asked by Maheu to stay until the end of his own term, which meant adding two more years. It was not easy to agree. We had seen many people who had stayed too long in the international civil service and ended their lives rootless, somewhere in the South of France. I wanted to get back to the U.K. whilst there was still time for a long stint of interesting work. But in the end two more years seemed possible, so we agreed.

This meant that we were due to leave in January 1975. As the fifth year drew to its close and the Senegalese Amadou–Mahtar M'Bow was about to be elected DG (by the Paris General Conference of Autumn 1974) he asked me to stay a further six months, until mid-75, so as to help along his early days. I agreed to that also.

In the event, I left after only three months of this last extension; and the choice was entirely mine. The major issue before the Organisation in M'Bow's first year was the Arab–Israeli dispute as this was exemplified in the anti-Israel Resolutions which I have described at length. That preoccupied the DG, should have preoccupied the Direction Générale, and among the ADGs particularly preoccupied me since my Sector was directly involved with two of the three Resolutions.

It would not have been easy for any Director General to handle the issue. It was quite particularly difficult for M'Bow who is black, African, from a developing country and Muslim. It is easy to see the criss-crossing of loyalties and pressures which would be inherent in any move he made on the three Resolutions. But some of us were ready to help him as much as we could. It soon seemed clear, to me at least, that under M'Bow the Direction Générale was going to be no more a reality than it had been under Maheu; and that the advice of an ADG from the developed white West would be regarded as likely to be tainted politically; that, in short, senior responsible officials would be bypassed not so much out of a Maheu'ian arrogance as because few actions were assumed to be disinterested.

After two or three months of these circumstances I decided that there was no point in staying on the extra few months just so as to mind the rest of my shop; better to go home earlier and start work on this book. I chose the manner and the time of my going carefully. I do not like melodramatic gestures; but I did want the reasons for my going to be known exactly to M'Bow himself and to a few close friends at UNESCO; and I did not want it to be made easy, for those who were disposed to do so, to write off my premature resignation as a safe gesture by someone who had already found a billet back home.

In early Spring of 1975, Goldsmiths' College in the University of London called me for interview for their Warden's (Principal's) post. I was one of five or six short-listed from a few score applicants; there was obviously no assurance that I would be the one they chose. Still, if they did choose me any force my subsequent resignation might have could have been neutralised. So I resigned one hour before I left Headquarters for Orly and the Goldsmiths' interview, thus making myself jobless. It was not a big gesture. I knew I would get a job somewhere in the U.K., if not at Goldsmiths'; and I had a six-months' Leverhulme Fellowship at Sussex University to tide me over. Few are so fortunate or so free.

My letter of resignation to M'Bow was confidential and I took special steps to keep it that way. It was carefully worded, without heat, and polite; and so was his response. Among the few close friends who were aware of all these goings-on, some felt that I should have made my letter public since it might have had more exemplary force within the Secretariat and outside. That might well have been a reasonable procedure. I decided against it because I wanted to give M'Bow, in those early days of his command, a chance of seeing that it is possible for an individual to take an uncomfortable decision out of personal principle, that not every such action is taken either under political pressure or to make private capital out of a public gesture. I do not know whether the point came home to him. As I've said, his job in those early months was exceptionally difficult. Incidentally, he seems to have gained ground since. In mid-1976, he was faced with that flouting by Rumania of the rights as an international civil servant of one of their nationals to which I referred earlier. From the beginning of that episode which, as I write, has dragged on for sixteen months, M'Bow seems to have acted firmly, and exactly as a Head of Agency should when faced by a government which reneges on its own commitments to the international service.

In both good and bad senses, our last days at UNESCO passed characteristically. We were not offered the usual public courtesies of farewell which even modestly-graded officials who have served fewer years than I had can usually expect. Blurred reasons were offered for the omission but there can be little doubt that it was prompted by a fear that, since I was going early, I must surely (it was wrongly assumed) have had a very violent disagreement with M'Bow about how to handle the Israel issue. Might not anyone who was seen to be in any way 'honouring' me or offering me a platform for a political farewell speech subsequently suffer?

That did not matter at all. What did matter was the great number of private farewell gestures made to us in those last weeks by all sorts of people, and in particular the friendly letters from all parts and levels of the place.

We left, as we came, at a weekend. Our home in Paris for the last few months had been that same Avenue de Saxe, which runs from the side of the UNESCO building, in which we had passed our very first month there. We had arrived in a bitter winter weekend; we left on a lambent spring Sunday. The furniture was already in England. We filled the car until it creaked with all the smaller, more precious bits and pieces which help make a home, with all the things we'd picked up or been given along the way and which now in England speak to us of Paris and of many other places around the world and, even more, of friends. The Spanish messenger from my office insisted on giving up the heart of his Sunday to helping us pack and load, and waved all the way down the Avenue until we turned the corner en route for Le Havre. It was not a bad way to be seen off.

This time too we travelled, at first, largely in silence. There was still too much to say and sort out, and we were deeply torn. We had no doubt that it was right to go and to go then. But of course we would miss Paris intensely; it is not easily lovable but it is a tonic place to live in—brilliant, harsh, energetic, a great public assertion on both national and international levels, and at the same time a honeycomb of areas in which urban life can still be lived on a most imaginatively human scale. We would miss friends and colleagues; and we would most of all miss UNESCO. We had, both of us, invested over the years so much energy, thought, emotion in that fantastic bureaucracy that to leave it was like cutting off a limb. Still, we knew that with part of ourselves we would never leave it. Both the idea and the reality of UNESCO— the one so idealistic and imaginative, the other so complex a tapestry of human failings and virtues—will be with us until we die; and we would not at all wish it otherwise.

APPENDIX

CONSTITUTION OF THE UNITED NATIONS
EDUCATIONAL, SCIENTIFIC AND CULTURAL ORGANIZATION

Adopted in London on 16 November 1945 and amended by the General Conference at its second, third, fourth, fifth, sixth, seventh, eighth, ninth, tenth, twelfth, fifteenth, seventeenth and nineteenth sessions.

The Governments of the States Parties to this Constitution on behalf of their peoples declare:

That since wars begin in the minds of men, it is in the minds of men that the defences of peace must be constructed;

That ignorance of each other's ways and lives has been a common cause, throughout the history of mankind, of that suspicion and mistrust between the peoples of the world through which their differences have all too often broken into war;

That the great and terrible war which has now ended was a war made possible by the denial of the democratic principles of the dignity, equality and mutual respect of men, and by the propagation, in their place, through ignorance and prejudice, of the doctrine of the inequality of men and races;

That the wide diffusion of culture, and the education of humanity for justice and liberty and peace are indispensable to the dignity of man and constitute a sacred duty which all the nations must fulfil in a spirit of mutual assistance and concern;

That a peace based exclusively upon the political and economic arrangements of governments would not be a peace which could secure the unanimous, lasting and sincere support of the peoples of the world, and that the peace must therefore be founded, if it is not to fail, upon the intellectual and moral solidarity of mankind.

For these reasons, the States Parties to this Constitution, believing in full and equal opportunities for education for all, in the unrestricted pursuit of objective truth, and in the free exchange of ideas and knowledge, are agreed and determined to develop and to increase the means of communication between their peoples and to employ these means for the purposes of mutual understanding and a truer and more perfect knowledge of each other's lives;

In consequence whereof they do hereby create the United Nations Educational, Scientific and Cultural Organization for the purpose of advancing, through the educational and scientific and cultural relations of the peoples of the world, the objectives of international peace and of the common welfare of mankind for which the United Nations Organization was established and which its Charter proclaims.

Article I *Purposes and functions*

1. The purpose of the Organization is to contribute to peace and security by promoting collaboration among the nations through education, science and culture in order to further universal respect for justice, for the rule of law and for the human rights and fundamental freedoms which are affirmed for the peoples of the world, without distinction of race, sex, language or religion, by the Charter of the United Nations.

2. To realize this purpose the Organization will:

   a. Collaborate in the work of advancing the mutual knowledge and understanding of peoples, through all means of mass communication and to that end recommend such international agreements as may be necessary to promote the free flow of ideas by word and image;

   b. Give fresh impulse to popular education and to the spread of culture;

   By collaborating with Members, at their request, in the development of educational activities;

   By instituting collaboration among the nations to advance the ideal of equality of educational opportunity without regard to race, sex or any distinctions, economic or social;

   By suggesting educational methods best suited to prepare the children of the world for the responsibilities of freedom;

   c. Maintain, increase and diffuse knowledge;

   By assuring the conservation and protection of the world's inheritance of books, works of art and monuments of history and science, and recommending to the nations concerned the necessary international conventions;

   By encouraging co-operation among the nations in all branches of intellectual activity, including the international exchange of persons active in the fields of education, science and culture and the exchange of publications, objects of artistic and scientific interest and other materials of information;

   By initiating methods of international co-operation calculated to give the people of all countries access to the printed and published materials produced by any of them.

3. With a view to preserving the independence, integrity and fruitful diversity of the cultures and educational systems of the States members of this Organization, the Organization is prohibited from intervening in matters which are essentially within their domestic jurisdiction.

Article II *Membership*

1. Membership of the United Nations Organization shall carry with it the right to membership of the United Nations Educational, Scientific and Cultural Organization.
2. Subject to the conditions of the Agreement between this Organization and the United Nations Organization, approved pursuant to Article X of this Constitution, States not members of the United Nations Organization may be admitted to membership of the Organization, upon recommendation of the Executive Board, by a two-thirds majority vote of the General Conference.
3. Territories or groups of territories which are not responsible for the conduct of their international relations may be admitted as Associate Members by the General Conference by a two-thirds majority of Members present and voting, upon application made on behalf of such territory or group of territories by the Member or other authority having responsibility for their international relations. The nature and extent of the rights and obligations of Associate Members shall be determined by the General Conference.[1]
4. Members of the Organization which are suspended from the exercise of the rights and privileges of membership of the United Nations Organization shall, upon the request of the latter, be suspended from the rights and privileges of this Organization.
5. Members of the Organization which are expelled from the United Nations Organization shall automatically cease to be members of this Organization.
6. Any Member State or Associate Member of the Organization may withdraw from the Organization by notice addressed to the Director-General. Such notice shall take effect on 31 December of the year following that during which the notice was given. No such withdrawal shall affect the financial obligations owed to the Organization on the date the withdrawal takes effect. Notice of withdrawal by an Associate Member shall be given on its behalf by the Member

1. Paragraph adopted by the General Conference at its sixth session (1951) (6C/Resolutions, p. 83). See below, p. 21, resolution 41.2, concerning the rights and obligations of Associate Members, adopted by the General Conference.

State or other authority having responsibility for its international relations.[2]

Article III   *Organs*
The Organization shall include a General Conference, an Executive Board and a Secretariat.

Article IV   *The General Conference*
A. *Composition*
1. The General Conference shall consist of the representatives of the States members of the Organization. The Government of each Member State shall appoint not more than five delegates, who shall be selected after consultation with the National Commission, if established, or with educational, scientific and cultural bodies.

B. *Functions*
2. The General Conference shall determine the policies and the main lines of work of the Organization. It shall take decisions on programmes submitted to it by the Executive Board.[3]
3. The General Conference shall, when it deems desirable and in accordance with the regulations to be made by it, summon international conferences of States on education, the sciences and humanities or the dissemination of knowledge; non-governmental conferences on the same subjects may be summoned by the General Conference or by the Executive Board in accordance with such regulations.[4]
4. The General Conference shall, in adopting proposals for submission to the Member States, distinguish between recommendations and international conventions submitted for their approval. In the former case a majority vote shall suffice; in the latter case a two-thirds majority shall be required. Each of the Member States shall submit recommendations or conventions to its competent authorities within a period of one year from the close of the session of the General Conference at which they were adopted.
5. Subject to the provisions of Article V, paragraph 5(c), the General Conference shall advise the United Nations Organization on the educational, scientific and cultural aspects of matters of concern to

2. Paragraph adopted by the General Conference at its eighth session (1954) (8C/Resolutions, p. 12).
3. Paragraph amended by the General Conference at its seventh session (1952) (7C/Resolutions, p. 103).
4. Paragraph amended by the General Conference at its seventh session (1952) (7C/Resolutions, pp. 103–4).

the latter; in accordance with the terms and procedure agreed upon between the appropriate authorities of the two Organizations.[5]

6. The General Conference shall receive and consider the reports sent to the Organization by Member States on the action taken upon the recommendations and conventions referred to in paragraph 4 above or, if it so decides, analytical summaries of these reports.[6]

7. The General Conference shall elect the members of the Executive Board and, on the recommendation of the Board, shall appoint the Director-General.

C. *Voting*

8. **a** Each Member State shall have one vote in the General Conference. Decisions shall be made by a simple majority except in cases in which a two-thirds majority is required by the provisions of this Constitution,[7] or of the Rules of Procedure of the General Conference.[8] A majority shall be a majority of the Members present and voting.[9]

b A Member State shall have no vote in the General Conference if the total amount of contributions due from it exceeds the total amount of contributions payable by it for the current year and the immediately preceding calendar year.[10]

c The General Conference may nevertheless permit such a Member State to vote, if it is satisfied that failure to pay is due to conditions beyond the control of the Member Nation.[11]

5. Paragraph amended by the General Conference at its seventh session (1952) (7C/Resolutions, p. 104).
6. Paragraph amended by the General Conference at its seventeenth session (1972) (17C/Resolutions, 13.3, p. 114).
7. These provisions are the following: Article II.2 (admission of new Member States which are not members of the United Nations, on the recommendation of the Executive Board); II.3 (admission of Associate Members); IV.4 (adoption of international conventions submitted for approval of Member States); IV.13 (admission of observers of non-governmental or semi-governmental organizations); XIII.1 (amendments to the Constitution); XIII.2 (adoption of regulations governing the procedure for amendments of the Constitution).
8. See Rule 81, paragraph 2, of the Rules of Procedure of the General Conference.
9. Sub-paragraph amended by the General Conference at its tenth session (1958) (10C/Resolutions, p. 61).
10. Sub-paragraph adopted by the General Conference at its fourth session (1949) and amended at its sixth (1951) and seventh (1952) sessions (4C/Resolutions, p. 9, 6C/Resolutions, p. 85 and 7C/Resolutions, p. 104).
11. Sub-paragraph adopted by the General Conference at its fourth session (1949) 4C/Resolutions, p. 9).

D. *Procedure*

9. a The General Conference shall meet in ordinary session every two
years. It may meet in extraordinary session if it decides to do so
itself or if summoned by the Executive Board, or on the demand
of at least one-third of the Member States.[12]

   b At each session the location of its next ordinary session shall be
   designated by the General Conference. The location of an
   extraordinary session shall be decided by the General Conference
   if the session is summoned by it, or otherwise by the Executive
   Board.[13]

10. The General Conference shall adopt its own rules of procedure. It
shall at each session elect a President and other officers.[14]

11. The General Conference shall set up special and technical committees and such other subordinate bodies as may be necessary
for its purposes.

12. The General Conference shall cause arrangements to be made for
public access to meetings, subject to such regulations as it shall
prescribe.

E. *Observers*

13. The General Conference, on the recommendation of the Executive
Board and by a two-thirds majority may, subject to its rules of
procedure, invite as observers at specified sessions of the Conference
or of its Commissions representatives of international organizations,
such as those referred to in Article XI, paragraph 4.

14. When consultative arrangements have been approved by the Executive Board for such international non-governmental or semi-governmental organizations in the manner provided in Article XI, paragraph 4, those organizations shall be invited to send observers to
sessions of the General Conference and its Commissions.[15]

Article V   *Executive Board*
A. *Composition*

1. The Executive Board shall be elected by the General Conference from
among the delegates appointed by the Member States and shall

12. Sub-paragraphs (a) and (b) amended by the General Conference at its
third (1948) and seventh (1952) sessions (3C/110, p. 113 and 7C/Resolu-
tions, p. 104).
13. Sub-paragraphs (a) and (b) amended by the General Conference at
its third (1948) and seventh (1952) sessions (3C/110, p. 113 and 7C/Reso-
lutions, p. 104).
14. Paragraph amended by the General Conference at its second session
(1947) (2C/132, p. 63).
15. Paragraph adopted by the General Conference at its third session
(1948) (3C/110, p. 113).

consist of forty-five members each of whom shall represent the Government of the State of which he is a national. The President of the General Conference shall sit ex officio in an advisory capacity on the Executive Board.[16]

2. In electing the members of the Executive Board the General Conference shall endeavour to include persons competent in the arts, the humanities, the sciences, education and the diffusion of ideas, and qualified by their experience and capacity to fulfil the administrative and executive duties of the Board. It shall also have regard to the diversity of cultures and a balanced geographical distribution. Not more than one national of any Member State shall serve on the Board at any one time, the President of the Conference excepted.

3. Members of the Board shall serve from the close of the session of the General Conference which elected them until the close of the second ordinary session of the General Conference following that election. They shall not be immediately eligible for a second term. The General Conference shall, at each of its ordinary sessions, elect the number of members required to fill vacancies occurring at the end of the session.[17]

4.a In the event of the death or resignation of a member of the Executive Board, his replacement for the remainder of his term shall be appointed by the Executive Board on the nomination of the Government of the State the former member represented.

b The Government making the nomination and the Executive Board shall have regard to the factors set forth in paragraph 2 of this Article.

c When exceptional circumstances arise, which, in the considered opinion of the represented State, make it indispensable for its representative to be replaced, even if he does not tender his resignation, measures shall be taken in accordance with the provisions of sub-paragraph (a) above.[18]

16. Paragraph amended by the General Conference at its seventh (1952), eighth (1954), ninth (1956), twelfth (1962), fifteenth (1968), seventeenth (1972), and nineteenth (1976) sessions (7C/Resolutions, p. 104, 8C/Resolutions, p. 12, 9C/Resolutions, p. 70, 12C/Resolutions, p. 95, and 15/C Resolutions, p. 103, 17C/Resolutions, 13.1, p. 133, 19C/Resolutions, p. 93).

17. Paragraph amended by the General Conference at its fifth (1950), seventh (1952), fifteenth (1968) and seventeenth (1972) sessions (5C/Resolutions, pp. 9–10, 7C/Resolutions, p. 104 and 15C/Resolutions, p. 103, 17C/Resolutions, 13.2, p. 113).

18. Paragraph amended by the General Conference at its eighth (1954) and nineteenth (1976) sessions (8C/Resolutions, p. 12, and 19C/Resolutions, p. 93).

B. *Functions*

5.a The Executive Board shall prepare the agenda for the General Conference. It shall examine the programme of work for the Organization and corresponding budget estimates submitted to it by the Director-General in accordance with paragraph 3 of Article VI and shall submit them with such recommendations as it considers desirable to the General Conference.[19]

b The Executive Board, acting under the authority of the General Conference, shall be responsible for the execution of the programme adopted by the Conference. In accordance with the decisions of the General Conference and having regard to circumstances arising between two ordinary sessions, the Executive Board shall take all necessary measures to ensure the effective and rational execution of the programme by the Director-General.[19]

c Between ordinary sessions of the General Conference, the Board may discharge the functions of adviser to the United Nations, set forth in Article IV, paragraph 5, whenever the problem upon which advice is sought has already been dealt with in principle by the Conference, or when the solution is implicit in decisions of the Conference.[19]

6. The Executive Board shall recommend to the General Conference the admission of new Members to the Organization.

7. Subject to the decisions of the General Conference, the Executive Board shall adopt its own rules of procedure. It shall elect its officers from among its members.

8. The Executive Board shall meet in regular session at least twice a year and may meet in special session if convoked by the Chairman on his own initiative or upon the request of six members of the Board.

9. The Chairman of the Executive Board shall present, on behalf of the Board, to each ordinary session of the General Conference, with or without comments, the reports on the activities of the Organization which the Director-General is required to prepare in accordance with the provisions of Article VI.3(b).[20]

10. The Executive Board shall make all necessary arrangements to consult the representatives of international organizations or qualified persons concerned with questions within its competence.

11. Between sessions of the General Conference, the Executive Board

19. Sub-paragraphs (a), (b) and (c) amended by the General Conference at its seventh session (1952) (7C/Resolutions, p. 104).
20. Paragraph amended by the General Conference at its seventh (1952) and eighth (1954) sessions (7C/Resolutions, pp. 104–5 and 8C/Resolutions, p. 13).

may request advisory opinions from the International Court of Justice on legal questions arising within the field of the Organization's activities.[21]

12. Although the members of the Executive Board are representative of their respective Governments they shall exercise the powers delegated to them by the General Conference on behalf of the Conference as a whole.[22]

C. *Transitional provisions*

13. Notwithstanding the provisions of paragraph 3 of this Article,

   a Members of the Executive Board elected prior to the seventeenth session of the General Conference shall serve until the end of the term for which they were elected.

   b Members of the Executive Board appointed, prior to the seventeenth session of the General Conference, by the Board in accordance with the provisions of paragraph 4 of this Article to replace members with a four-year term shall be eligible for a second term of four years.[23]

Article VI *Secretariat*

1. The Secretariat shall consist of a Director-General and such staff as may be required.

2. The Director-General shall be nominated by the Executive Board and appointed by the General Conference for a period of six years, under such conditions as the Conference may approve, and shall be eligible for reappointment. He shall be the chief administrative officer of the Organization.

3. **a** The Director-General, or a deputy designated by him, shall participate, without the right to vote, in all meetings of the General Conference, of the Executive Board, and of the Committees of the Organization. He shall formulate proposals for appropriate action by the Conference and the Board, and shall prepare for submission to the Board a draft programme of work for the Organization with corresponding budget estimates.[24]

   b The Director-General shall prepare and communicate to Member States and to the Executive Board periodical reports on the

21. Paragraph adopted by the General Conference at its seventh session (1952) (7C/Resolutions, p. 105).
22. Paragraph amended by the General Conference at its eighth session (1954) (8C/Resolutions, p. 12).
23. Paragraph adopted by the General Conference at its seventeenth session (1972) (17C/Resolutions, 13.2, p. 113).
24. Sub-paragraph amended by the General Conference at its seventh session (1952) (7C/Resolutions, p. 113).

activities of the Organization. The General Conference shall determine the periods to be covered by these reports.[25]

4. The Director-General shall appoint the staff of the Secretariat in accordance with staff regulations to be approved by the General Conference. Subject to the paramount consideration of securing the highest standards of integrity, efficiency and technical competence, appointment to the staff shall be on as wide a geographical basis as possible.

5. The responsibilities of the Director-General and of the staff shall be exclusively international in character. In the discharge of their duties they shall not seek or receive instructions from any Government or from any authority external to the Organization. They shall refrain from any action which might prejudice their position as international officials. Each State member of the Organization undertakes to respect the international character of the responsibilities of the Director-General and the staff, and not to seek to influence them in the discharge of their duties.

6. Nothing in this Article shall preclude the Organization from entering into special arrangements within the United Nations Organization for common services and staff and for the interchange of personnel.

Article VII *National Co-operating Bodies*

1. Each Member State shall make such arrangements as suit its particular conditions for the purpose of associating its principal bodies interested in educational, scientific and cultural matters with the work of the Organization, preferably by the formation of a National Commission broadly representative of the Government and such bodies.

2. National Commissions or National Co-operating Bodies, where they exist, shall act in an advisory capacity to their respective delegations to the General Conference and to their Governments in matters relating to the Organization and shall function as agencies of liaison in all matters of interest to it.

3. The Organization may, on the request of a Member State, delegate, either temporarily or permanently, a member of its Secretariat to serve on the National Commission of that State, in order to assist in the development of its work.

Article VIII *Reports by Member States*

Each Member State shall submit to the Organization, at such times and in such manner as shall be determined by the General Conference,

25. Sub-paragraph adopted by the General Conference at its eighth session (1954) (8C/Resolutions, p. 13).

reports on the laws, regulations and statistics relating to its educational, scientific and cultural institutions and activities, and on the action taken upon the recommendations and conventions referred to in Article IV, paragraph 4.[26]

Article IX *Budget*

1. The Budget shall be administered by the Organization.
2. The General Conference shall approve and give final effect to the budget and to the apportionment of financial responsibility among the States members of the Organization subject to such arrangement with the United Nations as may be provided in the agreement to be entered into pursuant to Article X.
3. The Director-General, with the approval of the Executive Board, may receive gifts, bequests, and subventions directly from Governments, public and private institutions, associations and private persons.

Article X *Relations with the United Nations Organization*

This Organization shall be brought into relation with the United Nations Organization, as soon as practicable, as one of the Specialized Agencies referred to in Article 57 of the Charter of the United Nations. This relationship shall be effected through an agreement with the United Nations Organization under Article 63 of the Charter, which agreement shall be subject to the approval of the General Conference of this Organization. The agreement shall provide for effective co-operation between the two Organizations in the pursuit of their common purposes, and at the same time shall recognize the autonomy of this Organization, within the fields of its competence as defined in this Constitution. Such agreement may, among other matters, provide for the approval and financing of the budget of the Organization by the General Assembly of the United Nations.

Article XI *Relations with other Specialized International Organizations and Agencies*

1. This Organization may co-operate with other specialized inter-governmental organizations and agencies whose interests and activities are related to its purposes. To this end the Director-General, acting under the general authority of the Executive Board, may establish effective working relationships with such organizations and agencies and establish such joint committees as may be necessary to assure effective co-operation. Any formal arrangements

26. Article amended by the General Conference at its seventeenth session (1972) (17C/Resolutions, 13.3, p. 114).

entered into with such organizations or agencies shall be subject to the approval of the Executive Board.

2. Whenever the General Conference of this Organization and the competent authorities of any other specialized intergovernmental organizations or agencies whose purpose and functions lie within the competence of this Organization, deem it desirable to effect a transfer of their resources and activities to this Organisation, the Director-General, subject to the approval of the Conference, may enter into mutually acceptable arrangements for this purpose.

3. This Organization may make appropriate arrangements with other intergovernmental organizations for reciprocal representation at meetings.

4. The United Nations Educational, Scientific and Cultural Organization may make suitable arrangements for consultation and co-operation with non-governmental international organizations concerned with matters within its competence, and may invite them to undertake specific tasks. Such co-operation may also include appropriate participation by representatives of such organizations on advisory committees set up by the General Conference.

Article XII   *Legal status of the Organization*

The provisions of Articles 104 and 105 of the Charter of the United Nations Organization[27] concerning the legal status of that Organization, its privileges and immunities, shall apply in the same way to this Organization.

Article XIII   *Amendments*

1. Proposals for amendments to this Constitution shall become effective upon receiving the approval of the General Conference by a two-thirds majority; provided, however, that those amendments which involve fundamental alterations in the aims of the Organization or new obligations for the Member States shall require subsequent acceptance on the part of two-thirds of the Member States before

27. Article 104. The Organization shall enjoy in the territory of each of its Members such legal capacity as may be necessary for the exercise of its functions and the fulfilment of its purposes. Article 105. 1. The Organization shall enjoy in the territory of each of its Members such privileges and immunities as are necessary for the fulfilment of its purposes. 2. Representatives of the Members of the United Nations and officials of the Organization shall similarly enjoy such privileges and immunities as are necessary for the independent exercise of their functions in connexion with the Organization. 3. The General Assembly may make recommendation with a view to determining the details of the application of paragraphs 1 and 2 of this Article or may propose conventions to the Members of the United Nations for this purpose.

they come into force. The draft texts of proposed amendments shall be communicated by the Director-General to the Member States at least six months in advance of their consideration by the General Conference.

2. The General Conference shall have power to adopt by a two-thirds majority rules of procedure for carrying out the provisions of this Article.

Article XIV *Interpretation*

1. The English and French texts of this Constitution shall be regarded as equally authoritative.

2. Any question or dispute concerning the interpretation of this Constitution shall be referred for determination to the International Court of Justice or to an arbitral tribunal, as the General Conference may determine under its rules of procedure.

Article XV *Entry into force*

1. This Constitution shall be subject to acceptance. The instrument of acceptance shall be deposited with the Government of the United Kingdom.

2. This Constitution shall remain open for signature in the archives of the Government of the United Kingdom. Signature may take place either before or after the deposit of the instrument of acceptance. No acceptance shall be valid unless preceded or followed by signature.

3. This Constitution shall come into force when it has been accepted by twenty of its signatories. Subsequent acceptances shall take effect immediately.

4. The Government of the United Kingdom will inform all Members of the United Nations of the receipt of all instruments of acceptance and of the date on which the Constitution comes into force in accordance with the preceding paragraph.

In faith whereof, the undersigned, duly authorized to that effect, have signed this Constitution in the English and French languages, both texts being equally authentic. Done in London the sixteenth day of November, one thousand nine hundred and forty-five, in a single copy, in the English and French languages, of which certified copies will be communicated by the Government of the United Kingdom to the Governments of all the Members of the United Nations.

SELECTIVE BIBLIOGRAPHY

ARON, Raymond, *The Opium of the Intellectuals*, trans. T. Kilmartin, London, 1957.

ASCHER, Charles S., *The Development of UNESCO's Programme*, International Organisation, Vol. IV, No. 1, Feb. 1950.

ASHER, Robert E., BROWN, William Adams, Jr., KOTSCHNIG, Walter M., *The U.N. and Economic and Social Co-operation*, Washington—Brookings Institute, 1957.

BOYD, Andrew *United Nations : Piety, Myth and Truth*, Penguin Special, Harmondsworth, Middlesex, 1962; revised edition, Pelican, 1964.

BROADLEY, Sir Herbert, *Can There Be an International Civil Service?* UNA Pamphlet No. 34.

BUCKLEY, William F., *U.N. Journal*, London, 1975.

CALVOCORESSI, Peter, *World Order and New States*, Chatto & Windus for Institute for Strategic Studies, London, 1962.

CAPELLO, H. H. Krill de *The Creation of the U.N. Educational, Scientific and Cultural Organisation*, International Organisation, Vol. XXIV, No. 1, 1970.

CARNEGIE ENDOWMENT FOR INTERNATIONAL PEACE AND ISIO *Functionalism : Final Report of the Conference, Bellaggio, 20–24 November 1969*, 1970.

CECIL, Viscount (Lord David Cecil), *A Great Experiment*, London, 1941.

CHOSSUDOVSKY, E. M., *The International Civil Servant : His Role and Vocation—An Inside View*, Co-Existence, Vol. II, Glasgow, 1977.

CLAUDE, Inis L., Jr., *The Changing U.N.*, New York, 1967. *Swords into Plowshares : The Problems and Progress of International Organisation*, 3rd ed., New York, 1964.

CLEVELAND, Harlan, Ed., *The Promise of World Tensions*, New York, 1961.

COWELL, F. R., *Planning the Organisation of UNESCO, 1942–1946 : A Personal Record*, Journal of World History, 1966, Vol. 10, pp. 210–56.

COX, Robert, W., JACOBSON, Harold, K., *The Anatomy of Influence : Decision Making in International Organisation*, New Haven and London, 1973.

COX, Robert W., *International Organisations : Their Historical and*

Political Context, International Institute for Labour Studies, Geneva, 1964.

The Executive Head: An Essay on Leadership in International Organisations, International Organisation, 23–2.

The International System and the Prospects of World Organisation, International Institute for Labour Studies, Geneva, 1965.

ed. *International Organisation: World Politics Studies in Economic and Social Agencies,* London, 1969.

CRANSTON, Maurice, *What Are Human Rights?,* New York, 1962.

CROCE, Benedetto, *Should UNESCO Die?,* Manchester Guardian, 18 & 19 July, 1950.

DALLIN, Alexander, *The Soviet Union at the U.N.,* New York, 1962, and Methuen ed. of 1962.

EICHELBERGER, Clark M., *New Dimensions for the U.N.: The Problems of the Next Decade* (Commission to study the Organisation of Peace), New York, 1966.

ELVIN, H. L., *An International Civil Service? What Should Be Done?,* Fabian Journal, July 1957.

FAWCETT, D. E. S., and HIGGINS, R., *International Organisation: Law in Movement,* O.U.P. 1974.

GORDENKER, Leon, *The U.N. Secretary General and the Maintenance of Peace,* New York & London, O.U.P. 1967.

HAAS, Ernst B., *Beyond the Nation State: Functionalism and International Organisation,* Stanford, California, 1964.

HADWEN, John G., and KAUFMANN, Johan, *How United Nations Decisions Are Made,* Leyden & New York, 1961, 2nd revised edition, 1962.

HAMMARSKJÖLD, Dag, *"Two Differing Concepts of United Nations Assayed",* International Organisation XV, 1961.

The International Civil Service in Law and in Fact, Oxford, 1961.

The Servant of Peace (speeches and statements ed. Wilder Foote), Bodley Head, London, 1962.

The U.N. and the Major Challenges Which Face the World Community, U.N. Review (New York) 4 (12) June 1958.

The Vital Role of the U.N. in a Diplomacy of Reconciliation, U.N. Review, Vol. IV, May 1958.

HARROD, Jeffrey, *Problems of the U.N. Specialised Agencies at the Quarter Century,* Yearbook of World Affairs, 1974.

HAZZARD, Shirley, *Defeat of an Ideal: The Self-Destruction of the U.N.,* London, 1973.

HESSE, Herman, Letter to Max Brod, 25 May, 1948, in *If The War Goes On—Reflections on War and Politics.*

HUXLEY, J., and BODET, J. Torres, *This Is our Power,* The U.N. Educational, Scientific and Cultural Organisation, Paris, 1948.

HUXLEY, Julian, *Memories II,* London, 1973.

UNESCO : The Purpose of its Philosophy, The Public Affairs Press, Washington, 1947; UNESCO document C/6, 15 Sept. 1946.

UNESCO : The First Phase, I—The Two Views, II—An Appraisal of its Success, Manchester Guardian, 10 & 11 August, 1950.

INCE, Basil A., *Decolonisation and Conflict in the U.N.,* Guyana's Struggle for Independence, Cambridge, Mass., 1974.

ISIO Seminar 1970, *The International Crisis,* Ditchley.

JAMES, R. R., *Britain's Role in the U.N.,* U.N.A. of Great Britain and Northern Ireland, 1970.

JENKS, C. W., *A New World of Law,* London, 1969.
Law in the World Community, London, 1967.
The World Beyond the Charter, London, 1969.
Some Problems of an International Civil Service, Public Administration Review, Spring 1943, Vol. III, No. 2, p. 94.

JORDAN, Robert S. ed., *International Administration, its Evolution and Contemporary Applications,* New York, 1971.

KAY, David A., *The New Nations in the U.N., 1960–67,* New York, 1970.

LANGROD, Georges, *The International Civil Service : Its Origins, Its Nature, Its Evolution,* Leyden and New York, 1963. Trans. F. G. Berthoud.

LIE, Trygve, *In the Cause of Peace,* London, 1954.

LINDSAY, Kenneth, *The Future of UNESCO,* Spectator, 13 Dec. 1946.

LOVEDAY, A., *Reflections on International Administration,* Oxford, Clarendon Press, 1956.

LUARD, Evan, *The Evolution of International Organisations,* London, 1966.
ed. *The International Protection of Human Rights,* London, 1967.

MANNING, C. A. W., *The Nature of International Society,* London and New York, 1962.

MARITAIN, Jacques, Address as retiring President in 1947 at UNESCO's General Conference (2nd), Mexico.

MINISTRY OF EDUCATION Pamphlet No. 12, *UNESCO and a World Society,* HMSO 1948.

MITRANY, David, *A Working Peace System,* Chicago, 1966.
The Functional Approach to International Organisation, International Affairs, July 1948.

MORGENTHAU, Hans J., Testimony before a Committee of the House of Representatives, 4 Feb. 1975, cit. in The Arab Grand Design in the U.N., William Korey, Midstream, October, 1975.

MOYNIHAN, Daniel P., *The U.S. in Opposition,* Commentary, March 1975.

MYRDAL, Gunnar, *The International Organisations and the Role of Their*

Secretariats, 1969, Institute of Public Administration of Canada——Toronto.

Realities and Illusions in Regard to Inter-Governmental Organisations, Hobhouse Memorial Lecture, London, 1955.

MYRDAL, Gunnar, *Twenty Years of the U.N. E.C.A.,* International Organisation XXII, 3 Nov. 1968.

NICHOLAS, H. G., *The U.N. As a Political Institution,* O.U.P. 1959, revised in O.U.P. paperback, 1962.

NIEBUHR, Reinhold, *Peace Through Cultural Cooperation,* in Christianity and Crisis, 17 Oct., 1949.

O'BRIEN, Conor Cruise, *To Katanga and Back,* London, 1962.

O'BRIEN, Conor Cruise and TOPOLSKI, Feliks, *The United Nations: Sacred Drama,* London, 1968.

PADELFORD, N. J. and GOODRICH, L. M., *The U.N.: Accomplishments and Prospects,* International Organisation, Vol. XIX, No. 3, Boston, Mass., Summer 1965.

The United Nations in the Balance, New York, 1965.

PARRY, Clive, *The International Crisis,* The Listener, 18 August 1955, pp. 243–245.

PHELAN, E. J., *Yes and Albert Thomas,* London, 1936.

PICKARD, B., *The Greater U.N.: An Essay Concerning the Place and Significance of International NGOs,* New York, 1956.

PURVES, Chester, *The International Administration of an International Secretariat,* London, 1945.

RUBINSTEIN, Alvin Z., *The Soviets in International Organisations,* Princeton U.P., 1964.

SATHYAMURTHY, T. V., *Twenty Years of UNESCO: An Interpretation,* International Organisation, Summer 1967.

SCHACHTER, et al. (for UNITAR), *Towards Wider Acceptance of U.N. Treaties,* New York, 1971.

SEWELL, James P., *UNESCO and World Politics,* Princeton Univ. Press, 1975.

SHILS, Edward, *The Intellectuals in the Political Development of the New States,* World Politics, XII, No. 3, pp. 329–368, April 1960.

SHONFIELD, A., *The Attack on World Poverty,* London, 1960.

SHUSTER, George W., *UNESCO, Assessment and Promise,* New York, 1963.

SIOTIS, Jean, *Essai sur le Secrétariat International,* Geneva, 1963.

SOBAKIN, V., *L'UNESCO: Problèmes et Perspectives,* Moscow.

SUTER, K. D., *International Machinery for the Protection of Human Rights,* for United Nations Assoc.

SYMONDS, R. and CARDER, M., *The U.N. and the Population Question,* London, 1973.

TAVARES DE SÀ, Hernane, *The Play within the Play,* New York, 1966.

THOMAS, Jean, *L'UNESCO*, Paris, 1962.

TOWNLEY, Ralph, *The U.N.: A View From Within*, New York, 1968.

U.N., International Civil Service Advisory Board: *Report on Standards of Conduct in the International Civil Service*, New York, 1954.

A New U.N. Structure for Global Economic Cooperation, report of the group of experts . . . U.N., New York, 1975.

UNESCO, *Human Rights: Comments and Interpretations*, a symposium introduced by J. Maritain, London, 1949.

URQUHART, Brian, *Hammarskjöld*, London, 1973.

YOUNG, T. C., *International Civil Service: Principles and Problems*, Brussels, 1958.

The International Civl Service Re-examined, Public Administration Review, Vol. XXX, no. 3, May/June 1970.

ZIMMERN, Sir Alfred, *The League of Nations and the Rule of Law, 1918–35*, London, 1936, 2nd. ed. 1939.

INDEX OF NAMES